Many Voices / Many Lands

Anthology of Poetry

VOLUME II, NUMBER 1
Spring 1988

Edited by

Will Stratford

And the Editorial Staff of *The Poetry Center*

Orinda, California
1988

Published by The Poetry Center Press, Orinda, California

INTRODUCTION

This volume of *Many Voices/Many Lands* includes poems from every state, Canada and many foreign countries. Represented are poets from all walks of life.

The reader may properly expect diversity here and you will not be disappointed. Included are some of the more imaginative poetry being written today. The range of themes, the emotions revealed, the regrets, anger, love, memories, humor—all the experiences of everyday living—are included. On any page you may discover some crisp image, some phrase turned just so, some insight that seems to have been written for your eyes alone.

Frequently I will jot down random thoughts on slips of paper and drop them into my desk drawer. Some eventually become poems. On one slip I wrote: "Poetry is Petals Assembled."

John Ruskin perhaps said it more elegantly:

> A poet, or creator, is therefore a person who puts things together,
> not as a watchmaker steel, or a shoemaker leather,
> but who puts life into them.

Many of the poems in this volume were created by poets not previously published. Perhaps their work, like the slips of paper in my desk drawer, had been hidden away. At The Poetry Center, we take great pleasure in publishing their poems for all to appreciate. We hope you enjoy reading them.

W.S.

ABOUT THE ILLUSTRATIONS AND QUOTATIONS

From the archives of the respected publication, *The Magazine of ART*, we are pleased to include selected drawings to illustrate the poems. The exceptional detail of the engravings and etchings, the variety of subject matter, the artistic skill of artists working over one hundred years ago combine to add much interest to the pages of this volume.

The aphorisms and quotations included have been selected by the staff.

SWANS.

A poet is the translator of the silent language of nature to the world.

—Rufus W. Griswold

THE POET QUEEN.

Grand Prize Winner

Golden

I hear her sing O them golden slippers,
only she sings it slow,
taking ten seconds
on the first half of golden,
lingering the melody
to suit her mood,
then she sings those four words again,
this time saying golden
about fifteen times,
up the scale, down, shouts it,
whispers it like the night hard love,
breaks it down until it sounds
like Gregorian chants, then marching,
and next the Vienna Choir Boys
are living in her throat,
and all the while
she's elbow deep in bread dough,
flour falling snow-like when
she tosses a handful in the air
on a fast golden,
and she looks up laughing
while all the skin of her neck goes smooth as notes,
and her not knowing I'm here watching.
—For my mother who, fearing cameras, left no photographs.

Judy Ruiz

Second Prize Winner

Who will Remember, Who will Forget?

They are in theirs and I am in mine.
I want to scream, yet I am quiet. I drink more.
I think suddenly about the house;
About the future;
About those I know and those I don't know.
Where am I and where am I going?
Where will I rest and who will care?
There is a companion,
But there is no love.
And when there is love,
There is no companion.
When there is love and companion,
there exists separation and divorce.

Love and needs.
Just a beer, a notebook, and a pencil;
And an imagination.
An imagination running far and one that returns.
A tragic imagination and one that is colorful.
Thoughts occupying the imagination at all times.
There is no peace from them.
Like you can explode.
And if there is an explosion,
Who will remember and who will forget?

Idan Sharon,   *Tel-Aviv, Israel*

First Prize Winner

Lichees

Through the open French window the swimming pool
holds the emerald day. She arranges fruit,

a pyramid in the porcelain dish: ornamental gourd,
snow pears from China, Philippine melons

and on the peak, delicately balanced, lichees:
small grenades. Uniformly subdued, Japanese kids

arrive from school, strip and assault the pool.
Their rapid metallic voices ricochet.

Emerald fragments scatter. Last night,
she heard them through the balcony's jungle

of bougainvilleas and palms. Nearer,
the afternoon battle rages on. A parakeet

flashes yellow alarm between eucalyptus leaves
—overhead, someone's playing Brahms.

She closes the smoked-glass doors to listen
—bullets rattle on—takes a lichee

in her hand, squeezes it, imagines herself:
pith-helmeted, crepuscular, armed.

Adrienne Brady   *Singapore*

Time

The moment I realized I really loved you
the days I spent thinking of no one but you
The night you asked me, your wife to be
the moment I realized you needed me
The years we spent sharing our love
knowing that it was sent from above
Time is my gift, only to say
time stops for me when you are away

Tami Diana Peterson

Into the Gentle Way of Day

Into the gentle way of day,
a cold cold whining weep,
throughout this cold winter stay.

Awaken I, from a winter sleep,
to find no spring outside,
no pretty roses to keep,

No wooden horse to fake a ride,
or green greenish leas
I can lay on or beside.

Not even swarms of feasting bees
or songs of singing danes,
just cold leaf and lifeless trees.

Spring! Spring! Spring! to relieve the pains
of this aching body
and of these cold winter strains.

Robert McNeely

Merry-Go-Round of Colors

A merry-go-round of colors black brown and white.
A merry-go-round of colors fighting for what's right.
Children on the horses in a race where no one wins.
Children in a circle paying for parent's sins.
Kids hiding in shadows scared of their friends.
Because their different colors mean their friendship ends.
A merry-go-round of colors goes round and round.
A merry-go-round of colors so love can be found.
The merry-go-round of colors is only in my mind.
But if it were real peace is what we'd find.

Colin Drake

Nature is the art of God.

2—Latin

Train Ride

The train sped past the station
I thought it was going to stop.
I stood by the door
Bag in one hand, coat in the other,
But it slowed just enough to mislead me.
It's not important now,
But at the time it seemed to matter.

Did I ascend the wrong track or
Was the schedule in error, or misread
or did some force unseen
Direct my path to the next station.
Forces unseen have such habits;
We meet, and are met by, certain people
To engage in certain events
Sometimes to gain
Sometimes to lose
Because of forces unseen.

Sometimes we cry out against such fates only to find
It's too late to change.

Another day, the train stops in the station
And I watch those embarking and disembarking.
But I know I'll ride on,
At least for one more stop.

John Michael Carroll
Included in **About The Poets** Section

Helen to the Stars

Into the night where the stars shine bright
Where her eyes gleam forth into the dusty air
Against the filling void there is a single light
An image of wonder that glows so fair
And he closed his eyes to see his Helen to the stars

And in the blackness beyond mortal plight
Like the glimpse of a falling star love is gone
Dreams of her gracefulness vanish where hearts cannot reunite
And the firmament above cries out for its anguished son
And he closed his eyes to see his Helen to the stars

He opened his heart to the panoramic darkness
Lifting his soul to the fates that keeps them apart
Where words and beauty once filled her with happiness
When the warmth of days slide from men's hearts
When she becomes sad and melancholy beyond her years
May she know that she is loved eternity if only from afar
And ease her restless soul and erase her fears
And he searched by night for his Helen to the stars
Smiling sadly he looks across the way
Whispering someday perhaps one day

Baine Jung II

Listen To The Wind

Stop awhile and listen to the wind.
He's telling you something if you comprehend.
There's a message to every breath he blows.
Just stop and listen to the wind.

Listen to the wind whistle and moan.
He sounds so sad, mournful and all alone.
The leaves seem to know what he's saying,
For they flee from the place where they were laying.

Listen to the wind, the trees all do.
They all bowed to every breath he blew.
He knows he's the king upon this earth,
that's why he sometimes blows with such mirth.

Listen and watch what he's capable of.
Even the clouds seem to scatter above.
He's telling us that God still lives,
even though we can't see Him, listen just
listen to the wind and with your heart you
should be willing to give.

B. K. Cole

Inheritance

Born with a love of beauty and a sense of pride,
I have dignity, great desire to learn,
And a genuine love of life.
From my mother I received this dignity,
Her love of beauty, her refined manner,
Her kind heart and her subdued sophistication.
From my father I learned integrity, hard work,
A rugged nature, a love for the world around me,
And that underneath hard can be soft.

Tamera Twitchell Smith

A Tropic Land Not Too Far

A tropic land not too far from the distant shore of Florida,
Across this deep silver crystal-like blue ocean here stands a
    land, a place, a state of perfection and happiness
Where all people on God's green earth should like to sail to
    discover and know this paradise
Propaganda that twists and turns the true wonders of this
    paradise rule, so near to home the American shore should
    not detour your voyage sail to discover this paradise land:
    Jamaica

A state of the tropic sun not too far from—a distant American
    shore.

George Morrison

Fall
Dedicated to my sister & friend, Janet Beardslee Carter

Fall is a beautiful thing,
much more prettier than spring.
Golden trees all around,
dropping leaves at every sound.

Trees of every different color,
all differ from the other.
Leaves lying all around,
the trees have shed them to the ground.

Soon the trees shall all be bare,
is the weather being fair,
to take these things of such great beauty,
or is it just its duty?

Fall will soon reach its end,
but I just want to pretend
that fall will never go away
and everyday will be like today.

Janice Beardslee Scafetta

Take Time

I awake to a beautiful spring day
drinking in every precious hour that passes away.
Right from the first brilliant light of dawn
To noon's warm rays, to the very last light of the twilight haze.

All this beauty in one small place,
a robin perched on the garden gate.
flowers of all different hues strewn among the ferns
of green lace, a beautiful peacock calling its mate.
Wake up and see all these things before it's too late.

I've had plenty of bliss and pain and sorrow, with all
these problems I've grown sorely tired.
But soon my heart sings and jumps for joy, for I know
with God's blessings there will surely be a tomorrow.

So we must think of better times,
and not take our lives for granted.
Beauty lies all around us, don't look at this
world as though it were slanted.

B. K. Cole

Honorable Mention

Thumperpumper*

b
i
t
t
e
r
n
  so
  still

stand-
   ing
camou-
flaged
   among
the cattails.
Skyward point-
ing his yellow
bill. Watching
and waiting until
he plucks a fish
for his meal.—
Satisfied, he
issues forth a
thumping squeal.
   T   t
   h   o
   e
   n   h
         i
   f   s
   l
   i   n
   e   e
   s   s
         t
to   roost.

Patricia B. Cabrinety
Included in **About The Poets** Section

Author's note: Thunderpumper, along with Stake-driver, are nicknames for the American Bittern. Both names are in reference to his song which sounds like a sledgehammer striking a stake. This is produced by his taking several gulps of air in his throat and then violently constricting the neck muscles. The expelling air produces the pumping sound.

Rainbows and Stars

Rainbows and stars and comets and things
Fine silken clothes and diamond rings
All have their way of touching some one
To make life brighter and have a little fun
The trouble we take to search and to reach
For the branch on the tree with the ripest peach
We each have to know our greatest need
Whether we follow the crowd or choose to lead
May we find the best for each of us
There's so much to live for, so much to trust
In a power that's waiting to come inside
When we open the door invitingly wide
Forget the anger—there is no need
As we listen to that still small voice and heed
The best of our being and let it flow
Encompassing our spirit with a rich warm glow.

Louise McPhail

About Thoughts

Do thoughts stack up
Like layers in a sandwich?
Or do they spread out
Like a hand of cards
Waiting to be played?

Do they pound against the mind shore
In constant bouts of power?
Or do they wait like new cut hay
To be raked up and bundled?
Gwendolyn Graine

Zoo Animals

Do you know what animals are at a zoo?
Or what the animals ever do?
They have lions and elephants to name a few,
Also tigers, seals, and chimpanzees, too.

Did you ever talk to the animals?
Or wonder what they'd say to you?
Birds of beautiful colors,
Red, orange, and blue.
But birds can talk,
They say "Hello, how do you do?"

Zoos have alligators, bears, and drakes,
Polar bears and water snakes.

I have named many,
But there are many more you can see.
So come to the great zoo one day,
And enjoy the animals with me

Christine Fantacone

Images

Images cripple,
More than winter winds,
Enveloping our being,
At society's whim.

Images are cruel emulations,
Confining our souls, Robbing us of wholeness,
Making us strangers to ourselves.

Our world is only a contemptuous image,
Where the strongest survive,
Supermen prey upon the meek,
Their emulated image is revived.

The essence of life is imagery,
False and malign
Lacking hope, lacking compassion,
Creating a prison of false pride.

Without any hope of ever being free,
Why survive this plastic existence?
Please liberate me.

Larry Robert Riddle

Wise Eyes

We'd have said, "You're crazy!"
Had they looked ahead and said,
"You'll not be a foursome
'Cause your marriages are dead,

"You'll all be going separate ways
And not too long ahead,
And none of you today will say
What's really in your head."

We four thought our marriages
Were strong and staunch and stable,
And we four shared some happy times,
"Friends forever, if we're able!"

But the times we shared were only
Windows to what was true,
Doubts and questions of reality,
Or rosy glasses looking through...

It's odd to remember times of ours
When we'd philosophize
In front of your fire so cozy and warm
In the room with the tiger's wise eyes

Looking down upon us four,
Maybe seeing what we couldn't,
Maybe knowing what was to come,
Seeing...when we wouldn't.

Ruth G. De Atley

From whence did Terra come to be?
How long is an eternity?
Why must I die before I'm born?
Between these questions I am torn.

I could sit and think for hours
Of the wonders men call "flowers,"
Of the faces people mask,
Or of the questions children ask.

Is life just one big mystery
Unsolved as yet but meant to be?
If it is, then men shall find
The answer in philosophy.

Cathy Roscoe

PORTION OF FRESCO OF AURORA, IN THE ROSPIGLIOSI PALACE.
(By Guido Reni)

Me, Myself and I

When one finds fault with a friend
It will bring that friendship to an end
For to have a friend, you must be one
Always quickly right a wrong when done

Remember with me, myself and I loving you
You leave no room to love others too
Eat your cake and frosting too
Soon you'll have only crumbs around you

When you make up this package, it is small
It does not take up much room at all
Self love does not reflect very far
You're the one that'll carry the scar.

Lee Wells

God Bless Us

God bless us, your children.
For we are your children
Both in Heaven above,
And here on Earth.
We ask?
We pray:
  God love everyone.
  God love the good and the bad ones.
  God love the fat and the thin ones.
  God love the rich and the poor ones.
  God love the old and the young ones.
  God love the tall and the short ones.
  God love the man and the woman.
  God love everyone.

God bless us, your children.
For we are your children
Both in Heaven above,
And here on Earth.
We ask?
We pray:
  GOD grant us...PEACE.
  GOD give us...COMFORT.
  GOD grant us...REST.
  GOD bless us...your children.

Giulia F. Paladino

Tale of Old St. Marys

Tell a tale of old St. Marys, as she nestles near
  the sea;
of her deep and curious past, that's so rich in
  history.

Some tell of clipper ships sailing silently
  into port,
smugglers removed their contraband, and found
  other lands to court.

They whisper of french Huguenots, who are resting
  in their graves;
murdered by the Spanish, they await
  Resurrection Day.

We hear of ancient churches, one the oldest of
  its kind,
a Presbyterian church, boasting of her scene
  in time.

Orange Hall's another marvel, how stately she
  remains,
a staunch reminder of the past; bequeathing
  memories that never wane.

She's proud of her old houses, precious gems
  for all to see,
more relics of another time in
  St. Marys' history.

Ramona L. Smith

Little Rocking Horse

Silent he stands beneath the pennants on the wall;
His paint is chipped in spots, a broken ear,
And hair in patches missing from his mane.
Long has he waited here, but not alone,
For loving hands have brushed the dust away
While memories often brought a silent tear.
Where is his rider now, that lusty lad
Who rode him, whooping joyously, 'crost the lawn,
His "San Juan Hill" the shaded patio,
Waving his hat it circles round his head
While summer breezes rippled through his curls?
God only knows! For those who deal in hate
And greed for gain and lust for power
Called him to wars he never understood
And that he knew that he could never win!
"Missing in action!" Who knows what it means?
Fading away in some slave labor camp
Or buried deeply under Asian mud?
So may this lonely little horse one day
Join others in a mighty cavalry
That, sweeping over barricades of power,
Conquers, and ushers in the dawn of Peace!

George N. Heflick

Flowers have the glances of children and the mouths of old men.

—Chazal

Sonnet to David

Come down, young David, and bring your slayer
Goliath is raging, plaguing the world—
Deadly weapons without pity, he hurls
at our life fount, our chief defense player.

Virulent giants pirate our red sea,
plunder its extent to siphon our source—
contaminated life entered by force
scorning their efforts all the while in me.

Highest of minds ignore simplicity,
scrambling for grants while our world turns grayer—
Display your bravery, slay the life slayer
perchance a mere stone will be the right key—

to purge life's fluid, Nature's Deity;
Come, young David, defend futurity.

Mary A. Neimann

SALAMIS.

Thoughts

I know how much I love you
And how much you love me
And I think that's all I need in life.
But other times I think I need more.
I need your patience
And understanding
When everything right seems wrong.
I need you through the good times,
And the bad times,
And the times that seem like nothing at all.
I don't mean to pressure you
Or make demands on you
If you ever feel that way.
Sometimes I think I love you too much,
And that's why things go wrong,
But that's when I need you the most.
We need to work to keep things right—
When I seem hurt or angry
Have patience
And understand
And know I will always love you.

Deborah A. Weaver

Come Home

I wish in all my dreams you were here to hold;
Here I sit all alone, the house is bare and cold,
So far away you are in the long days and nights;
I hope that you will return so that I can make things right.
Where are you my dear on this cold and dark night?
Out drinking with your buddies and checking out the sights.
You appear to eyes and all of my dreams
You are all that I need and wish for it seems,
Please return from that far away place
And make me your own.
Please return back to these roads you used to call home.
Can't you see darling I love you with all of my heart
And that I have nothing to do since we are apart,
You will be back and I will be waiting.
You did return home from that far away place.
Come here my darling let me dry that tear from your face,
I know not why I had that fight with you
I'll make it up honey in all that I do,
Come with me now and let's go to bed
We'll wake up tomorrow and start fresh again.
    I—Love—You.

Brigette L. Fry

For I Dance Too

Humming, murmuring by the hour
it nudges
And then powerfully, like an eagle,
it descends
Sucked by its beak into the very
bowels of another flower
The humming bird dances in delight
a rainbow painted bubble
In its animated suspension by nature
knows no trouble
A thousand feathers in a thousand
movements
Co-ordinated to catch each infinite
spectrum of the sun in a moment
Then, the bubble comes to life
It dances dazzlingly in the morning
light
At that moment the rivers of my senses
cease to run
And I know the senselessness of emotion
For I too dance, the ecstatic dance of
procreation.

Babooram Rambissoon

Changes
(Pantoun)

As this child inside me grows, I wonder.
I wonder will this bring us closer or tear us apart.
Over twenty years of memories, just us.
Just us, becoming one another; Can we share?

I wonder will this bring us closer or tear us apart.
A bond set in time, now threatened.
Just us, becoming one another; Can we share?
Can we share and make our bond grow stronger?

A bond set in time, now threatened.
We lost each other once, never again.
Can we share and make our bond grow stronger?
Stronger, as changes consume our lives.

We lost each other once, never again.
May our hands join never to be parted.
Stronger, as changes consume our lives.
Three not two making memories to be shared in life's twilight.

Tedna Taylor

Alone

I am alone, for no one cares.
I am alone, for I will not dare.
I am alone, because I am scared,
to face myself and my problems.

I am alone, for there is no one there.
I am alone, and it's just not fair!

For a day will come and then they will care.

I am alone, and I'll shed my tears.
I am alone, led by my fears.

But it doesn't matter, because some night,
I'll lie in bed,
and get out my only true friend, and then
I'll be dead.

So much for life.
Thank you knife.

Why now I'm not here for anyone to tell
me they cared all along,
what you showed me was I did not belong.

The day has come,
now do you care?

Misty Tallant

So Special

There comes not often to any man
The touch of beauty I have had;
An electric flash which awed the sun
Stirred my heart and made me glad.

Blessed am I for this gift to behold
Which spurred a fire deep in my soul;
A vision more lovely than any poem;
A sweet sweet vision, I know, of heaven.

Felt have I the tenderest touch,
And basked in light so truly fine;
Been given something I treasure much;
Something, so special, so very much mine.

Darkness and fear dissolve in thin air
In the search for life, for love so fair;
And the light of truth leads me on;
I see the sun, now comes my dawn.

Whatever may happen, wherever I'm led,
My footsteps are guarded as forward I tread.
My life is no longer clouded in mist;
It does have a purpose, I more than exist.

Jeff Woodward

Truly Free

I used to see a plane flying above
Wondering where it was going
Then, not really caring...
Just wishing I was on it.
I'd watch until it disappeared
Into the clouds
Taking with it all my hopes and dreams.
Still I'd gaze at the sky
As if I could still see it...

Now, I see the mighty hawks
As they hover, circling, high above.
I see the fast moving clouds, splashes of blue
Beneath the cottony masses
And then, a single plane, moving
Toward its destination.
There's no feeling of sadness or
Longing to be aboard,
For I've finally found
My freedom, on the ground.

Elaine Christie

Untitled

People said he had been walking for a long time
His brown feet and sandals
  cracked and caked with dust
  left light patches in the sand

  vanishing like

  the notes of his flute

  in the distance

When he grew tired
  children picked up flowers
  and lay them by his feet

Twilight lit the well-trodden path
They followed it
Petals blew after them in the breeze

Heather Mildvan

MOUNTAIN GLOOM.

Waters

A harbor of guilt
Waits patiently on a sea of sorrow
A forlorn stream of anterior action
Thunders over the falls of unlived tomorrows
Fathomless tides of unnurtured dreams
Forever crash upon shores
Filled with myriads of unresolved hopes,
Smashed and broken fantasies

Place me not in the numbing body
Of emotion-filled waters
For I can not resist them,
I can not yield to them,
I have drowned in them before—
        Though I live—
I never learned to swim

    Marcus M. Draves

The Great American Family?

Mommy, Mommy come look at me!
Not now dear I'm looking at TV
Daddy, Daddy listen to me rhyme!
Sorry darling I don't have time.
Mommy, Mommy come read me a book!
No time dear I have to cook.
Daddy, Daddy help me with my shoes!
Sorry baby I'm reading the news.
Mommy! Daddy! there's a hole in my head!!!
Not now sugar we're in the bed.

    Ronald D. Robinson

Untitled

Skirts in peacock plummage
  swirl sweet around the floor,
    fanning rainbow visions
    lifting high above the roar.
Jazz and Jesus soaring,
  souls saved in a heat of skin.
    In the beat of wild calliope,
    southern lights are born again.
Please pay the prancing preacher,
  blood flush in his sweating face.
    He's cajoled and led the sinners home.
    He has loved without a trace.
Tomorrow when the silence comes,
  verses crumpled in the seats,
    when the smell of flesh and fear are stale.
    garbage littering the streets,
  old janitor will sweep and clean,
  then take the altar down,
  and pin up shining poster cues:
"The Circus is Coming to Town!"

    Catherine A. Bennehoff

Scripts

Woman who handed me my life,
what agony I tossed carelessly on you.
The years sauntered by,
I casually acknowledged your existence.
Locked in your quiet corner of desperation,
you cried silently into the night.

Could I call back the years,
I would do so now.
I see with crushed heart,
the loneliness, the uselessness,
  the hopelessness,
I allowed you to feel.
Is there some way I could have taught
my daughter to slash this pattern?
She perpetuated this savage ritual.

She must be the final contestant
  in this game.

    Shanee

---

*Pleasures are transient,
honors are immortal.*

        —Greek

Dark Side

Oh Princess of Providence
Gloom of Dark and Golden Tassel.
Anger was given up in 1971. But
The world is still in orgy 1988.
Mercy is needed more than ever.
For man to kill man is a terrible thing,
For man to die is not.

The animal is not going to rule,
Man is.
And the Man is Discipline with Jesus Christ and His Love.

May the Cross of Christ,
Foolishness to the worldly, be
Salvation from understanding Jesus' precepts.
For He who rides is True.
He rode from the beginning,
Became flesh,
And rose to ride again.
He is special, His Disciples are special.
But these He picks from among the men and women.
All I know is that He chooses you—you cannot really choose
  Him.
But your hope is that He will.
And He will,
If you obey His Precepts.

    Damien R. Hutar

Life

Little do you know today
    what might take place tomorrow.
        lots of things along the way
            could bring either joy or sorrow.

You certainly have to plan
    and hope for the best.
        you do the best you can
            and leave to God the rest!

Those testing times will come
    when things seem to fall apart!
        at times you'd like to run
            and you wonder where to start!

There is one thing for sure!
    there is just no place to quit!
        so you start in once more
            because you have true grit!

Arthur F. Ward

No wise man ever wished to be younger.

—Jonathan Swift

Tribute

I had a friend! He passed away!
I knew him all my life, and in a way
part of me died on that fateful day.

He was a man, no doubt of that.
With a craggy grin and sweat stained hat.
A patriot! An American who heard the call
and never let fear make him stray or fall.

His courage was a banner proud. He was a
man among men, a cut above the crowd.
This friend I was proud to know, and will
always let my friendship show.

Brave in battle! Gentle in love!
Now he is gone to God above.
He set us goals by his example.
A guide for those who would adventure sample.

This friend of mine I never met.
But by his star my goals I set.

So until at last when we shall meet.
Near the stars by the judgment seat,
and together we will explore the path
that leads to universal peace at last.

So my friend until that day, I'll live
life better for your stay.

God bless you! John Wayne

W. L. Earp

Detectives

Reading the great detectives
I am not selective
black thoughts and black pulp
makes me stare and gulp
    All the stories start the same
    with a distressed and beautiful dame
    she's a bundle of nerves
    and has dangerous curves
And she goes to a seedy Detective Agency
where there's a special flagrancy
of cheap whiskey, cigars and broken dreams
and the dame isn't as innocent as she seems
    The whimsy, flimsy Lord Peter
    drove away in a two-seater
    And Ed McBain was looking for Evan Hunter
    and finding Lord Peter's butler Bunter
Outside the office of Marlow & Chandler
it was full of confidence men and panhandlers
trouble is the detective's business
and it makes him hapless and listless
so he calls up Father Brown
saying, you better come around
because it's all a mystery.

L. C. Helming   Sweden

While Sitting Here

While sitting here, I suddenly realize that
My every thought, my whole being is thinking of you.
I'm in a daze, the people, the noise, the wind,
I no longer hear any of them.
I see you, I hear your voice,
All this so suddenly while sitting here.

I feel the sun on my face,
The trees part and I can see into space.
But as far as I see, your name stretches across the sky.
I blink at the sun and the skies explode!
Or is it my heart thumping at the joy of my thoughts.
A sweet cool breeze whistles your name through my thoughts.
My tension relaxes, and while sitting here
I began to say your name.

I look back on my day, the tension on my face goes away.
I feel better now; the day doesn't seem so bad.
The decisions I had to make don't seem so big now,
My every thought is still on you.
And all seems better now; because while sitting here,
I thought of you!

Samuel C. Gregory

Untitled

Shiny white, with dark grey shadows
atop a bright blue sky
Clouds of cotton, big and small
dance and float on by
Creating creatures, animals alike
or pillows they seem to be
A friendly face with outstretched hands
reaching out to me
Inviting me to come along
a freedom-filled ride
"Oh come with us to paradise
please, please do not hide"
I stand up,from under the tree
which protects me from the wind
and reach to them with outstretched hands
floating with a whim
Oh, what a ride I am on
I can clearly see the ground
Feeling so much movement
but hearing not a sound
I think that I feel happy here
my feet can't touch the ground
And now I come to realize
Yes, paradise, I have found

Michelle Napoli
Included in **About The Poets** Section

The Beach

The trip was pleasant and upon arriving, I threw open the
  blinds and slid open the door and what did I hear but one
  sweet roar, the waves were rolling and the air was calm, I
  jumped in my sweatsuit and like a bomb,
I raced to the beach and wet my toes and the feeling I had no
  one knows.
That night, I had dreams of a sunrise and water glistening
  and to voices in my head, I kept listening...so the next
  morn, early I rose, I jumped in the shower and put on my
  clothes. I dashed to the beach for an early morning walk
  and before I knew it, it was twelve o'clock. My pockets full
  of shell and rock.
My body was free, my thoughts were flowing, I felt like a bird
  soaring, soaring, soaring...

Linda Bond Byrd

Ideas

Ideas are whispers from another plane.
They come to us for birth.
We breathe a form around their force
And give them life on earth.
Some grow well and some grow wild.
What we nurture is our child.

Margaret Kelly

The North Wind

*Written for my niece Christine Noelle for the occasion
of her eighth birthday, 7 December, 1987*

Whip up, wail, Old North Wind,
  Winter's on its way!
Whistle in the woodlands where
  Whining branches switch and sway.

Blow,blow the clouds a-yonder,
  Chill the air and make it bite.
Sting each leaf to color a-wonder
  Set a frost in morning white.

Life's now nearly wound full circle:
  Age shows us its flaw
When wet winter's Godsweet waters
  Send bold birth with Springing thaw.

Susan Lynn McPherson

This World

What's wrong with this world?
Crime abounds in its streets
It appears from murder to robbery
These crimes fall upon you without word

The media cries out these crimes
You hear it on television
It is read each day in the newspapers
It's a wonder it's not done with chimes

What about its good points?
The birds that fly in the skies
Wild creatures that live on the ground
Plant life that our spirits anoint

Think about its good people
All those that commit no crimes
After all aren't these the majority?
Many congregate under a steeple

Think about the forest tall
All the deep blue waters around us
Can there be better pleasure than nature brings?
Isn't it a good world after all?

Gerald H. McKelvey

The Greatest Laugh of All

Laughter comes in assorted styles,
From big laughs to small
And from shallow to deep,
But none is superior to the greatest of all

It comes from inside
And it bursts through real clear.
When a true one arises,
All present will cheer.

No words may describe
This internal gutterance
That bursts forms of sorrow
With one solo utterance.

Problems are solved,
Or at least momentarily lost,
When this giant laugh
Appears at no cost.

Francis Thomsa Russo Jr.

Please Leave the Dishes

I love to have you visit me,
I like to cook and stew,
But as you can see, my kitchen's small,
There's hardly room for two.

So won't you sit and chat with me
While I put the food away,
And stack the dishes neatly—
Tomorrow's another day.

Eldora Rose Yensen

Pursuit

Within the noise of traffic
    And construction works
I, finally, take a break from distress
    Never I thought one day I would
Exert my untrained body
    But, here I am...Almost a year without
Other than the solace of THE BOOK
    Enjoying fine literature
Only sunburning
    Strained muscles, callused hands
Averse mornings, long days
    Short night—and leisure

In the midst of my misery
    Dad's words echo in my mind,
"Son, be valiant...don't be a coward
    For only through courage you'll be able
To overcome your battles..."

Well thanks, pa!
    With renewed strength, I reflect,
From now on
    I am in pursuit
        Of a better turn

J. Duenas

Oh, To Be a Bird

Oh, to be a bird and fly away!
    To be free to flitter, to sputter, and twedder,
To be of sparkling color, to chirp, to sing,
    A desire of thirst to taste of springs and spring,
To feel the shelter the dark bending limbs can bring,
    To be free to quickly vanish when trouble nears
Never to truly fear,

To see a shadow in the brook,
    To share and be a part of that shady crook,
To be light and gay and of feathery touch,
    To eat freely of seeds that grow so much,
To be oh so very neat and sleek,
    Always wiping that browny beak,

Oh, how it must feel to be a bird
    With a bouncy downytail a flippin, floppin, and a bobbin.
Oh, how it must feel to be a bird
    To feast of summer delight all winter long,
And fill the air with nature's song.
    Oh, to be a bird!

Helen Dent

To Rose From Your New Dad
(To a new daughter-in-law)

Here is a special message on a very special day,
For a lovely young lady, charming in every way.

I can imagine the years when you were very small,
How sweet, cute, and lovable you were to all.

I can see your proud parents in those growing years,
But now the little girl is gone and a woman appears.

You're not looking over your shoulder at the past,
For you've found your knight on white horse at last.

As you take wedding vows and into the sunset ride,
May you keep your knight forever at your side.

You'll be part of a new family tree for life,
As the minister proclaims you both as man and wife.

Be careful in your journey, as I know you will
For the ground can be rough over valley and hill.

Travel as a team, and compromise when you must;
Whatever crisis you face, remember to have trust.

Your man in shining armor will struggle, it seems;
Of those pots of gold at rainbow's end, he dreams.

He will serve you well, my dear, in more ways than one;
I should know because, you see, he is my only son.

He's given me precious you, a new daughter I can love;
And grandchildren, I'm sure, thank the Lord above.

So here's the beauty of pride and praise so glad;
Here's to you, my flowering Rose, from your new dad!

Win Kelley

*Included in **About The Poets** Section*

Conquest of Space

Space vehicle poised on planet earth,
Man of faith occupies its berth,
His choice was great, his name shall also be,
Succeed or fail in his passage to immortality
So call him mighty! Inscribe his name first,
In the bright valhalla of the universe!

Countdown ended, zero hour arrives,
Astronaut begins his conquest of the skies!
The giant spaceship escapes its mooring,
Destination-worlds ripe for man's exploring!
With rumblings that echo thru the launching site,
Vulcan's flaming spacecraft begins its flight!

Then with its movement faster than eye can trace,
The space traveler streaks upward into space!
Beyond gravity's pull, driven by nature's force,
Earth's satellite follows its circuitous course.
The celestial pilgrim stirs with high elation,
Encircling the earth, embracing God's creation!

Infinite God! Indomitable man!
Man reached up, God grasped his hand!

Herbert F. Lair
Included in **About The Poets** *Section*

Mature Childhood

I remember World War II, Pearl Harbor, Hitler, relatives going
away to war, and "blackouts."

I remember making a New Year's Eve trip to Dallas alone at age
six on the Super Chief, which was packed with soldiers,
sailors, WACS and WAVES.

I remember the drinking, singing, crying and kissing at
midnight; and all the attention I enjoyed by being the only
kid on the train.

I remember homes with flags hanging in the window with stars
representing family members who were serving in the
military.

I remember savings stamps and victory gardens; and taking a
sprouted bean in a sardine can to school for "show and
tell" as my contribution to the war effort.

I remember ration stamps for almost everything, including
shoes, and wearing ugly brown oxfords because my feet
were narrow and the selection was also slim.

I remember sadness, photographs of handsome young men in
uniform and folded flags.

I remember unity in America, serious talk about the war,
sacrifice, going to church, and praying a lot that the war would
end; and

I remember the war ended...there was great joy, and the world
began to live in peace.

Coleen Gibson
Included in **About The Poets** *Section*

The United States

Oh, the splendor of the United States!
God's country, freedom's noble land.
Where freedom of speech and expression
Are making man's dignity grand.

Striving to end man's oppressions,
Bravely with valor it stands,
Offering freedom with justice to all
In its peaceful, bountiful lands.

Lord bless with grace the United States,
The noblest land of the free,
Protecting, defending for all generations
Man's right and freedom through Thee.

Lewis E. Babbidge

A NEAPOLITAN WATER-CARRIER FROM MERGELLINA.

A Joy to Reminisce

The golden glow of the sunset
Steals across the patio,
Awakening me to memories
Of a long time ago.
Oh, how we used to sit and laugh,
About the things we used to do
And the silly mistakes that we made,
And no one never knew.

The flowers now are blooming,
That you planted in the border-bed.
You chose only your favorite,
For they all had to be red.
The tandem swing is still in the garden
That you painted white and green.
How many times in the moonlight
We sat there and planned our dreams?

I still see you stand so tall and fair,
With your arms open wide
There to enfold me,
Ever close to your side.
We had our children,
Our home God did bless.
Now, in the golden glow of the sunset
A joy to reminisce.

    Verna Wantnuk   *Canada*

Time to Choose Our Leader

Yes, it's time—the presidential election year
Is coming to the U.S. voters, both far and near.
We've read the newspapers, attended political
meetings and watched T.V.
But now, I ask, why is the choice so hard for me?

We have an ample supply of candidates, from
both parties, 'tis true,
But after many days of study and deliberation,
how do we know who
Will be the best man to make our country strong,
To guide us and to keep us from going wrong?

So, we continue to read, listen and evaluate
The statements and promises of each candidate,
On election day, we go to the polls and our vote is cast,
Trusting that we have put the right man
in office, at last.

Election day is over, and whether our
choice or another candidate won
the presidential post,
Doesn't really matter to the utmost;
You see, one man can't do it all,
He will be our leader, but we must stand tall.

By faith, cooperation and dedication
We can help our president make a better nation,
By first seeking help from God Above,
And asking for guidance for our
new president and the country we love.

    Grace Freestone

Settled

Pearl gray shadows cascade
Through an eastern window.
Golden Jubilee blossoms lace air currents.
Warm kisses from wet lips
Settle silently on my skin.
In the easiness of her breath
I can find a spot of heaven
      And wonder.
Eastern shadows and spring
Scents of heaven. I too, Adam,
Found my rib settled by my side.

    James R. Sharp, Jr.

Untitled

I've written lines in Reference to,
   This Game that we call life.
I've written lines on Relationships,
   where man names lady his wife.
I've written some on special friends,
   on how tough they are to find.
I've written lines to certain people,
   wishing friends they would be mine.
All! of these lines that I have written,
   Come from deep within my brain.
Most! of these writings bring Happiness and Joy.
   While some of them do bring pain.
Writing for me expresses my feelings,
   Much better! than I could Speak.
It does not matter if I'm feeling low,
   or if life is at a Peak.
Writing for me allows me to say, whatever is on my mind.
   I Hope! The people who read these writings,
   will be able to find.
The Reasons that I write these lines to friends and friends to b
   To answer this Question the Best that I can?
   I'll Just Say,
     That's me.

    Scotte

Gentle Wind

Sabrina
Washington Square, New York City
Fall—Gentle wind

Wonderment
New experience
Hands outstretched
Fingers separated—
   reaching toward the movement
The quiet gush of air
   between her fingers

Sabrina
Totally enmeshed in the dance
   slowly billowing around her

Sabrina and her new playmate

   Sari Robinson-Goldstein

True Colors

The bluest blue belongs to the sea
And cannot be produced synthetically

The greenest green belongs to the grasses
And cannot be concocted from chemicals and gases

The reddest red belongs to the rose
And not to the end of a reindeer's nose

The goldest gold belongs to the sun
And its beauty can never be undone

The blackest black belongs to the night
And can hide the bad things from our sight

The whitest white belongs to the dove
And is the true symbol of God's perfect love

   Stacy Lawson

Honorable Mention
Still Life

Searing heat touching skin translucent
tiny tears of water
arranged on a still canvas
the locusts and the red ants
they knew, they screamed
they lived furiously
those moments when every color was brilliant
the red dust cold in my mouth
no outward movement discernible
while the warmth raged inside
rushing forward through every pore
escaping this blank canvas
to meet a motif of more significance
of every palpable palette ever contained
in one life
the locusts and the red ants,
only witnesses to an artist's commitment to a
still life.

   Diane Robinson

Psychic Exposure

Softly blended colors reflecting earthtones,
   spelled *me* and *my place* called home.
This abstract painting was a perfect touch—
   so I bought it—"I loved it so much."
After I hung it on my living room wall,
   my home shouted "Welcome! *you have it all.*"
Mystical abstracts of this painting,
   compelled me to some heavy thinking.
I questioned *who* could have known *me*
   to expose that part for *others* to see?
I took a trip back to the Studio Place—
   I wanted a good look at this *Know-it-All's*
Easel—art board—the smell of paint
   colored my senses—all familiar and faint.
As he stood up and turned around,
   I knew at once—*my equal* I'd found—
Through hand brushed images of his mind—
JUST ONE EXCEPTION—*The Artist* was blind.

   Thelma mb Kucharas
   Included in **About The Poets** Section

All that is good in man lies in youthful feeling and mature thought.

   —Joubert

Unwelcome Vigil

Alone I hover by the window
An eon passes in the silent night
and still I wait.
Ears strained for the crunch of tires on gravel
the whispered shuffle of your weary feet,
your careless gait.
Worry gnaws, a companion to doubt
perhaps you have been rendered helpless
alone yourself.
Frustration triumphs over both as
this vigil robs my body of rest,l
my mind of health.
Suddenly, I stir upon my perch
As at last your key turns in the lock
you have returned
Relief is soon replaced with ire,
as stealthily you emerge into the hall
you have not learned.
"I wasn't waiting up for you," I lie
My voice a traitor quakes with every word
from tears unshed
Engrossed in some imagined labor
Abruptly having found the task complete
I go to bed.

   Joan Dower Kosmachuk   Canada

Heart Eyes

Heart eyes
glow soft, and questing
and warm.

Heart eyes
see with a rainbow
of feelings,
and touch
with the pungent joy
of nearness.

Heart eyes
first find life
in the womb of timelessness,
and learn to see
by watching the stars.

Heart eyes
blush when rendered deep
with tenderness.

As long as life exists
these eyes
will seek to find
another's good,
and answer
with its own.

Heart eyes...heart eyes.

Mary Dockens-Lillejord

This Was Meant To Be

For you my darlings I do grieve,
In a few days I must leave.
Then with God I will be.

You both are truly grown now,
And soon my pain will take a bow.
For no more will it torture me.

Away from you I shed a tear,
But you go on without a fear.
For my love is always near.

Never let them tell you so,
That God's true love does not flow.
For he gave me life to cherish you.

I know it will be hard at times,
In the outcome you'll be fine.
For God not only loves you,
He will show you what to do.

Please never show Him anger,
From taking me away.
For true love, life, and laughter,
He gave along the way.

For now my darling children,
Forever may you see,
That this was meant to be.

I LOVE YOU.

Deborah Brown

Mountain Vacation

As steam rises from the hot
cup of coffee you're sipping;
the early morning fog is
slowly lifting. The
sun, over the top of the
mountains, is peeping!

The quiet serene stillness
gives you a feeling of completeness!
The whole world seems at peace!

As the mist and fog are burned
away, by the brightness of the sun;
your mind lazily drifts away.
You find yourself wishing, that
forever you could stay!
Here your worries are at bay;
postponed until another time!

Before you're willing,
you must go back to
the everyday, hustle and bustle!
It would be easy to delay,
and you must tear yourself away!
But starting now, you look
forward to returning to the
mountains next year!

Doris Richards
Included in *About The Poets* Section

Silk and Heaven

Lying naked in a bed
or fully clothed in a crowd,
I feel so close to you,
a closeness we share.

Your body feels like silk,,
you love like heaven.
I love the feel of silk,
and I'd die to get to heaven.

Tom King

Pollyanna

Where did the years go?
Wasn't it only yesterday
That I was young
Believing in
Happily ever after?
Where did the years go?
How did they slip away
Without my knowledge
Or consent
Without living them?
Where did the years go?
What happened to
Happily ever after?

Shirley Carvalho

Puppy Love

Puppy love,
how do you know?
If it'll stay,
or it it'll go?
Is it for real,
or is it a game?
When it's over,
will memories remain?
When it's for real,
can you be for sure?
That it won't die,
that it will endure?
All of your feelings,
deep down inside;
Are they acknowledged,
or do they still hide?
Well...if ever,
it happens to me;
I hope I'm awake,
enough to see.
This miracle of love,
bright and alive.
So I can be,
a wonderful wife.

Tricia Henry

Movement

He looked around and saw her laugh
the woman with her lover.
She has a way of knowing
the world is hers to love.
Moving through life
like waves hitting the sand
she met him in the hallway
and held him with her eyes.
The wind got louder
the earth disappeared.
His heart lost its vision
as he awoke from his dream.

Leonard Ginsberg

SPANISH PATIO.

Poetic Blues

Their poetic blues
in rhythmic rhymes,
The expression of a heart
I developed through time.
I can scream on paper
and no one will hear,
except the eyes of a reader
as they read these tears.
A cry so loud
in poetic blues,
is the release I found
and come to use.
For my colorful heart
to bleed in rhymes,
to empty on paper
between each line.
It spills in ink
In moments of pain,
finding comfort through hell
and keeps me so sane.

Barbara Garcia

Atoms

You cast spells
without knowing their meaning
What would you ask Satan anyway?

Tony Simmons

Love Is

Love is
    sharing breakfast, for two.
Love is
    patience, making peace, loving you.
Love is
    soft music trapped by your perfume.
Love is
    caring, let's toast till noon.
Love is
    your smile comfort by the rain.
Love is
    my armor, to protect my queen.
Love is
    your passion, I am your king.
Love is
    freedom.
Love is
    clean.
Love is
    Every lover's dream.

Ronald Beau

Honorable Mention

The Loon

She rises high near birches
to fly
the Chippewa River bend
tapered front, back
flapping dark missile
crazy call
searching
my dream recurs
floating on grey space
alone
I fear falls that do not come
held instead
by loving drafts
cotton tree currents
she feels wet lands
moist worlds in misty drops
seeks convergence
through clouds
she grows small
all
wing now
disappears around the bend
with Northern Spirit answers.

Carol Albrecht-Schrantz

For My Wife

Reaching for a dream
A realm of lasting love
Finding that which holds
the bonds of forever

You my love are that dream
Always there throughout the
trying times a beacon of love
The pillar of tenderness
The dream I care not to
Live without, for you are
My life.

James R. Hayes

We Are One

We are one together
We are one another
We are one forever
We are one.

We have one mission
With just one vision
And for one reason
To be one.

We make one vow
To achieve it now
And we will somehow
To have peace.

When we share one love
When we share the above
When we share a peace dove
We have peace.

Madame Muorie

Joey

Tell me, my love,
my sweet young boy.
What is it I can do
to open you like
the flower that
you are?

I open your hand,
and slowly, softly,
kiss the tender
hollow of your palm.

If only you
could be opened like
a hand, or a flower,
would you tell me?
Could you whisper
it...gently?

(i know better than to ask)
Barbara Whetstone

Untitled

Today I cried a silent tear
for all the times we've fought
for all the times I wanted to talk
and simply just forgot

Today I cried a silent tear
for all the times we've been apart
for all the times that I was wrong
and knew it in my heart

Today I cried a silent tear
for knowing what lies ahead
for all the times I've doubted us
for all the words left unsaid

Today I cried a silent tear
for getting upset about your past
for holding it against you
and thinking that we won't last

Today I cried a silent tear
and put it all behind
tucked in a little corner
far in the back of my mind.

Tina Sarette

Maybe...

I wander through the night,
Searching for a memory,
A part of me that is lost,
Buried deep within me.
I watch the starry night sky,
I wonder if it's worth it,
Living the way I do,
Feeling so empty inside.
It all seems so meaningless,
So cold and worthless,
The way I'm living life,
Somehow incomplete.
It is so lonely, so very lonely,
Sometimes I think it's useless,
To go on living like this,
Missing a part of me.
I feel so very alone,
A lost forgotten soul,
But somehow I can't stop hoping,
That this will someday change.
Maybe in some distant future,
I will find what I've been looking for,
The memory that I lost,
And I won't feel so empty anymore.

Sabrina M. Burke

Cain and Abel

I am terraced
  climbing the night's
gaping womb,
  I creep in slither,
witness to a new sky.
I have brought you
  here to follow
So you will leave
  other names.
Should sleep cause pain
  in our thought—
  or will we rest hollow
  by aurals silver beam
Should light leave
  us severed,
separate obscurities, oddities
  alone on the planet
in a clinging battle for
    oneness.
I loose my darker brother.
Disintegration
  is imminent.

Broken Star
Included in **About The Poets** Section

Moonbeams

Free and moving she follows my every step.
Far above the clearing she is an astral ship
  Floating free among buoys of light.
  But here she is still, nestled in dark
  Arboreal extensions. I see her as the
Jewel in a Crown of Thorns. Her Beams
Rain down beyond the Permeable Flesh.
  Deep in the mind's eye, that is where
    She acquires her Luster.
  Oh! How my eyes must shine with an
    Internal Light.
Chrisopher Erickson

Spirals and Cycles

Gay were our steps
when entering our bright new home,
with happy dreams
exciting echoes of future joys.

Sparkling sunrays
drew me toward the outside world,
where chipmunks raced
and squirrels begged for toasted bread

Pleasant was this time indeed
until I saw it lying, stiff,
in frozen quietness;
That little bird would sing no more.

Bleakness overshadowed, joy abruptly
changed, I sensed,
  I felt this pain of sadness,

Like cold, unfeeling fingers
gripping my very soul, forewarning,
some unknown sorrow yet
in nature's constantly changing plan.

Then I, hearing his voice,
chose to bury this sign
that slowed my heart,
Before returning to his broad,
    unknowing smile.

B. Mae Taylor-Clifton

Divided

Two become one
Can one be three?

One for all I owe
And am and ask anticipate
Who's been and seen
And doesn't wince to
Be and see again.

Two for times in a box
When my arms are lead
Whose arms never tire
And I can sleep.

Three for fast wind speed
and words and fear
Whose darkness floats to
Me and run for fear
that there is real
Adultery.

Claudia Tagliasacchi *Canada*

The River

The water flows
  so smoothly on top
But the fury underneath
  will never stop.
All life believes
  what is seen is real
And nothing can make
  the raging still.
The power that takes
  all reason away
May destroy
  your life one day.

Bobbie Powell

If You Miss Me

If you miss me sometime
then call me anytime,
I shall fly to your arms
in every hour of the day
and night.

If you miss me sometime
call me day or night,
I shall go to you, not in
my mind, but with my heart:
to kiss you the whole night.

If you miss me sometime
  me day and night,
I shall be with you in love
in every day and every night;
that you never miss me again
in your life....

M. Tamas Tomay-Ybly

"Smile"

Just smile at someone and watch
  their face.
It's very "catchy" to human race.
Most everyone will smile back
  at you.
The number of people who don't
  are few.

A smile makes you feel so much
  better than a frown any day.
Seems to lift your spirits in no
  other way.
It's good for every one to see.
Make me happy as can be.

So, put on a great big smile now.
  Never does hurt any how.
No more frowning—keep that
  smile.
  Even for a little while.

Helen Barrante

My Lincoln Continental

Oh, Lord, I prayed one day,
I want a Lincoln Continental.
Can't You hear me up there, Lord?
'Cause You know I've asked You
  this before!

You say I should be content with
An old Chevy or Ford?
Now, I don't mean to sass You, Lord,
But, gosh, why? Are Your funds
  running low, too?

You say I should take a number
  like all the rest?
But, listen Lord, I've got corns
On my toes and bunions on my feet;
And, I'm nearing the twilight years.

Yes, I know I can *walk* up the
  golden stairs,
But, please Lord, couldn't I just
Have my Lincoln Continental now
So I can drive it Home?

Beth Bristow

VERMILION TOWER, ALHAMBRA.

"Ode to Death"

Please do not trudge in front of me
  Lest I stumble and I fall
And do not slink behind me
  Casting shadows strange and tall

But come near and walk beside me
  Then place your hand in mine
For life and death melt into one
  And both can be sublime

Matters not if some say "dark as night"
  For some have other themes
A tunnel with a light so bright
Beyond their wildest dreams

It guides their dear departed souls
  To a place of light and love
Therefore I shall not be afraid
  But trust in God's great love.

Gladys Groendal

Lovers, Friends

Since I met you
  you've shown me
    happiness
I lost long ago.

You've given me
  the kind of love,
I was
  looking for;

tender, loving,
  honest, sincere.
I have no fear
  when I'm in
    your arms.

You may be
  my lover,
But, more importantly
  to me
You are my friend.

Wendy M. Souder

How Sad the Song

How sad the song
  My aching heart sings,
A thorn,
  Torn deeply
    Within...
Would sweeter relief bring;

Cry on, then my soul,
  Cry on...
For the night
  Is sorrow on wings,
And tomorrow,
  Tomorrow...
Sweet fragrance of song
  My soul at last
    Doth sing;
    Death,
Oh death...
  Where is thy sting?

D. Jeanne Peterson

Old John Bean

He dreamed away the hours in school,
He idly sat in absent air,
The master took him for a fool,
And gave up in despair.

When everyone else was working away,
You'd find him loafing near a stream,
He'd slip away and sit all day,
He'd read and idly dream

When all others passed him in the race,
And his brothers won the prize,
He wore the same expression on his face,
And lingered beneath the evening skies.

He lived alone, he spoke of few,
Loafingly through life he went,
And what he dreamed of, no one knew,
To be so content.

I saw him when he was old and gray,
His eyes were dim,
As I stood beside his bed that day,
Somehow I envied him.

When at last beside his bed,
"And life is short, so soon?" he sighed,
"It's been so rich and good," he said,
"I've love it all,"—and he died.

Rosanna Hanning

Till The End of Time

Your memory, forever in my mind sweet enlightenment,
You were one of a kind, you shared with me, moments
of lasting joy you'll always be remembered, till the
end of time.

We shared the good times, and the bad ones just as
well. But when you were there, everything just
seemed swell. But now you are gone, and I'm so all
alone you'll always be remembered, till the end of
time.

Till the end of time, Till the end of time. Your
memory lasts forever, for you were always mine you'll
never depart from me, I'm always thinking of you.
But if that should ever happened, you know that I
would be through.

Think of me always, no matter where you should be.
We'll always be together from here to eternity. You
were always my favorite, to you I send this rhyme.
You'll always be remembered, till the end of time.

Till the end of time, till the end of time. Your
memory lasts forever, for you were always mine, you'll
never depart from me, I'm always thinking of you.
But if that should ever happened, you know that I
would be through.

Richard Rosales

The Search

We're all looking for something;
    something we can't find.
We're all searching for someone;
    while there's something dying deep inside.
We need something to believe in, something like ourselves.
    We used to believe in our country and God;
now people are believing in rocks.
    Crystals, the occult, where will it end?
With fictional heroes and fictional friends?
    We're living in make believe worlds.
Living a lie, living in fear;
    We're living in cages that aren't really there.
We've got to learn to accept our lives;
    we will have to take it from there.
Can't you accept me the way that I am?
    Where are we going, where have we been;
let your chains go, don't lock yourself in.
    There are beautiful people in this beautiful world;
you've got to get out, see for yourself.
    Then you will see what you really need.
When this happens we'll all be freed.
    Then together we will find what we all really need.
Friendship: Life's most pleasant aspect.

Michael A. Steben

Patterns

We met our tomorrow, yesterdays ago,
the drummer we heard, obscured,
in the world's cave of sounds, where
passing each other we nod at oblivion.
Noting TV's celebrations, God-like cars,
business matters, and little else,
our lives, running on parallel tracks,
seldom intersect.

We find an agony we can't explain,
traveling in life's fast lane, while we wrap ourselves in others
        cocoons,
and butterfly, towards the known, the safe,
plumbing the tip of eternity's fingernail,
hoping that our tomorrows will drown today's
banalities.

John L. Kirkhoff

In the Quiet Dawn

Before the rising sun splits
through the naked trees, only duck-
swishing sounds bridge the breeze—
banistered on either side by
filigreed chirping of crickets.

Up from swampy thickets
extending across the bog
comes the massive, supporting croaks
of a lone bullfrog

Peering past these punctuations
of silence, while the sun etches
a path across this inland sea
V-ing thoughts land from
migration—to build, nest and
hatch for conservation.

Lola Beall Graham

The Greening of the Land

'Tis the time of the year
  For a change in the land,
For flowers to peep from the earth,
  The birds on the wing
To come Northward to nest,
  And to chirp to all—
It is Spring! It is Spring! It is Spring!

Tiny birds on the trees
  Peep out from snug nests,
To enjoy the warmth of the sun;
  And they joyously shout
Spring is here, everyone,
  It is Spring! It is Spring! It is Spring!

The fields, and the yards change their color
  From brown to a brighter green,
For they, too, must change with the season—
  The change makes a beautiful scene.
    For it is Spring!
It is Spring! It is Spring! It is Spring!

Vivian Craun

Hegira Cancelled

In so many caverns I have searched
For that special reason to believe in myself
And many times, too, I've been trapped
Caught by my inability to cope with life
And I've been tempted just to end it all

But I remembered my soul
And a dream I keep there
God, how I need a dream
Just one lousy dream
To help me hold on
To all the good in me
That I had nearly forgotten

Maryel Backstrom

If you think the words "night" and "evening" have the same meaning, note the different effect they have on a gown.

—Tuzette

The World

The world is a planet,
A member of the solar system,
Gravitating around the sun it spins
With its sister worlds as its kin,
It is a small water body
Having a moon and the most advanced,
Divided into northern and southern hemispheres,
Of western and eastern nations and peoples
Under respective leaders and governments,
Dominated by the United Nations,
There are varied democracies and constitutions.
The supernatural world is the dome
Of the life, vegetation and mineral home,
Countries are states of every race,
The scientific age is the space epoch,
Marking the zenith of our Earth,
We own the lands as our heritage,
and they are monarchies and republics
Denominations of kings and presidents.
The globe began as a dust nebulous
Far away in the cloud of time,
The planet has a life span
Of billions of years of existence
Making a spiral orbit in the atmosphere,
A part of the deep stratosphere.

Manion E. McMahon   *Australia*

My Demon Lover

Into my room at night he does come,
At the stroke of twelve, he must have my blood.
Gentle and tender, he is never rough,
He comes to make love, oh why, oh why is it never enough?

I want to fly with him, to soar through the air
But how can I go, when I'm practically bare?
Around my shoulders, his cloak he does throw,
And into his eyes, comes a love's glow.

Off we go, up into the night sky
When I am with him, I always fly high.
Over the mountains right up to the sea,
He tells me he loves me, and longs only for me.

He says though we may be miles away,
Deep in his heart, he hears what I say.
But the eternal darkness that keeps us apart,
Won't let us be together and says we must part.

So down from the night sky, and back to my room,
He places me gently, on the bed where I swoon.
He commands me to sleep, and so I obey,
I want to go with him, but no I must stay.

He kisses me with longing, and says he must fly,
All alone in my room, am I left to cry.
In restless dreams I toss and I turn,
And impatiently wait, for his promised return.

Mary Fields
Included in **About The Poets** Section

A Lost Hope

The walls were cold as water dripped down,
    searching for a soft place to land.
The spot of gleaming sunshine that layed ahead,
    grew larger as my steps brought me closer to my goal.

My eyes starved for the warm glow of light,
    as it dawned upon the grass land.
My mind was excited for fresh air and new visions,
    to see and remember.

Yet, that single spot of sunshine,
    grew farther and farther away.
As I walked towards it,
    I picked up my speed.

    unfortunately,

To my surprise that spot of sunshine,
    grew dimmer and dimmer,
        never to be seen again.
As I looked far ahead,
    I saw a wall that looked cold as water dripped down.

My gleaming spot of sunshine and hope turned into,
    dark cold nothingness.

Serenta McDonald

ELIJAH WALTON'S "GREAT ST. BERNARD, MONT VELAN."

The Black Web

Kissing under the sparkling city lights.
Yearning to be loved on those cold, chilly nights.

Asking you to the Senior dance.
Never receiving my first chance.
Deep inside, my candle would dance and flicker.
Needing someone to light your wicker.

Satin hats and ribbons weren't for a city slicker like you.
not seeing white, pink, or red; life was black and blue.
And so you went to the Masquerade Ball.
Caressing long legs and wanting them tall.

Watching the tall, slender lady dancing with long, blue, black
        hair.
Preferring an experienced woman with a natural flair.
She danced away the cobwebs in your head,
Pulling out your insides with a black-silver thread.

Seeing her long, silk,black dress like a frail weed—swaying.
Shadows dancing on the wall; tonight her music was playing.
finally drinking from her silver flask.
You couldn't see beyond her black, satin mask.

Behind her mask she was hollow and old.
Long ago her ideals were lost and sold.
In the night you'll cry, never realizing what's the matter.
She's the black widow who'll have your head on a silver platter.

Trapped in a spider's web; you're entwined in her black shawl.
She takes off her mask after the Masquerade Ball.

Sonya J. Berman
Included in **About The Poets** Section

22

On Your Wedding Day

Today is your wedding day
a day to cherish and remember;
it's the day you choose to be united
and live together forever.
You have joined in love before your friends
and your family too,
they have all come to see your marriage,
a bond of love between you two.
I don't know what tomorrow will bring,
but i hope it brings both of you love.
May the joys of love be with you
and God look on you from above.
I wish the both of you the best of luck
and a happy and prosperous life together,
may the joys of love be yours today
and always be yours forever.
May your years together be the best of times
and always be filled with love,
and from my heart i truly say,
I hope you both have a long and lasting love.

Tracy Lee Barger

Love does not dominate; it cultivates.

—*Goethe*

Nine Years

Nine years of love and joy have passed
Though many have said our love would not last
Through troubled times, our love has braved
Through sorrow and grief, yet love still remains

When life was hard and love should have broke
We fought together, with faith, trust, and hope
And now we see, as the years roll by
We have a love that shall never die

But the precious memories I choose to share
Are the walks in the mountains,
        as sunlight glistens in your hair
Of starlit nights, as a gentle breeze would blow
Or the fun-filled walks, through the pines covered with snow

For three beautiful children, you brought into this earth
The love that we shared, through the pains of their birth
The love that you give me, as we share our life
Outweighs the sorrow, troubles and strife

Nine years ago, in a meadow of hay
We swore our vows, on this our wedding day
Nine years of love and joy have passed
But we proved to many that our love will last

James D. Puckett II

Remember

My skin burns where you touched me
Like small drops of acid
Does your skin remember me?

My mouth is dry since you kissed me
No matter what I drink
Does your mouth remember me?

My ears ring since you spoke to me
Like far away fairy bells
Do your ears remember me?

My eyes tear since I looked at you
Rivers of love and pain
Do your eyes remember me?

Do you remember me?

Pamela Anthony

For Married Folks Only!

Shattering glass bursting into
simultaneous pieces
Exploding firecrackers against
a midnight sky sending
single rainbows falling
to the ground.
Groans, like a wounded animal
two entwined, now one
wrapped in sweet ecstasy
        Coitus.

Paris Jenkins

My True Valentine

You are all the world to me
Your wisdom makes a light for me to see
Your cheerful words make my heart smile
And when I need you near to listen awhile
I know you will always be waiting for me

I cherish your sweet kiss and hug
And all your kind and thoughtful deeds
I only hope that in me you can plant seeds
That I may grow to be good, kind and true
And bring happiness to others as you do

My wish for you on this Valentine's Day
Is love, health and happiness always
But not just for one single day
Every minute of every hour of everyday
I love you more than words can say

Georgia Horsfall

Loss of Compassion

Caring is a lost passion;
A feeling gone out of fashion,
And I wonder why.

We're too concerned with our self-esteem
To help others who are in need,
Which makes me want to cry.

If we'd give concerns to others
As if they were our brothers
The world would be better.

Our policies are no solution
And blaming can bring no resolution
For our many flaws and errors.

So all we can do is blame ourselves,
With our selfish subconscious of self,
And wonder why many starve and die.

Jeremy Gilbert

---

*Who bravely dares must
sometimes risk a fall.*

—Tobias George Smollett

The Voice of the Wind

I listen to the voice of the wind,
Calling, calling, calling to mankind.
Speaking to each new generation,
In a language it can understand.

It called to my Grandmother in her youth,
Moaning, moaning, moaning down the chimney.
Speaking to her through rattling grain,
And the creak of the swaying Sycamore.

It spoke to my Mother in her day,
Banging, banging, banging on the door.
Speaking to her through rustling leaves,
And the crack of linen on the line.

At night it sings at my window,
Knocking, knocking, knocking on the pane.
Speaking to me through squeaking hinges,
And the clink of an empty soda can.

How will it speak to my Daughter?
Singing, singing, singing in her tongue.
Does the Solar Wind make noise against a space ship;
Or the wind of Mars whistle through its red dunes?

Will the voice she hears be one of mourning?
Wailing, wailing, wailing through bombed out ruins.
Speaking to her through crackling fire storms,
And the stench of the unburied dead?

Neva F. Darbe

The Well

They pulled a baby from a well tonight, and I cried, alone.
36 hours—looking into a dark heaven only a child can see.,
while a man with no clavicle crawled down to greet her,
and her first word was "no."

Spock just nods—it's the right thing to say at her age.

It just goes to show that everything makes me think of you
waiting for my rescue practicing my response
as you slip into my darkness, as you squeeze through the
         narrow opening
where I fell deep into myself; eighteen years ago, maybe
         thirty-six.

Paramedics immobilized her head,
one arm free to wave good-bye to her second womb,
free to wave hello to the world of greedy eyes and bright lights.

She will never be the same, though they'll work to calm their
         fears but
she'll never be the same because she knows
something different than the rest
and the rest will ask and pry and poke her until the day she
         cries.

But she'll never tell what she saw; she won't have the words.
         Even
these aren't her words, they're mine. And if you really want to
         see my heart
get the whole town together, poke a flashlight down the shaft

but remember, you're looking for a little boy, hidden by a large
         chunk of time
and when you find him, better immobilize his head and bring
         him slowly
out of his night because he knows the greedy eyes and bright
         lights
and he's not coming out for them.

He's coming out for you.

Peter Cooper

Journey of Love

There is a spot, unspoiled, where love is found throughout;
it's here we're free of worry, or wrangling fears, and doubt.
Beneath the steadfast oak we'll sit and contemplate the sky,
while breezes soft as God's breath sound an ancient lonely sigh
Slowly now, let's close our eyes, the journey will begin;
our hearts are drawn to soar upon the sound and light within.
beyond our world of solid form there lies a greater plane,
where melody and splendored lights pour down on us like rain
Explorers of the light and sound is what we truly are;
we'll trek the worlds within ourselves, so near, and yet so far.

Glenn D. Woolum
*Included in **About The Poets** Section*

ST. CHRISTOPHER.
(From an Alto-relievo in Wood.)

God's Garden

The flowers in his garden,
   are beyond compare.
describing all their beauties,
   is gentle and so rare;

Each petal you caress,
   each fragrance that you smell,
Are touches that he's added,
   and added, quite well;

With each their own color,
   own shape and size.
Deserves a big blue ribbon,
   the (best) of the prize;

They grow with all the love he has,
   through his mercy and tenderness.
The effect they have on everyone,
   is as it is I guess;

He plants them in,
   and out of season.
There is purpose,
   there is reason;

Such beauty to us all, they are.
   A gift they bring, to both near and far.

   Veronica Mullins

Can't Hold Back the Tears

Every time I think of all the wonders
The Lord has done in my life,
An unimaginable joy builds deep in the pit of my soul;
Words can't define the feeling
Nor can I express to your understanding;
The indefinable emotion that engulfs my soul.
His touch is always so gentle,
His voice is always so soothing;
Guiding me; telling me that I'm His very own.
Though some may jump and dance;
Others may shout out loud,
But I can't hold back the tears,
When I think of the joy in serving the Lord.
He's been my counselor in times of trouble,
My comforter when the dark clouds appear,
My father when I need an understanding ear.
He's my friend when others have left me,
A companion when I'm alone;
He's all things and everything, yet He's still my Lord.
Although others may shout and dance
At the touch of my Savior's hand,
But I can't hold back the tears,
When I think of the joy in serving the Lord.
   AMEN

   Lawrence V. Crenshaw

Bessie's Best Help

How nice it would be
If once, you and me,
Thanked God for trouble
That cause us to grumble.

Poor, Pitiful me! I'm smart as can be!
I know what I want!
I know what I need!
No matter HE doesn't agree!

How can I know the true meaning of FAITH,
'Til in a twinkling, I have no Houseplace.
Fire has destroyed the material things,
Now I feel the comfort of GOD'S wings.

How can I know the true meaning of HOPE,
'Til my loved one says, "Don't worry,
   we can cope."

You tell me this is trivial, trite and untrue.
I   *'m so glad GOD blessed me this way—*
'Stead of you.

The PEACE that I feel,
No mortal can give,
For I know in my heart,
My GOD LIVES!!

   Bessie Hedrick

Four Angels On Four Corners

The third part of the sun, the moon, and the stars shined brightly upon the earth. All was quiet. No sound of the voices of the trumpet.

We were standing on the four corners of the earth, dressed in white like we were told by our Father. The wind had blown onto the earth. This was not the tradition we were taught.

In the same hour, we waited for an earthquake, the tenth part of the city to fall, and the slain of seven thousand men. It never happened. But you see, it wasn't supposed to be like that.

The thrones sat to the center, yet empty. Multitudes, nations, and different tongues were together as one. Their souls were to be beheaded before the witness, but the witness was nowhere in sight. Where is our Father?

The trumpet sounded. The third part of the sun, moon, and the stars were smitten and darkened; the day shone not for a third part of it and the night likewise. The wind had come to a halt. Then we realized what we were waiting for had now come.

Tonja Davis

We must attain wisdom as we go up stairs—one step at a time.

—Tsze-Kung

Honorable Mention
Stark
They look like such strong hands;
Callous hard and wrinkle rough.
I see them shake at the loss of a son.
He buries himself in his fields,
My father. Finds solace in soil,
Finds growing things remind him
Of a boy...Mother dusts the box
Holding her young man's medal once,
Then leaves this place forever.
Father lingers in an empty room,
Watches the sun change patterns
On the floor and finally
On the East wall.
I stand on the porch,
Watch a thunderstorm sweep wet
The wide fields. It unites the soil
And my father's sweat. I see him walk
Into the rain, toward the wheat
Which bends and blows, and grows
Out of the salt with which he watered the earth.

Jacqueline M. Schaefer
Included in About The Poets Section

Perspective of a Child

Get down on your knees and see how big a tree looks from the
    perspective of a child.
It is a totally different world down among the knees of the big
    people who have forgotten the perspective of a child.
While you are down on your knees trey looking through an
    old fashioned keyhole to see what I get to see from the
    perspective of a child.
You get to see gum stuck underneath the tables and greasy-
    dirty handprints underneath there as you look from the
    perspective of a child.
There is a lot of dust that can be seen all over so, if you don't
    understand my not being concerned with cleaning it is
    because my world down here fails to meet inspection.
I don't really care. I'd rather go on playing but I had rather
    you understand me and all the little people around that
    see from the perspective of a child.
I don't like what I see when I see the dirt on the floor, the
    things in the carpet but I go on a playing on them just the
    same.
So, when I make a mess, I don't understand the fuss because I
    feel I live in a mess as I view it from the perspective of a
    child.

Deloris Wood
Included in About The Poets Section

The Dream

I'm sitting in this lonely room
Looking at the bright full moon,
A million stars are twinkling in the sky
Reflecting off the tears falling from my eyes.
I see the couples walking by hand in hand
This night was made for lovers throughout the land,
As I sit alone and softly weep
I close my eyes and drift off to sleep.
Softly I hear the floor boards creak
I feel your lips gently brush my cheek,
I hear you softly whisper my name
My heart soars, my passions flame.
You take me in your arms and hold me tight
The pain flies away, everything seems so right,
Finally as our bodies meet
I've never know love to be so sweet.
With passion spent, into your eyes I gaze
By the light of the early morning haze,
Slowly I see you start to fade
The pain returns and cuts like a blade,
I close my eyes and start to scream
I realize now, it was only a dream.

Cynthia Brand

Denial

He is very smart and I
relate to his views—but he's kind of loud.
He's articulate and I'm
moved by his speeches—but he rhymes a lot.
He's interesting and I
admire his guts—but he's a preacher.
He knows the issues and I
like his positions—but he couldn't win.
He's a strong person and I
think he's a leader—but I just don't know.
We never stopped to listen
to ourselves groveling for excuses.
We could not bring ourselves to
stop saying "but" and start stating "therefore."
And now we cajole ourselves:
"Maybe next year,"—as if it were the Cubs.
He's honest, decent, and I
like his attitude—but he is a black.
We could not have done better,
But God knows, we should have been able to.

R. Buongirno

SCHEVENINGEN.

Hold Back the Judgment Day

Hold back the judgment day until I find my soul. Wait awhile
please before I grow too old. I'll always give the best, that's
within my heart. So hold back the judgment day and
remember me to God. There are amendments that I must
make. So hold back the judgment day, if Heaven can only
wait.

Down all my avenues. Down all my boulevards, into a world I
have bravely known. Freedom rings and freedom sings;
but if I shall lose my soul, so wait awhile please; before I
grow too old.

A world that is beautiful, hopefully as human beings. An
American dream.

So hold back the judgment day until I find my soul. Wait awhile
please, before I grow too old.

Charles Lee Terrell

Dr. Martin Luther King Jr.

So beautiful to see
A blessed victory;
In the memory of someone
That's gone; That fought
For so many things he knew
Were wrong.

From the hearts of you and me,
We loved you so, Dr. Martin Luther King.

It hurts so bad to see
It's a WHITE AND BLACK
Reality;
But, It's a big accomplishment
You were sent from our descendants;
To have a special day;
To make a better way;

So many things in your life
Seems like they were done in strife;
But you showed us the best of
Everything;
We loved you so,
Dr. Martin Luther King!

Anthony P. Mitchell

---

*No author can be as moral as
his works, as no preacher is
as pious as his sermons.*

—Jean Paul Richer

To Be Good

To Be Good, you must be good in everything you do
or say, all around person moves along a course, all
the way.

To live in parallels of life, will be the hardest
thing to do, you must satisfy those around you and
yourself.

You must be at your very best, since it's you who will
strive for the ultimate level of success.

There is no need to be upset, when things go wrong,
life is in your favor, be alert, be brave.

Being good in your way can help improve conditions
another day.

We hope to do things that are possible, things that
are near perfect in front of judges sitting nearby.
Their high standards and morals makes it very hard
for us to reach the sky.

Gilda Gray Manley

Let Us Be Happy With Each Other

When you were just a little tot,
Hugs and kisses you gave a lot,
But, oh, can't you see?
How much you are hurting me?

Why have we grown so far apart?
So much pain is in my heart.
There is no meaning for me in this world,
Until the bitterness in your heart will be uncurled.

You used to climb upon my knee,
Oh, how happy I used to be,
'Cause "I love you all the much in the whole wide world"
    I would hear,
How I wish I heard that now, but I won't, I fear.

Of you I have always been so proud,
Even though I may not have always said it aloud,
But I'm ready—to all the world I'll shout,
This is my daughter—That's what my life is all about.

Let's stop the tears we shed,
Time grows short, it has oft been said,
And learn to laugh together,
Because you won't have me forever.

Now, that you, too, have been blessed with a daughter,
Don't you think that you ougher,
Let us be happy with each other,
As one mother to another.

Mollie Hoffman

Upside Over, Inside Out and Backwards

Rebecca of Sunny Brook Farms,
Has burrs in her meadow,
The cows have gone dry,
And the chickens won't lay.

Pollyanna has a hole in her stocking,
And jam on her best dress.
Her smiles have turned to frowns,
And she is given to having tantrums.

Mary Poppins' umbrella has turned wrong side out,
And she has been grounded for violating military air space.
Her magic is all wet,
And she can't nanny anymore.

Then I met a smiling face,
With a kind word and a warm heart.

The burrs bloomed into flowers,
And the chickens began to lay.
Pollyanna's Granny bought her a new dress and stockings,
And her disposition became radiant again.
Mary Poppins found a new umbrella,
And her flying license was restored.
Her magic returned,
Because it only flourishes in loving hearts.

Joan Lowe

Converging Courses

There is a lasting endearment which can arise
when two whose paths happen to cross
begin first by knowing the sharp and irregular
sides of each other's nature,
and not the ultimate 'til further on;
initiating the development of a glowing ember
that will burn forever,
the tenderness growing up in the
interstices of a mass of dull and commonplace reality.
This communion of body, mind, and soul
usually taking place through common pursuits,
is, however, unfortunately seldom superimposed upon love
between a man and a woman
simply because they associate,
not in their everyday tasks,
but in their pleasures chiefly.
When, however, fortunate conditions permit its occurrence,
the resultant combination of feeling proves itself to be
the only attachment which is strong as death—
that love which the floods cannot drown,
nor many waters extinguish,
beside which the passion usually called by
that name is as ephemeral as steam.

Wanda Gardner
Included in **About The Poets** Section

THE AGE OF INNOCENCE.
(By Sir Joshua Reynolds.)

Televised Truth

Each glance through the luminescent window
Sends the poet's hopes to the death row.
A man of one thousand pounds is a hero,
Guatemala children die in sorrow.
Heroin swells the cheeks of a young girl,
Nausea makes her intelligence swirl.
Love makes its way through hallucinations,
Rainbow after a storm of abjections.
The trembling double-chin of a senator
Gorges itself with the people's candor.
A minister with business suit and tie
Stigmatizes any kind of a lie.
A material girl is named Madonna,
Poverty makes the Earth a gehenna.

Emmanuel Pierreuse
Included in **About The Poets** Section

---

*Lessons are not given, they
are taken.*

—*Pavese*

Eddie and the Magnificent Magnifying Glass

LLLLuminous virtu-
    osity,

Through a magnifying glass!
Is a bleached stain of brilliant monotony,
Wielded by pudgy hands.
What virtuous luminosity,
To crush a spot and play light along the sidewalk cracks.
Watch it tango with the scribbled walls!
and fool around the neighbor's cat, (we call him Siggy,
            he has no tail).

But fleshy insistence has a curious existence, and
Virtuous luminosity, what a restless virtuosity!
That sends the blinding spot upon a blue skirted crotch.
Cascading jello giggles and several kicks
(with flying grass!) incorporate inconsistence with
fleshy insistence. For now, (watch her skip behind
            a fire hydrant!)

the ant would assume any responsibility, and focusing
luminous attention on its beaded body, satisfaction
twines with ant vapor.
What a brilliant stain of bleached monotony!
leaving behind an ashy shell for the sun's
buttery fingers to prod shadows
from.

David Dieni

Secular Tree

Sky, the earth and I are three

Sky above
Earth below
In the middle I stand alone.

A flower?
A fruit of sorrow?

Storms
Rains
Burning of sunshines
and even war.
Sometime they disappear, I see
Sometime they take place
Around me.

Through happiness to sadness
Of guests staying all day and night
In the morning Mr. Sun says hello to me
While the Young Wind and I are getting exercise
In the evening Lady Moon advises me to go to bed early
as I am telling the stars the old stories of life.

The Old Wave comes and asks me angrily
—Why are you standing here for a long time?

To calm him down and answer quickly
—I am waiting for a friend from another planet!

Damthanh Nguyen

The Mirth

Snows stained sanguine lilt and
Cringe; the snows assuage.

i can't forget the little boy who said he'd skate home.
(You've come colossal in a year, Boy)
rushing and raging the blanched dark
crackling-thing, water clear.
it came in buckets like a cow's milk (and pucks)
that day and you loped with that darned stick bumping behind,
wearing, glaring behind.
busses and motors wouldn't do, 'cause you could fly
with mirror blades, two razor blades.
and (so you say), "I flew to Colorado," you do.
well, i can fly too, you.

had i believed your music myths, your
octagonal nightmares on a dream-thin shallow plane,
i might have eschewed your monster fire,
pained passion as you chased
that thing you and all tried to rape; like
crimson moonlight Chandra (or better still) chased
chaste little girls, little boy.

And scarlet ice sings dirges, as you flee
dove-like peaceful and dive to the puddled
red spot where blood was spilled, was chilled, Yours.

hark. the narcissus.

Kathryn Maris

All My Children

I have a son who's #1
He's handsome, dark, and tall
A heart of gold for all I'm told
If you need him he's right on the ball
And there's #2 He's honest and true
The Bible is his way
He is the one whose work's never done
But always takes time to pray
Then #3 whose face you must see
Looks happy, smart, and kind
Even though he's away you might say
He's always on your mind
Look at #4 he is one more
Who is tall and thin but witty
When he's around he is the clown
Who makes your day most pretty
Now take #5 he wouldn't survive
If he couldn't give love to us all
Along with the rest he's one of the best
That makes mothers like me stand tall
There's more I can say that brightens my day
The daughters I have number two
One short and one tall but best of all
These girls are good mothers too

   Marion Gilbert

Youth

Youth, the leaders of tomorrow
   Struggling each day with sorrow
Youth, the forerunners of the 21st Century
   Brave hearts enduring stormy seas
Youth, take a stand, and courageously right the wrongs
   Implanting happiness of humanity where it belongs
Youth, stop the fighting between each other
   And realize we are all sisters and brothers.
Youth, challenge your weakness and boldly stand
   Take charge of your life in full command
Youth, banish the evils of weapons and crime
   Cut the ropes of suffering with wisdom divine
Youth, stop slandering the body with drug pollution
   And enjoy your own magnificent Human Revolution
Youth, Together travel the emerald road hand-'n-hand
   Envisioning World harmony and peace within our land.

   Shirley D. Zagorec

À Guillmette

Ma chère petite Guillmette,
Je pense a vous, et Chantal.

Comme je suis triste, que
Vous etes sans de Papa (de
Votre tout coeur, tous les deux)
Que vous fait a des remonstrances.

Comme je suis triste, pour
Mes très petite
Poupées, il y a long temps,
Aussi comme ce que
Vous avez me donner, (de la
Parte de Robin) et
Quelle reste, solidement, toute
Seule, lelong du fondement du
Bureau de musique;
En face: devant mon peînture de
Bretagne; notre petite
Guillmette, de Rennes
(Je me rappler, comme enfant
D'amour, avec
Son frère, Jean-Claude plus grande)
Aussi, l'enfant,
D'amour, ma
Cher, cher, petite,
Guillmette.

   Geneve Baley

Included in About The Poets Section

To You, My Child
(For Jessica)

I'm writing this to you, my child,
That someday you might know
How much you've come to mean to me,
How much I love you so.
It seems I've waited a lifetime
To hold you in my arms.
I vow to you my life and love,
To protect you from all harms.
And as I watch you grow each day
And discover many things,
I hope that you will know the joys
And happiness life brings.
The most important thing of all,
I pray for you each day,
That you will come to know God's love
And that Jesus is the way.
For He will lead you through this life,
He'll never let you down.
And if you ever feel afraid
In Him, your strength is found.
And so my child, I give to you
My never-ending love.
And then my child, I give you to My Savior up above.

   Darla Horner Menking

Search Seek and Receive

You may search a lifetime for something that
You don't really understand,
God knows exactly what you need
The gift of salvation is offered to all of man.
There is a yearning within the soul of man to have
Fellowship with the Son,
Until you have a personal experience with Christ
Then satisfaction will never come.
Nothing else can give us the peace we seek
Listen to me, my children, to the words that I speak.
With Christ you'll be strong instead of being weak.
These words were given to me by the Father, that a
Soul might find its way,
Why wait until tomorrow or next week when you
Could find Jesus today.
You must be lost before you can be found
You must seek before you can find,
Jesus dies not just for you or just for me
He died for all mankind.
Come today before you grow feeble and gray,
Why won't you come willing
Come let Christ show you the way
Come while the Spirit is dealing.

Patty C. Jaynes

A POST OF CONTENTION.

Love
Based on Matthew 22: 37-40

When asked the greatest commandment, Jesus said,

> "Love the Lord your God with all your heart
> And all your soul and all your mind," and then
> Second, "Love your neighbor as yourself.
> On these two commandments depend all the law
>   and the prophets."

Love your neighbor as yourself.
   God says your neighbor must be loved.
   God says that you must do the loving.
   God's love embraces all mankind.
   Man's love must follow his example.

   God is beyond our comprehension.
   This is something all can understand.
   This is God's law for mankind to follow.
   This will let us live by God's commands.

   Love instead of hate and fear and anguish.
   Think of all the things that it would solve.
   This is what The Understander, Jesus,
   Tried to tell us all so long ago.

   This love encompasses all God's creation,
   Its application everything in life.
   It sums up all the words of explanation,
   A simple word which covers all that's right.

Juliet Ashley Lesch

That's God

See the sunshine, shining bright
giving Mother Earth nourishing light
See the flowers that bloom each spring,
The roses, tulips and violets
Aren't they pretty little things?
See the green grass that you play on each day,
dodging and darting, wherever you may
That's God, my child, that's God.

Hear the robins singing each morn,
Now who do you think my boy taught them their song?
Hear the crickets as they chirp at night
The moon and the stars give off their light.
Hear the children as they sing at play
Listen to their song my boy,
Oh, don't they sound gay
That's God, my child, that's God.

See your mama and daddy too
Now who do you think my boy made you?
Remember the animals that we saw at the zoo,
The lions and tigers and the elephants too.
Well all of these things are a part of Him
And those who don't believe in Him will someday be condemned
That's God, my child, that's God.

Jacqueline P. Taylor

31

Touch of Life

You gave Me life...
with a scream of a wounded pigeon
fighting for open sky
You let the world to grab and pull
the roots of Your heart...

Without a tear in Your eye
You said—This is My child...
and let the darkness cover Your body
with warmth,
      You were ready to Fly...

The Universe seemed so small
Stars so near
The coldness of the moon cut Your tired face
like a knife

You wanted to touch me
I was too ignorant, conquering My own fear
You reached for Me and Flew
      for Your life...

I shut My eyes, trying to cover My shame
with a cry...
You reached for Me again
I pushed Your hand away

I looked into Your face
seen Your life going by...
I touched Your body...gave You life...killed the pain...

Violetta Colman

DuValier's Dream

DuValier was a bitter man, who cursed the morning sun
That brought a new betrayal every day.
He shunned the world of mortals, and the sound of human
      tongue
And blessed the night that chased that side away.

A disillusioned dreamer, who would never love again
Who tried a bit, and found that it was rotten.
Preferring perfect strangers, to the company of friends,
Cause Strangers are so easily forgotten.

DuValier took the fickle turns of fortune, and in stride
Expecting next to nothing out of life.
Ill fortune found a girl, and a flame that caught her dying,
Whose burning beauty cut him like a knife.
She touched him thru the senses,
That his mind could not control.
Then smiling, stepped aside to watch him fall
Betrayed by his own body, and the hunger in his soul
Duvalier wasn't dreaming, after all.

Oh, It's hard to keep believing,
When you know you've been deceived.
To face a lie, and dare to try again.
And there is nothing like a woman,
And her spell of make-believe,
To make a new believer, of a man.

Bruce W. Parker

*The more a work is admired,
the more beautiful it grows
for the multitude.*

—Gourmont

Golden Radiance

A golden radiance seen from afar;
that shines as brightly as a star.
A beauty so fragile as a light;
that illuminates the darkest night.
The first time i noticed was by chance;
as i turned my head and caught a glance.
In awe of this beauty i had to see more;
so i patiently waited by my front door.
Needing to see what that brightness could be;
that vision of loveliness i need close to me.
To my surprise and sheer delight;
this vision of womanhood came into sight.
With beauty and grace, she came close to me;
until so close that her radiance i see.
My passions rise from far within;
as i wish for a conversation to begin.
We talk endlessly, but seems like a day;
this new love of mine is here to stay.

Robert C. Raineri

Fingers Of My Mind

Fingers of my mind paint a picture of long ago;
When life was love and on the go,
Before there was a tinct of indigo,
Bringing about a parting of the ways...
Breathe deeply my soul the clean air of lost springs,
Bearing a substance for strengthening,
A forever searching but tired being; an eager one,
Pacing, the unraveling road of life...
Gamble not my heart, when the essence of life can be sought,
Out of beautiful meanings that yesterdays brought,
By pressing the values that lie in thought,
Laying bare, the tieings of the times...
Sources of reminiscence, carry me to a land of joy,
When all was just a girl and boy;
The future was something with which to toy,
That wonderful world of once upon a time...
For the whole of life is just one conglomeration,
Of countless yesterdays, no formations
A very deceiving figuration,
Leaning, towards that one and only, tomorrow...

Furman Clarke

Love

When you see the out-stretched "hand,"
As it starts to come your way,
Grab it up right then,
And keep it every day.

Once in your heart,
It'll never go away,
No matter how much you use it,
Forever it will stay.

Let it all come out,
Show everyone you care,
For this is a common language,
A language we all share.

Wondering what it's called?
It's something you know of,
It is a unique feeling,
The wonderful feeling of love.

Angela Rogers

BIRTHPLACE OF DANTE.

Hours of Love

While I stroll through a meadow of blue and yellow flowers
My thoughts drift back to you.
I hear the wind whisper as it entangled your hair;
your bubbly laugh as we chased one another at play,
fetched water from a well—
waded in a stream
gathered wild violets near the trunk of a tree.
May my memories of you never end.

Virginia Goland

How Do I Know I Love You?

It scampers across my mind,
Whenever, angry words cross our lips,

It's hard to explain, my silent meditations,
Whenever, you plead for my silence to be explained.

How do I know I love you?

For a time, I wander away from the present,
To the past; to the future; away to better times,

When we laughed; we smiled; we hoped,
We danced with joy, because we loved.

How do I know I love you?

There was none before you,
And none ever can follow you.

Once, my heart was opened by you,
Now it is closed; never to be opened again.

How do I know I love you?

The stars are brighter; the sun shinier;
The days shorter; the nights longer; when I'm with you.

You are with me wherever I go—
All thoughts, words and deeds; occupied by you.

How do I know I love you?

You are you; the word of love is you to me,
That's the way it will always be,

Because you have become the essence of my spirit,
our love has inspired my love for you!

Virginia A. Camplese
Included in **About The Poets** Section

Three Little Words

Three little words are all I said,
but they were enough to turn her head.
A smile she gave, so light, so gay,
I offered my hand as she stepped my way.

I talked, she laughed, as we trod the by-way,
The fields were covered with flowers of may.
The sun's golden rays gave her hair radiant light
and a breeze through her curls gave me delight.

I dreamed of Jeanie, of the light brown hair,
but found another ever so fair.
The girl I married swept me off my feet
and I think often of the way we did meet.

As a rainbow rises within my view,
I say once again, "I love you."

Morris Eldon Ward

Honorable Mention

The Robotics of a Cashier

My boss plugs me in at five every day.
With a mechanical smile upon my lips,
I join the ranks of mindless machines
sporting ponytails and blushing-red smocks.
Our souls wait in the parking lot.

Across the keys
　　　Checking 1, 2, 3...
Our fingers fly,
stained green from excessive caressing
of Washington's capitalist countenance.

There's a beat to checking—a dull, mechanical pulse.
You can't dance to it, but it's there—
　　　a clicking and clanging
from nickels dumped in the register drawer,
　　　a rustling and snapping
as brown paper bags are flapped open for filling,
　　　a computerized whirring and babbling
as registers flash eerie green numbers and vomit receipts,
　　　a beep and a digital shudder
as I accidentally unplug my co-worker's register,
　　　and her bright, teen-age eyes
　　　　　go blank.

　　Teresa J. Talerico

PEVERIL CASTLE.

---

*Folks who claim it can't be
done are a dime a doesn't.*

Listening

Is it really so very hard
just to listen with all your heart?
Not to judge or be insincere,
only to try and really hear.

The person you are speaking to
may be finding it hard to do.
I need for you to hear me,
I have a need to really share.
I need for you to hear me.
I need for someone to be there.

We see it in each other's faces,
throughout the years we see the traces,
of the blindness and lack of care,
that show our hearts weren't really there.

When we listen we lose so much
if our hearts are out of touch
with the feelings our families share
because they need us to be there.
Is it really so very hard
just to listen with all your heart?

　　Sheri A. Jones

The Difference

I met an elf
　so very small,
I asked—
　If he'd be happier if he were a bit more tall.
He said, "I'm short and I'm small and,
　I am what I am,
If we were all alike
　the world would be so bland."
"I see everything and don't miss a single detail,
　For everyone notices my outer soul and;
　to see my inner they fail.
　For I love life and life loves me,
Even though for you I am hard to see."

I met an elf
　so very small,
I asked—
　If he'd be happier if he were a bit more tall.
He said, "Life is pitch black dark and then you die,
　Why should I worry about living at all—
why, why, why,
If I don't die the night; I'm angrier the next day,
If I die soon; It would be the answer to what I pray.
I'm not dead; I want to be alone; Get away from here."

Tomorrow he dies.

　　Steven Walters

The Fisherman

Down by the sea, the fisheries
reek bonita—reek
sea bass
and an ancient black fisherman
with a crab basket—full
brimming red snapper and flounder and perch.
Under the aged pier
patient fishery cats are waiting
      to ravage his "catch."

Squabbling sea gulls sit near
the once noble mariner.
And, dried up starfish,
washed up kelp,
litter the shore.

Over by the surf
in putrid holes, in rotting piles,
garbage—The ancient fisherman
tosses intestines, tails, heads
into the crimson dusk.

Janice Kollitz

Man

Man is so critical with his heavy judging eyes,
Always finding faults in everybody's lives.
Killing, hurting, and destroying one another,
Whatever happened to the universal brother?
When we speak of pain remember it's self inflicted,
To all these materialistic things we are addicted.
Why do we think we're so great?
Remember, we're only evolved apes!

Victoria E. Hardy

dark streets

have you ever walked on darkened street
where trees whisper to you
and every far away blinking light
are eyes coming for you?

have you heard on those lonely nights
the rustle of leaves in the wind
and do they sound like scraping feet
from a consciousness of sin?

do you shiver and shudder on eerie walks
at the scurry of a cat
did the awesome wind shout at you
"hurry and don't look back"?

and as you ran, without backward view
did inches become miles
did dreadful sounds, in dreadful flight
become your courage trials?...

Lorraine Soo Storck

Sounding Good

Good Health for 100 Years, at Least!
Financial Tranquillity!
Quiet Discussions!
A Home Environment Undivided!
Our National Anthem!
All Instruments Played in Tune!
Birds Chirping!
The Splashings of Swimmers!
The Laughter and Giggles of Children!
Sinks That Drain Well!
Budgets and Checkbooks That Balance!
Beautiful Music!
A Cat Purring!
All Ovens That Are Entirely Self-Cleaning!
A Car That Never Conks Out on a Left Turn!
Excitement of Packing to Travel—Any Place!
A Large Ship, with its Horns Blowing—Leaving its Moorings!
The First Cry of a Newborn!
Every Bill Paid, When Received!
The Sound of the Theater, with a Hit Show!
To Be Able to Love Your Neighbor, as You Do Yourself!
To Be Justified in Saying, "I'm Worth It"!

Alice Mary Rachels

> *A hero is no braver than the ordinary man, but is braver five minutes longer.*
>
> —Ralph Waldo Emerson

The Little Things

It isn't the distance that one has to walk,
Nor even the problems when one has to talk.
It isn't the loneliness or yet sense of loss
Nor even the rivers that one has to cross.
Neither the mountains one may have to climb
Nor the fact that we don't ever have enough time.
The hardest part of our living this life
Are the small things that bring the hurt and the strife.
They may seem small but given enough time
They take their toll in our peace of mind.
The multitudes of our little strains
Little worries about our loss or our gains
Can wear us down and pull us apart
Destroy our lives and even harden our heart.
We can handle hardship, tragedy and sorrow
Looking ahead toward a better tomorrow.
We can do it all with much poise and grace
But things that defeat us, cause to lose the race
Are the small things that we failed to do
Hurt, like walking with sand in our shoe.

Tim Estes

Night

All I see is the light
In the window, through the night.
Alone in this house so big
Depression comes setting in.

Give me light, give me day
Send my blues all away.
Come the morning, come the light
Come the people, come the life.

People moving all around
Fill my emptiness with sound.
Happy am I in the day
Life goes on its merry way.

Dusk comes falling down
People run for sheltered ground.
Some go home to family dear
Some go home alone in fear.

Everything so dark and bare
Life is gone now, but where.
Alone and locked away
Waiting for another day.

All I see is the light
In the window, through the night.

John F. Grimshaw

Awakened

Promises made on impulse
As solid as a whim
Seen as legal contract
Notarized by him.

Prospect grew from dreaming
Of all the words he said
Rewinding and replaying
Those pledges in my head.

Messages that flattered
Weren't what they implied
Captured me and loved me
Then switched—the other side.

Wrapped around the words
That only last a minute
Bound to lines that shared the hope
My world would have him in it.

Promises on impulse
Graffiti on the wall
Words of transient meaning
With no ownership at all.

Living in his fantasy
Now awakened to my pain
Restlessly counting falsehoods
When shall I sleep again?

Nance E. Keyes

Untitled

The figure stands,
its vision clouded by gray sadness.
Sharp silver points reflect the past
as the red pool grows,
engulfing its victim.
At the point of death
a sound escapes,
disappearing
into the silence of peace.

Michelle Vuckovich

Of An Ending

The other Wind
that blew in this morning air
came prowling as this last summer

And circled my shelled thoughts
as a windy cloud that drifts
from a garden of rain

If only to chain its chant
of merriment in a dream and
sort neatly away in my house

Yet is a wind,
whose name is un-named
and presence felt, beyond a dream?

For I, a man was left a man
to this morning breeze, as all
my fears came when it passed.

Wilson Jackson

My Own Goodbye

Take from me my sorrow,
This life so filled with pain,
I've fought so many battles,
All of which remain,

So frightened of the future,
Unknowing what will be,
Where can I turn for comfort,
My only friend is me,

Tears no longer have a reason,
Emotions turn to stone,
Losing inner feeling,
I now must die alone,

To think it all would end this way
At last my peace is found,
Sleep that's never ending,
A world without a sound.

Steven Carol
Included in **About The Poets** Section

Cackling Hen

A hen lays an egg,
then cackles with relief!
More room out than in!
Her creation was no sin.

Clodah G. Summer
Included in **About The Poets** Section

Keelboat

Panache of the voyageur,
Of Mike Fink (gouging eyes
and biting ears),
It carried 3,000 pounds of freight
In thirty inches of water

Sail, rudder and
Six pairs of oars,
Or, "sweat la cordelle,"
1,000 feet of towrope,
moved freight.

Poles of turned
St. Louis white ash,
Herculean labors,
Walking the *"passe avant,"*
  "A bas les perches"
  "Levez les perches"
And wooden shoes in the mud
Propelled the freight...

And St. Louis Creoles,
Filled with salt pork, hominy and beans
Fiddled and danced
French reels into the
Starlit Mississippi night.

Katherine Stevens

I Have Answered

I lift my head
to Your violet eyes.
I weep inside
as I look to the skies.

Why do I weep
when I have so much?
Why don't I thank You
for Your Healing Touch?

Time has worked his way
into many history books.
But not one states information
on Your Healing Look.

You are so great
but they love You not.
They do not appreciate
all they have got.

I will be your servant
Your Golden Child.
I will do Your Work
so precious and mild.

Manini Bhakta

Me

Where am I going
What have I done
Have I expected a fountain
When there is none
Where can I find
Just why I'm here
I must seek out forgiveness
He will shadow all fear
My faith will be tested
But my love for God
Has been thoroughly digested
Alleluia, I'll praise, I'll pray
Without you dear Lord
There would be no today
The dawn meets the sunset
The stars shine above
My thoughts turn to you Lord
I'll give you my love
For you are my shepherd
I'm one of your sheep
Dear Lord you have promised
This kingdom I seek.

Alvera Gartmann

The Caretaker

Over the windswept land he rides.
A daily task of need.
To oversee a kingdom built
by blood and sweat and prayers.

What is there here that draws the man
to servitude and toil?
That makes a man forsake all else
but the land for which he cares.

What is the burning need inside
to nourish, to build, to grow?
To reap from this unyielding place
a monument of worth.

That when his life has ended here.
When love and labors cease.
His mark upon the land will say,
he served well, his piece of earth.

And when at last the debts are paid
and all accounts are given.
When man releases up his soul
to be measured for its worth.

Will God reward the final toll,
a judgment of value met,
To the earth that nourished the man
or the man who nourished the earth?

Jo Ann Jones

Dear Lord

Dear Lord, of all the things
You are aware of
You know I have wasted
All these years

Dear Lord, you have given me
An arm to lean on
And a strong hand to hold me
When I stumble and fall

You have loved me
All these wasted years
And me, Dear Lord
Not loving you back

You have strengthened
My faulty spirit
And brought cheer
To this lonely heart of mine

Dear Lord, with your arm to lean on
And your strong hand to hold
I may stumble
But Dear Lord, I'll never fall

Shelcie Crawford

Life and Death

Death is like birth.
The baby has no choice
In the matter of his birth.
And for a while he is
In total darkness
Alone and lonely
Being conditioned and
Prepared to be born
And live in this world.
That is the way death is also.
Like the baby
We have no choice in the matter.
If we are born, we will also die.
The grave, like the womb
May be dark and lonely
But we are being conditioned
And prepared for life
With God forever.
We are born alone
We must die alone.
No one can do it for us.
And both are for our good
And for the glory of God.

Bonnie McGill Cohn

A Teacher's Bequest

Just bury my body by the side of the Sea
In a rough pine box cut out for me,
Where the wind and the waves and the leaves of a tree
Will deepen my sleep as they whisper to me.

Perhaps a green plant, or else a wild rose,
Will feed on my corpse as it buds and grows;
Or still my remains may ascend in a tree
With the birds and the squirrels for company.

My Spirit has flown from death and disease—
Let it wander abroad—don't stifle it, please;
Whatever was good let it grow with the years,
Whatever was bad please drown it with tears.

My image will live—you can't keep it down—
On the face of some child my smile or my frown.
I'll not be offended at mimicry,
That smile, that grimace was a part of me.

Ida Adell Swanson

The Key

Knowledge is your key
To the lock of success,
The ticket to your trip on earth;
The extent of your knowledge
Determines your path,
Your effort determines your worth.

Delphine LeDoux

Mist on the Mountain

When the mist is on the mountain and the breeze is in
the glade, when the moon and stars have said Good Morning
to the sun, but it's still too early to need the shade.

When the early workers are sipping coffee and the day's wheels
have started to turn, then the open road is calling
and my heart begins to yearn.

That's the time I start out walking as I know that "motion is life,"
and because of all this walking I may
avoid the surgeon's knife.

So, if there are those who doubt me and they do not fully
agree, this is definitely their privilege, but walking is
still the best for me.

For when the mist is on the mountain and the breeze is in
the glade, if your only experience of all this beauty is
from a car window, or through curtain paneled lace, you
are missing some of God's Greatest Beauty until you're
out there walking, and can behold it face-to-face.

Don Mauldin

Travelin' on the Galveston Tour Car Track

Travelin' on the Galveston Tour Car road,
Down the winding road track,
In the red pew, miniature, seats,
And clinging to the steel rails.

Under the canopied-top street-cars
We are holding fast on the rail-line,
Travelin' throughout the flowered streets:
Pink blooms, white blooms, feathery-shooted
Blossoms circle round the romance of
Ambiance: against the salty sea winds;

We're holding desperately on—
In the big wind.
With or without hats, on the tour
Of the road of history, churches, the
Long-gone gold coast, and
Jean La Fitte's pirating, for the poor—?

Geneve Baley

A Ride Down the Mountain

A ride down the mountain, treacherous.
The landmarks few,
the unknown holds
many curves.

But there, a spot familiar.
There, a spot retraced.
I'm still unsure on this spot,
There! Yes! I know this place!

This place that is my haven,
This place that is my home.
I beggar dreams and rest here,
But when I am alone

I think about the mountain,
The hard and winding mountain.
With dangerous curves
Beckoning near.

Robert Errera

On a Cloudy Summer Morn

On a cloudy summer morn
At a corner I stood forlorn
A handsome couple came my way
Many thoughts came into play

On they quietly passed with grace
I know my life can improve its pace
Their cross was heavy and great to bear
My misery was nothing to compare

And while Life is often dull or mean
This couple made me feel serene
To see the bond between this pair
Transcends the love we try to share

A moving lesson is there for free
You need only look and see
The blind man and his dog

Steven F. Hoff

A dog is the only thing on earth that loves you more than you love yourself.

—*Charles Darwin*

Interval Between Winter and Spring

When catkins of the pussy willow
In channels along the roadside swamp
Are soft and puffy like a pillow,
Spring is moving in in stately pomp.

Across the bedsprings of open fields
Fluffy wisps romp and race with the wind,
Where silver mattresses, tufted and filled,
Await harrow and plow to begin.

A green spread starts its quilting artwork
Upon strips and squares of grassy mounds
Where patterns of leftover snow lurk
As though awaiting the tractor's rounds.

Beneath a canopy of sunlight,
Patched by bouffant clouds of lacy blue,
A coverall of heaven's delight,
Hovering expectantly, shines through.

It's an interval between seasons
When winter unsheathes love's cradle berth
And makes way for the many reasons
Why the world stands still for earth's rebirth.

Naomi Sullivan Rhoades

Spring

The groundhog's shadow now, he fails to see,
of snow and frost, the world is free,.
The crocus tells, "The tale of spring!"
Now we can hear, the robin sing.
Forth cometh too, the daffodil,
with all her yellow petal fill,
She proclaims: the Easter-tidings!,
and brings all life, from out of hidings.
The lily of the valley, sprouts for us in May,
to brighten up our warmer day.
The tulips, so erect and proud, they say "It's Spring!,
and Summer too, is on his way."

Marion Blakeslee

All About April

April is rain,—
funneled, flowing,
over the leaves,
starting to sprout.

April's vernal refrain—
voice of the breeze blowing
kisses to her who heaves
soul sighs of trust, not doubt.

Since Now with spring love is the main
theme among others worth knowing—
a credo for him who believes
that this is what life's all about.

Marie F. Petrocelli

Winter

Happy young men, dancing on frozen lands
with bouncing balls and masks of joy
they hold in their hands

Alone I walk as people move around,
but nowhere is a friend to be found.

taking my own ball to play with, they soon snatch it away.
I start to dance, but they laugh and move away.
So I stop.
This is not a dream—not a city street.
No calm waters to rest my feet.
Just myself on the waves of judgment.

I play with my red plastic boat,
it sinks—I let go.

This scar shows it all.
Please go away, back to your snow.
And leave me with my boat in the waters,
just let it rest.

Andrew Troelsen

Gone With the Wind of Time

A deathly dust among the roses as matter
has no intelligence and no sensation,
because spirit is light & matter is darkness.
The stream rises without desire no higher than
its source. The radiant sun of virtue and truth,
and love coexists with being. Manhood is its
eternal noon, undimmed by a declining sun....
Man governed by immortal mind is always beautiful
and grand. Each succeeding year unfolds beauty,
wisdom and holiness. Life and goodness are
immortal.... It is divine love that paints the
petal with myriad hues in flowers, and arches
the clouds with the bow of beauty: beauty, as well
as truth is eternal....
Blazing the night with starry gems; so is
morning light, star of revelation and progress.
Spiritus est lux, materia autem est tenebra.
*Post tenebras lux. Lux lucet in tenebris in
novissimo die.*

Allan De Fiori, P.N.

Untitled

I blow a kiss to the moon so bright
That shiny orb that lights the night
The clouds drift by, the shadows form
Is it a witch, a plane, a storm?
I watch intently as the clouds disappear
And the light returns that I hold so dear
Once again I smile as I look to the sky
The stars wink in unison as I wave goodbye

Beverly Jean Williams

Rustic Queen

Your heart of stone replaced the crown upon your head;
Flames of love are quickly put out
By your unfeeling rage.
With daggers of ice, you send away those who love you...
Building walls around you stronger than the castle in which you live.
With dispassion, you explode with no mercy for those in your kingdom.
Your throne of honor has chilled the blood in your veins.
In desperation you try to conquer,
In outbursts of rage, your love is shown to be hate.
Your robes of splendor are turned blood red...
This kingdom must be hell to you upon this earth.
With mental suffering, and sorrow, how you must grieve for your lost scepter...
Rustic Queen look for the Morning Star there in the east;
May it bring you peace
May it awake you before you fall asleep.
That we may remember your love;
And be released from the prey of your domain.
Yet my Rustic Queen, even now I do love you
Though to me you are dying.
Breasts full of milk;
Even now full of poison to drink.
I would to see you happy before I am dead.

Robert O. Pugh

Today Our Heavens Are Empty of Goddesses

Today our heavens are empty of goddesses,
Yet I only need to look upon you to find
The spur my heart needs to write not in impulses,
But in deep sincerity of your greatness over the nine:
Of only you can I write the epics of Calliope,
Feel love only expressed by enduring Erato,
And set it to music high enough for Euterpe,
So that it may be entered into the books of Clio.
In the sacred songs sung by Polymnia,
We will laugh and dance with Thalia and Terpsichore.
As the stars celebrate with Ruania,
Across the tales and fables of Greek folklore.
Perhaps I am only an old poet as you accuse,
But it is you, my goddess, who is the Muse.

Rob Bignell

Undefeated

If my line should die,
It dies with its teeth in the enemy's throat,
It dies with its name on the enemy's tongue.
For just as mere life is not victory,
Mere death is not defeat.
And in the next world I shall kill the foe a thousand times,
Laughing,
Undefeated.

Paul Costello

WINTERTIME.

To My Love

A precious heart beating next to mine
is what I hope for in time
breathing in the life of love
with grace, like an angel from above.

Emotions soaring, flying free
each thoughtful act does wonders for me,
We all hope true love comes to be
and this is what you are to thee.

A fountain of joy flowing free
be this, be this often for me
and may time find us lost
in the bliss of holy matrimony.

Tim Fritsch

The magic of first love is our ignorance that it can ever end.

—*Disraeli*

To Pisces, from Aries With Love

I am eternal youth,
the spark of life that
breathes in a newborn baby.
Mine are the eyes thru which it cries.
I am the rainbow after the storm,
the song of life that beckons to all.
Mine is the shining ray of hope
that flickers in every heart,
even into the darkest dark.
I am the wind that whistles thru the trees,
the mother of all things to be...

You are total, the grand sum
of all things that have come and gone.
Yours is the last step of the last mile.
In you we know we've fulfilled out lives.
Yours is the breath
reaching over oceans and plains,
carrying a promise of eternal inner peace.
Yours are the eyes that saw yesterday
and have seen past the morrow.

I am the beginning, you are the end.
Between us, we have everything...

Cathryn DeShields

Over You

It happens at the oddest times
    I think of you and

Sigh.

I think of you and cry
tears that cannot fall openly because I'm in an
elevator with people who wouldn't understand

Why.

I miss the moments spent with you,
I want to reach out and touch you,
to hear your voice, and to be with you

Again.

I would have loved your children, I said to you one
night as you cried tears that were made from lies
that entrapped you to me. You fell in love with me,
and I with you in love

Fell.

It happens at the oddest times
I think of you and hate you for the time we spent
together growing closer and only knowing now why
you had to leave me

Alone.

It happens at the oddest times,
    I think of you and sigh
    and ask myself

Why?

Jami Lynne Byron

Passing of Seasons

'Twas the season of our happiness
When Youth walked hand in hand
    With Cheerfulness for life's sweet sake,
And Joy reigned o'er the land.

    Sorrow was an unknown visage,
Whose presence was yet unfelt,
    And sunny days and starlit nights
Throughout the kingdom dwelt.

    Our hearts sang forth the song of life,
And we could ask no more;
    As Beauty danced with her sweet love
Across the ballroom floor.

    And yet the Ages sendeth forth
Her call to one and all;
    And soon Youth passes by us
With Beauty soon to fall.

    'Twas the season of our happiness
When Love and Life were free;
    And Laughter ruled a land of joy
That ne'er again shall be.

Doris Fulkersin Thomson

Untitled

As I looked out over the sky
I saw a little bird flying by,
Below the clouds, way up high
Flying by without a cry.

Walking round in fields of green
I notice things I've rarely seen,
A tiny squirrel, a little bird
They utter things I've seldom heard.

They do not worry about their food,
The Lord gives them things that are good.

Suddenly I heard a shot
All my fear I forgot,
I ran to where I heard the sound
The little bird on the ground.

I bent to see just how it was
But it was dead because,
It breathed is last, then expired
From the shot that was fired.

Oh, Lord! Oh, Lord! Please let it be
That I am not as cruel as he,
Who killed my friend just for pleasure
In an instance of justice I cannot measure.

Kathy Shearer

Anita, Eric, and the Owl

This morning as I lay
   warmly in my bed
the raucous cry of canada geese
sounded gladly overhead
I smiled, and in my mind I saw
   the majesty of the V

The grip of winter has loosened its hold

Later my son and daughter
   will walk the woods
to locate an owl heard calling
   in the noontime light

Song of eastern bluebird
   gladdened the hearts of my children,
and caused them to rejoice

They silently hiked a formidable hill
   and startled the errant owl—
He rose in the February light
   sun cast a golden glow on nonchalant wings

As their eyes followed his predictable flight
   he settled on a higher limb in a taller tree
calmly blinked, and disregarded their presence...
They smiled, and made their way home

Lillian S. Miller

Tragedy of the Daybird

Two small daybirds
Juxtaposed on the lowest limb of a tired willow
I take my gun a shoot the small one
And take the feathers and make me a pillow

Yet the other still sits there
Its mate beneath my sleepy head
And sometimes it would dream, I fear
And with that I were dead

Fly away little daybird
Or I will commit another crime
I want for you to know your friend
Will sleep with me throughout all time
And help me with my whirling mind
To chase away the dandelion
And listen for the children crying
Wondering if the bombs are flying
Praying that the day is dying
Hoping that the night is dead.

Walter J. Klimczak

TURTLE-DOVE

A Butterfly Died Today

A butterfly died today
during my coffee break on campus,
i spied a fallen Monarch
another one survived
skimmed the branches
of Eucalyptus;
my eyes address
the silent one
flattened by maintenance man's hose
some force tore off the wings
like tissue
moving me to be so moved,
and marvel
the arbitrary siege of nature
and we—also subordinate.
The hose continues.

Beth Ellen Jack

Harbor Town

A haze has settled over the island,
as we walk along the lulling harbor.
It's like a mist that wraps around us,
like the arms of love, drawing us near.
We come upon a tranquil green clearing,
and spread out our late night picnic.
You brought champagne and stolen glasses,
and we toast with an encompassing "thank you."
Eating cheese and crackers, sipping champagne,
we slip into quiet talk of ourselves.
Gazing up, we see our shooting star,
crossing the Milky Way like a message.
You rest your head in my lap,
as I speak slowly of our days together.
We share our innermost feelings,
and the moment becomes enchanting.
A calmness softly settles over us,
as we realize we have only hours left.
We speak of missing one another,
the difficulty of knowing we must part.
We know we'll hold fast to this time,
and the knowledge we'll be together soon.
As the dawn begins to filter through,
we know we've realized our dreams, together.

Debi Buettner

The Bringers Of The Morning Light

Towards evening's end
in the final corner of the August day
with the windchimes tinkling in the orange sunlight
we sat on the veranda swing ever so gently rocking to and fro.
The long, easy summer day
now so gradually diminishing into nightfall
seemed to be moving slow as a barge
and, in a sense, it felt just like we were passengers on board,
witnesses to the grandeur of great progression.
From within the pillared roof with the steps leading down
and above the banister, all around,
the moon and the stars were just faintly beginning to show
like islands in he seas of space.
And so it was that this was quite a time and quite a place
to have personally shared he stories of our separate lives
and to now have clearly seen how the child in each of us
had ventured to this particular place in time
where adults might appear sublime. In fact, how perfect it was
      to kiss you thereafter for the very first time
just as the night had appeared to settle in comfortably with
      good cheer
leaving the future to be the color clear.
Who would have guessed then as the swing came slowly to a
      halt
that this was the beginning of a lifetime we would spend
      together
and, later, an occasion in real life that we would exalt.

Gilbert Mowery

Missing You

Evening falls, my mind begins to wander.
A chuckle here.
A smile there.
From nowhere, the ache begins.
Deep inside, then it travels to the heart and lingers.
Slowly the hurt of missing appears, in silent streams of tears.
You hear nothing at all, but an old voice.
You listen, it becomes clearer.
It seems to be drawing nearer.
It's just as vivid as yesterday.
Pictured thoughts of you and he.
Your eyes closed, crying silently.
You are in that picture holding hands.
You speak, but the silence is deafening.
You squeeze tightly, but your hand is empty.
Love of missing is as strong, as the love of then before he was
gone
The picture begins to fade to grey.
As he turns to walk away.
"Please don't go, I want you to stay."
I know he can't hear a word I say.
I watch till the blackness slips in, and my dreams appear.
This is the only way I can keep him near.

Bonnie E. Nunes-Vendette
Included in **About The Poets** Section

Like the measles, love is most dangerous when it comes late in life.

—Robert Louis Stevenson

The Cool Blue Sea, Dreams and Sand Castles

While gazing out at the cool blue sea
Where Neptune's breeze still blows free,
Wondering where today will lead,
What will become of tomorrow's seed?
And as the waves come crashing to shore
I wonder who's keeping score.

The sea's tranquil sounds drift to the land,
Dreams and castles built of sand,
Visions reflect in the sun's light
Questions of who's wrong or who's right,
Remembering the past pains and sorrow
Dreaming about tomorrow.

Cheryl Ann Bryant

The Snow

I went to the snow,
One mourning alone,
Never to return
To the love of a mother,
Kiss of a lover,
Or embrace of a friend.
I left one cold day
Not planning to stay
For I took none of my clothes.
When I got there
I was tired and cold
They lay me to rest.
I brought no flowers
So they gave me some
For my long journey home.
The roses were as white as the drifted snow—
The carnations were as death.

Karen E. Snyder Schreck

A View Above

I donned my hat and coat
    to leave and take a walk
An inspiration came upon
    laid upon my very head
I sat and wrote, it came out good
I felt a luster, a feel of warmth
That I should be chosen
    to write a verse or two

I arose, went to the window
    removed my hat and looked up
    into the beauty of the sky
Said thanks a lot, that I've been chosen
    to write a verse or two

Bring to each a kind thought
    make life more grand, for all who read
Thanks a lot
    and I remain, your faithful servant
To serve until the end.

George E. Alexander

Mother, Mother Where Are You?
*I dedicate this poem to my beloved mother,
in wake of her passing.*

Mother, Mother where are you? ...with your face so pleasant
and your eyes so true. You were always loving, you were
always caring, Mother, Mother I won't be blue. But if I go
on sobbing and I'm forever sad, it's due to the depth of my
love for you. You gave so much of yourself, little did you
spare, and so much of yourself inspired everywhere. You
brought me in this world, showing me how to love; saying
thank the Lord for all I have and smile at the stars above;
live a fruitful life; try to be fair; and be good at the
things I do. Always do right and God will be there, to
shine his light on you. Oh Mother dear, I wish you were
here, for my love for you is so true, although you're distant
you still seem near, Mother, Mother where are you?

Kenneth M. Davis
*Included in **About The Poets** Section*

After Thoughts

If I had known the sorrow and depression
That would haunt me long after you had gone,
I would have been more loving and more caring,
And tried to bring you gladness with a song.
If I had only known.

If I had known these cold and wintry winds
Would chill me to the very bone,
I would have entreated you to linger,
And held you close and tried to keep you warm.
If only I had known.

If I had known the hurt which you had suffered,
Had understood the sorrow in your face,
I would have begged for your forgiveness
And tried to bring more warmth into our place.
If I had known.

I walk the streets and search the lonely faces,
Visit the favorite places where we used to go,
Call each day and night for word about you,
But spring is here and you have vanished like the driven snow.
If only I could have known.

Henry O'Grady

> *To expect more than your
> mother expected of you is
> expecting too much.*
>
> —William Feather

The Right Hand of God

Eighteen years, now I give her back to you
Well traveled, and now to your heavenly home
Just let her sit at your right side
Please God, she's got an urge to roam.

The rain will fall, I'll feel her touch
I'll see the snowbound fences, the snowflakes
she used to chase, I'll kick up leaves
the way she used to, cascading down her back...
I'll see her in every summer sky, lake, and
summer breeze, I'll hear her in the wind,
Every cloud becomes her face,,,she is everywhere
She walks with me,,,into, through,,,and beyond,,,,

She is not dead,,,not really gone
Just assumed a different form
In memory's chamber she lives with me
There is no pain,,,no age...nor time
Cremation, yes,,but your life force
Was God's love and energy,,,this can never be destroyed
Though changed in form, you help me fill the void
Loving you knows not of death,,,this cannot be destroyed.

Patricia M. Latzman

THE BEST OF FRIENDS.
(From the Painting by J. Charles.)

A Journalist's Guide to Friendship

A friend is one who, always,

Recognizes the what
Anticipates the when
Identifies the where
Understands the why

And, sympathizes with the how.

Anna-Rita Censi   Canada

Death of a Friend

I remember the day that Tinker died,
I called that morning to ask if she had survived the night;
Yes, but there was no improvement,
"We should put her to sleep," the Doctor said.

But could I do that?
To my friend, my constant companion of fifteen years?
Remembering the playful kitten only eight months old
Who had walked into my life and heart.

The girls said quietly, "Her heart stopped beating—just
    as I picked her up."
And I knew then that Tinker had held on just long enough
    for me to come.
Now, no need to say the dreaded words,
God knew I couldn't do that to this friend of all my years.

And Tinker, in her love, had spared me
The dreaded order she knew I could not give.
For suddenly, God had taken charge!
And there in that moment of our sad parting, I kissed her one
    last time;
And then like a slowly fading star, that dear little life
    quietly ebbed away,
And Tinker was in the arms of God.

Enid Mitchell
Included in **About The Poets** Section

Elegy

I reach back to rusty memories
and see her laughing eyes.
I try to imagine those eyes filled with rain,
but find only joy in the past.
She was born to laugh and love;
rainbows filled her days with gold—
        And Donna called to say
        Peggy's father died last night.

Way back in days of simple fun
when homework made us crazy,
life was rough, but we'd never cry (much);
we were young, and alive, and loved.
We never thought darkness could fall—
        But...Donna called to say
        Peggy's father died last night.

What should I give her? What can I say?
Words never seem to be what we feel.
How can I comfort when my soul is numb?
After words never said; after letters unwritten;
after all this time between places...
She's gotten along well all these years...
        Still...Donna called to say
        Peggy's father died last night.

Elizabeth Martin-Burk

*No bird soars too high, if he
soars with his own wings.*

—*Blake*

Memories

She knew the end was very near,
And her pleading voice, I can still hear.
I heard her, but tried to ignore,
by saying, things would be better, for sure.
But things were not better, only worse.
For soon, she was under the care of a nurse.
The days came, and the days went by,
And my rebellion to see her, outdid my try.
I was a coward, and I did feel a shame,
And here was no one else I could blame.
But the acts were obvious and very plain to me,
This fading side of her, I could not see.
I wanted to remember her and all of her dreams
And her great determination of life to its extreme.
Even through her pain, and pressure and strife,
And the verdict the Doctor put on her life
She gave of herself—Full and complete,
And challenged each day as a brand new feat.
She helped her neighbors, and kept in touch,
Until the strain of cancer became too much.
She tried and tried and made an effort to live,
But, finally, there was no effort to give.
then God came and claimed her soul,
Now she has peace, with Him in control.

Annie G. Federici

My Passion for Her

(from Journey)

My passion for her teemed my heart! I host her within, enhanced
   with beauty, My world in shine! Standing tall, as the origin
   of life, given birth to My soul, the suns, the stars! She is the
   mother of my earth! In her womb she carried my child! Time
   has come to trade in her past, and shine forth like a star!

Let the light spill forth a path through the doorway of her dreams!
   From here on black holes through white, shall give birth to
   life! She shall be adored as free! She shall splash the tears of
   hunger to extinguish! To drown all wars! Than trade in the
   warships for bread, to nourish the hunger-ridden millions!

Listen to the echoes of the moanings in the stillness of her heart!
   The petals of her soul shall not wither nor die! Gently dry the
   tears in her sheenless eyes! He! is churning your
   womanhood! Like weeds sprawling around your sprouting
   noble seeds! He turns in the young lives for warships, Death
   spinning his wheel!

He! Has failed to lead! Betrayed his world! Enslaved her noble soul,
   yet she whispered love in the dark! He! infringed on her life,
   still trespassing on her soul, her rights! I for one speak of her
   with love, only as a passerby! I call on you to take turns! Pass
   on to him your worn-out chains! Don't let him hammer
   more chains!

She must step forth to find her roots of strength! To reach out
   with workworn hands and lead! Disrobe his world from the
   fence and chain! My desire is to share the glorious liberty! To
   slip from sorrow into joy with all the women, shading the
   worn out chains!

Alien Star

Things Long Gone But Missed

As I sit in my favorite easy chair, I think back
about the decades of my life. I experienced true love
that endured through pain, tears, and strife.
I think about the things I miss since you passed away—
The sound of you and the children playing, outside during the day.
I'll never hear those wonderful sounds again.

The smell of your body, after a warm shower—
it lingered with me, for over an hour.
The sound of your voice, as it filled the room,
the dark and silence, is cruel in my desolate gloom.
For the years we were married, the good times will always shine.
I pray someday, it will once more be mine.

These tears, they mean nothing, as they fall from my eyes
to the ground, and land at my feet, without making one sound.
I will always cherish our love as it grew—
and never forget the joy of loving you.
These things, and so much more, are what I miss,
like the warmth of your arms, and the taste of your gentle kiss.

Rose M. Ruth

I Know He Cares For Me

I know there is someone beautiful out there who
cares deeply for me
When I feel desolate and uncertain—
Devastated by the onslaught of
loneliness and fear.
I have only to trust Him—
Stem the flow of tears—
And close the flood gate—
To know my God is near.

Though I can't see the warm smile on his gentle face—
I know he will always be there for me.
Silently and uniquely, plotting strategies—
in His mystifying way.
While couched in the bosom of His love—
God keeps a lonely vigil—
far up above.
To bridle any and all temptations—
That might tend to lead to some irrational or
unfavorable persuasion.
For my God is beautiful—
And He does care deeply—
for me.

Kate L. Buchanan

THE STILE.

Bluebonnets and God

I was lonesome one day, living all by myself,
So I thought I would just take a ride.
Along the Bluebonnet Trail I went,
And God was right there by my side.

The hills were ablaze with such splendor of color
By mere words simply cannot be told.
So I bowed my head and said, "Thank you, dear Lord,
For this beauty my eyes can behold."

I loved Him before, but since my Bluebonnet ride
I find myself loving Him more.
And joy fills my soul, knowing some happy day
I'll walk with Him on that Heavenly shore.

I cannot stop here, for there's work I must do
To tell everyone whom I see,
Christ will forgive all your sins,
Ask Him into your heart, and you'll be forever more free.

Mary Snow

Vietnam

The lovely green hills roll across the land;
Sweet and gentle is this earth of Vietnam;
A tender music guides me along the way;
A girl sits by the riverbank.

Her long black hair falls across her neck;
High cheekbones accent her almond eyes;
The water trickles by her quiet spot;
At peace with her graceful land.

The birds sing and swoop across the water;
A soft flute plays faintly in the distance;
La Vietnamiene—cô looks up at me;
A picture of eternal beauty is etched.

The setting is a cool and fragile scene;
A perpetual sight in the land called Vietnam.

Misha

The Burning Bush

When Moses tended sheep, and saw the burning bush
That burned incessantly, nor was consumed,
He fell upon his knees in consternation
And awe, to see the miracle.

    Through many years and many climes
    The burning bush came down to earth—
    A bush, consuming

        Woman, man, and child
        In fiery faggots of Inquisition
        And wars of conflagration.

And then the bush fell into evil hands again,
And swallowed children, mothers, fathers, maidens fair
In crematoria, in our times.

    But when the mightiest burning bush of all—
    At Nagasaki—
    Burned hordes of humans into cinders,
    It was itself consumed!

        I pray to God the world may never see the likes
        Of yet another burning bush!

Mary Schulman, Ph.D.

The Sermon

I should have remembered the lesson
that the minister was teaching, but
what I seem to remember is a tall
gentleman leaning back against the
snow white pew, slowly and majestically
sliding—
      Down,
          Down,
              Down.
Then suddenly his foot that was
awkwardly positioned on the corner
of the pew in front of him twisted,
then slipped; startling him, causing
him to snort and growl for it had
awakened him.
The awestriking experience provoked
the minister into losing his place
in the sermon. While he was frantically
rummaging through his notes, the minutes
seemed to take their time in passing
by the distinguished number twelve.
The seconds appeared to be afraid
of the bold, black number, almost
jumping back to escape his deadening grip.

April Morrison

Liquids

    The young poor misinformed black and
white men took off in the gray tin
cans to do what their government
said was obligatory to preserve the nation's democracy.

    So they lifted their guns and
killed the yellow men who were
trying to do the same as the white and
black; and then the yellow, black and
white merged with the blood red that found
itself seeping into the green divided land of Vietnam.

    Yet the red liquid was not the
only liquid to suffer from drying out,
as the clear tears began to run from the
eyes and roll down the cheeks of the white,
yellow and black children, women, men and, the
white middle and rich class students who
clamored and died at the hands of Nixon's idiotocracy.

    And today no one talks about why
the stain of blood and tears appeared—they
focus on the skeletal remains of MIA's—those
poor souls who never should have died in the
first place in that far away land of Vietnam.

Thomas Ward

Veteran's Day, 11 November 1987

The Rum Runner (In Birmingham, England)
...Steal away until the morning...

See the yielding red neon lights in the late evening
You walk through the mirrored entrance gates of the Rum Runner
and into the yard
Leading down to Birmingham's nightclub
Where you are deliberately blinded by the coloured lights
'cos they're so bright and they're shining it right in your eyes
Now caught in between fizzy smiles
All mesmerized by the video star on the screen
and the nite romantics spinning in the mirror ball
in lover's arms—hear the strains of music heavy in the air
Imaginary perhaps—but undeniable all the same
add a warm welcome to their isolation
so that they can call it paradise without occasion
Deep voices heave in the unreal silence as heady nights
of excited chatter and plots play around the doorman
Dark and brooding hazel eyes will overstay the official sign
Okay you just might be right this time
and break the warning siren
at last compromised by cocktail parties
and misty visions
When this all contrives one scheme
saved at their rum runner's expense

> *Tatjana S. Casvellun*
> Included in **About The Poets** Section

It Was Just One of Those Things

She was a pal, you know...the family friend, his wife?
We'd stolen moments once or twice, touching the dream
And even teased our flesh some, but only in a wish some
It was just one of those things

Well, the kids grew up and our lives grew weary
I fled my wife, as she fled me, and found a better story
And so my pal set out to seek her own riches, fame and glory
It was just one of those things

But her house needed mending and her kids needed tending
Her soul needed rending and her back, well...it needed bending
So she offered me her love but with nothing really pending
It was just one of those things

We stirred up words of long ago that warmed our souls
And joined as friends and lovers, nuzzled against the cold
But her quest for rainbows...well, it was greater than my hold
It was just one of those things

Now I have no friend no pal, my table's set for one
But behind she left a treasure, all the passion of our pleasure
So my heart recalls her rightly, my body yearns her nightly
It was just one of those things

John McAlister

The Blue Collar Goose

Looking down from the high tower of the ELECT
all barrels are pointed at the blue collar Goose
who they think Got Loose
and a move is on to kill,
The long suffering, laboring well plucked and fleeced,
blue collar goose that laid the proverbial Golden Egg,
is now in effect.
The last of the big time spenders
can never be big time lenders
with high interest rates knocking at the loan sharks gates
and with the economy in dire financial straits
Heaven will have to wait
Borne out of necessity,
the answer at the eleventh hour,
may have to be a stroke of fate.
God only knows the hour may already be too LATE.

> *James R. Peacock*

Silent Rage

Sometimes I get so angry, I just want to scream
and sometimes I do
Sometimes I get so upset, I just want to cry
and sometimes I do
Sometimes I feel so ugly, I just want to disappear
and sometimes I do
Sometimes I feel so alone, I just want to injure myself
and sometimes I do
Sometimes I feel so hurt, I just want to die
and sometimes—I don't

> *P.R. Young*

A STREET IN HELIGOLAND.

Daddy's Footsteps
(Dedicated to Ken Michael and the memory of his late father Paul)

Little boy on his daddy's knee
Air Force stories of medals glistening
Planes soaring like birds uncaged, and
Blue skies
Little boy listens...
Dreams of the day
He too becomes a hero
How proud Daddy will be
When he follows
in his footsteps.

Debi Barrett

The most important thing a father can do for his children is to love their mother.

—*Rev. Theodore Hesburgh*

Helping Him Grow

To look at the world with a child's point of view,
Is sometimes a task, not easy to do.
But try it just once. And you will agree,
A boy's trust and love can grow tall as a tree.

Encourage a boy to stand tall and erect.
And soon you will see you have gained his respect.
Be honest and firm, yet bend when you need.
He'll learn his self-worth, since you planted the seed.

Let a boy make mistakes, be allowed more than one,
By himself he'll discover, it's not too much fun.
He'll make his own path, he'll learn the right choices.
With patience and love he'll hear the right voices.

Teach a boy he can laugh, at himself, it's okay.
We all have our flaws, we'll outgrow them one day.
Be kind and be patient, don't ever ridicule.
By himself, you'll discover, he's learned the golden rule.

Teach a boy a set of values, not too high, not too low.
He'll feel good about himself, be a joy to watch grow.
If you do all these things, I promise one day,
A good man he'll be for you showed him the way.

Dorothy Litz

For Sean

I was there when you first appeared,
Among tense excitement, sweat, and tears;
Anxious of your coming
Into this world of violence and fear.

Then in my arms you were placed,
And I gazed upon that angelic face;
So meek and so mild,
Blessed with peaceful grace.

Eyes that sparkle at each new sight,
Little hands that squeeze me tight;
I will be at your side
As you grow and reach new heights.

You are the future,
You are a beginning;
To give the world hope,
And a chance for winning.

Ken Turner

Daddy

I remember the things you used to say
How you had your own special way
The color of your eyes so pure
The strength of your hands which made us secure

The sweat of your brow which kept us fed
The lessons you taught, the way you led
The integrity you kept throughout your life
The earned respect of your family and wife
Your love of nature and things of the earth
you valued life and knew its worth

Out of yourself, you gave us the best
Your hunger for life and all its zest
You taught us of things past and those to come
Where we were going and where we were from
You taught us your faith in God above
And showed us his grace by the depth of your love

You were busy at living and laughed at death
And probably smiled as you took your last breath
For the voice that called was one you knew
The kingdom of God was familiar to you
A place for you had long been prepared
The Glory of God was waiting to be shared

On especially bright days, as the wind flutters by
I wonder if its you giving your wings a try
And as the hour begins to get late
I long for the day we'll meet at the gate

Bonnie Spotts

The Substance of Our Connection

Because I could not stop for Death,
He kindly stopped for me;

She was a woman who birthed two children,
a corner of her mind always alert to them.
She would not back into corners of compromise.
Her life kept its rewards as long as she gave
to others, through love, through friendship.

The carriage held but just ourselves

I see our heritage, a line of women
believing in tomorrow. I see her pleased
once more with remembrance of international
alliances spanning generations, rendering
the present infinite.

And Immortality.

One moment she was lace as delicate as gossamer,
a woman who cherished dreams, self-reliant
in her will. Love unraveled thread by thread like
a tattered sweater, leaving formless shreds
which she gathered and rewove into knitted beauty.

Lois Young-Tulin

Smile at the Moon

The belligerent sky permeates our behavior
Inching mankind to the edge of precipice
All standing at a celestial crossroad.
The moon smiles down turning us to
A new perilous direction commanding that
True answers are in our souls.

In depth of despair we stand alone with God.
Mostly silenced as we gaze at the moon's changing colors.
Some of us only brushing with crisis
Others meeting it head-on.
So lower your expectations as you peer at the afflictions
In the sky with all its terrestrial activities.

The full moon is sprinkling the last of the evening's
Silvery moonbeams over our troubled sleeping places.
We gaze at the disc set in the heavenly blue.
It illicitly touches our emotions and thoughts
Helping our consciousness to become clearer.

Smile at the moon, as man and heaven proposes and disposes.
Then listen to the small voice within.
Smile at the moon for the great wheel of destiny
Does not stop turning as we gaze at the fading eclipse.
Bring more of yourself to life; for what you are
And what you can do will no longer govern your living.
So watch the terrestrial sky and smile at the moon.

Effie Ritsche
Included in **About The Poets** Section

Fisherman on the Wharf

Against a brilliant summer morning sky...
    a flock of geese
      encircles the marshes,

While the strong scent of the salty breeze mingles
    with that of the
      fishy bay waters...

It permeates my senses. Childhood memories of lapping waves...
    sand, seashells
      course through my mind,
And I think, "How time has flown...!"

Gulls still perch on the pilings, Pleasure-crafts gently rock
    at their moorings...to the rhythm of the flowing tides.

Haunched over the bulkhead, sits an old man...with a
    weather-beaten face, he hides under a worn fishing
      hat...firmly gripping the rod.

He gazes intently on the waters, expecting a tug on the line any
    moment...by an unwary fish eyeing the
      tasty morsel on the gleaming hook.

Absorbed in thoughts of his own.

A picture of peace...in his world of this moment...oblivious
    to the waking sounds
      of nearby businesses...

The scurrying feet of the working folk...or increasing sounds of
    traffic...that will soon...
      break this sense of tranquillity.

It is another dimension of time...for this solitary figure...at home
    with God...nature...the
      beauty of dawn.

Never aware...that he's not alone....!

Irene Passarella

LUTTERWORTH.

Lady Liberty

After many years of darkness
as Americans we knew.
Our lady in the harbor
cried out to me and you.

One hundred years have passed her by.
And the symbol for what she stood
was slowly crumbling, just falling apart
of neglect, from me and you.

So finally, in 1986 a campaign
throughout the land,
did raise enough, to rise the hand of,
Lady Liberty again.

Her torch, once more does light the way
to ships, that pass her by,
and in my mind, I know you felt,
the way I feel inside!

That, freedom is a great big word and
her torch will light the way,
to every man and woman in America today!

Dawn Henry

---

*Defeat is for those that
acknowledge it.*

Freedom

I sit. I think. I wonder.

The down trodden; the oppressed.

The last drop of blood,
the last fleeting breath,
the flashing of the blade,
as men went to their death.

For whom the fires of freedom must forever burn,
a lesson from history yet to be learned,
The stroke of freedom's blade shall forever be,
until freedom prevails, and all men are free.

Yet ignorant, heartless tyrants press on with vengeance.

Freedom sounds from the four winds that blow,
haunting every soul that it yet does not know,
With thundering war clouds seemingly far away,
ready to quickly gather most any day.

I shudder!

I cry.

Willard Lee Skelton

Christmas Joy

The animals all gather round,
Donkeys, cows, and sheep.
They somehow know this special night,
Not to make a peep.

For in the barn, amidst the hay,
A Child was born to Mary.
A special star lit up the sky,
So travelers need not be wary.

The Blessed Mother held her Child,
Tightly to her breast.
In the stable, cold and dark,
She was but a guest.

There's nothing like a newborn babe,
With skin so soft and sweet.
Downy hair and hungry cries,
Tiny hands and feet.

This Babe will be our Savior,
If the world would only see,
That little baby, Jesus,
Was born to set man free.

Margaret A. Grafton

Untitled

"Go to the mountain young man
go to the mountain, I say,
go young man, as fast as you can,
go to the mountain young man.

Fight with the lions
young man, if you can
and feed the sheep on your way;
charm all the snakes
that cross your path
but make sure you don't delay
and climb the mountain
as fast as you can
to reach the top, if you can."

I did heed the advice
of the old wise man
and climb the mountain I did.
When I reached the top
I felt like a man
and enjoyed the splendid view:
and I thought of the old and very wise man:
He had climbed the mountain too.

John Bookis

Untitled

How fast my heart was set for sail
Disillusion never entered my mind.
Never was the will to fail;
Love was hardly ever mine.

How graceful and free
Was my heart at sail.
Never was the harbor set in mind for me.
Never was the will to fail.

My heart was caught by the wave of honesty.
Winds of trust swept my away—
Trust filled my mast quickly
And sent me astray.

A new experience set in my heart
And the harbor came to view.
Soon my heart furled and from the sea I did depart
To stay in the harbor of love with you.

Soon, I knew my heart was fain.
How glad I was to go—
Hoping and praying to experience no pain
And stay in the harbor of love and never forgo.

Carrie Wells
Included in **About The Poets** Section

Love Is

Love has no limits like the hands of time.
Love is an ever growing feeling,
Seldom going 'round and 'round
Like the hands of a clock.
But growing stronger and stronger
Like the winds of the ocean.
Blowing the ship across its way.
The cool breeze,
The peaceful sunshine you make me feel each and everyday
No words could ever say the way I love you baby.
"I LOVE YOU!"

Renaldo Tyson

She Walks in Beauty

She walks with the fluid grace of nobility.
Ever caring, ever sharing her unboundless gift of love.
Eyes that shine like diamonds in a star lit sky.
As a breeze ripples through her soft flowing hair.
Her graceful captivating movement of splendor.
Her voice a gentle whisper in your ear.
The sound of heavenly music within her loving embrace.
She walks in beauty as though a celestial body
surrounded by heavenly Angels.
She walks in beauty this creature named love.

Dodie A. Nash

On the Edge of Forever

We were on the edge of forever
    until the distance pulled us
    from the edge.
From the moment I fell in love with you
    there was nothing that could pull me
    away from you.
But, you have weakened and let the
    negativism of distance prevail.
Each day my love for you has grown,
    it kept me believing and kept
    my spirits alive.
Why are you letting the distance win?
It has beaten you because you are
    no longer in love with me.
The distance has not beaten me,
    I am still in love with you
    and I'll never forget how we were...
    on the edge of forever.

Elizabeth Ann Stanciu

Immortal Love

The moments we shared were so precious,
    But few.

It seemed that our lives were joined,
    With an eternal glue,

Our souls exchanged voices,
    Our hearts were in unison.

We became one without ever knowing,
    When this merger had occurred.

It seems that neither time nor distance,
    Has permeated this bond,

Our love shall remain forever,
    Sheltered from extinction.

With our spirit and our flesh,
    Melted into a single co-existence.

We are soulmates, with our love taken
    Beyond the three-dimensional world.

We will love each other,
    With invisible passion.

From distant shores,
    We have come together.

Not wanting to say goodbye,
    During this finite life,

Only to look forward to the next
    From within our immortal love.

Anna Zacchia

BOLSOVER CASTLE.

My Castle Heart

In my heart,
There are many tiny little rooms,
Like the bedrooms of a castle.
Filled with memories, dreams, laughter, and tears,
That were shared with the people in my life.

But, in the living room of my heart,
Where the fireplace and hearth would be,
There's nothing left of the raging fire,,
Except, tiny burning embers.

My soul echoes,
Like empty chambers of a tomb.
I walk the empty halls,
Finding only fragments of what used to be.
For when you left,
You took the dreamer out of me,
And now—
I'm left with what used to be!

Marlene May
Included in **About The Poets** Section

Night Harmony

Falling to the west
Rising to the east
The contradictory suns meet.
In the same sky
Dark with red,
Lights dot the top over my head.
Gentle breeze blows through the night.
Silence falls, this is the still, with little light.
The grass settles,
Only slight movement by the wind.
Night animals stalk,
Day animals sleep,
Most is peaceful,
The world will keep.
Til tomorrow when the sun rises bright
Morning comes to wash away the night.

Shawn Daubert

Recollections of an Aftermath

I believed him to be my last refuge.
He looked like a Don of Dons.
This "Nine Days' Wonder" now yesterday's deluge.
I looked again, he's a John of Johns.
John-a-Nokes and John-a-Dreams
Had my leeward heart on her marrow-bones.
Eternally moribund that affair now seems,
But somewhere a faint echo carries past moans.
Bacchus and a Midsummer-Moon Madness conspired.
In harmonious unison they laughed in my sleeve.
My Knight o' the Post swore evil retired,
Then gave me "Anne's Fan" as he'd ready to leave.
A red herring was he who gently took my hand
And seduced me on the high road to Needham.
At sixes and sevens was I, and with nowhere to land.
So a Johnny Raw became I vowing someday to beat him.

Constance Warner

Time To Rumble

Round up the boys we're going to have a rumble tonight. Make sure you tell them to bring their bats, knives, and chains. We're going to show them how tough we really are.

So many times we've been assaulted by them, but tonight it'll all be changed when they invaded our turf, and took our women. That is too much it's time to rumble.

We are the stingers, and they are the creepers. We shall meet them in the park in the heat of the night. We're going to show them that we can't be pushed around.

Here I am walking down the streets as my gang gather behind me. People saw us come, and they got out of our way. No one was coward by the look of our faces to have a rumble.

They say the creepers outnumber us, but that doesn't mean we can beat them. This kind of gang fight will tell us who is a man, and who is a coward. We must fight to survive in the rumble.

Jesse Centeno

Finder

Finder oh where are you oh finder? I have lost myself within
dimensions of the earth, dimensions yet to be comprehended.
Understood only by finder for he is owner of these dimensions.
Play the strings with life oh finder, for my spirit weakens to
the sins of my past, present and future as it draws upon itself.

A. Blane Roberts

TWO NOODLING LUMPS OF FLUFF.

The Victors

They came in disordered files, appearing and disappearing
Within the boundless sweep and swell of a violent winter's
storm-scape;
Warriors astride shaggy ponies—kin to those of Aurignacian
times—
Riding as though no cold, of the deepest kind, could touch them.

Man and horse breathed an air too rarefied to fill their chests;
Hoar-frost ghosts danced from ice-crusted nostrils.
The creak of leather, brittle as the air.
Co-mingled with the sounds of beast and man gear,
Whispered and sang a muffled dirge midst horse crunch,
Darkening the deep snow mantle as they passed.

Tattered banners tangled by the whip of winter wind;
Men, weapons, ponies—all tattooed with talisman blood crusts.
Snow-peaked, grisly, medusa-like heads looked down from sky-
stabbing pikes.
Fierce death-faces watched as the victors marched from old
conquest to new battle.

Wending across the shadowless hills, blurring the near horizon
The victors, bearing their tokens of past battles,
Ride to other encounters, unending—
In columned ranks... Forever.

James T. Forrest

Untitled

In the darkness of the night
I creep

In the shadows of the after dusk
I am a thief

I slither into your sacred bedroom
I hiss

My hot fetid breath
causes a stir in your slumber

My black and rotting nails
brush against your young cheek

I slide the tooth
from beneath your pillow

To replace it with my pouch
of thirty silver dimes

Then hovering toward the window
I am a breath upon the sill

I unfurl my leathery black wings
and into the night I go

Sleeping children await me
They make payment with their teeth
for my thirty silver dimes

Shawn

Rags of Honor

Honor to the unarmed
And occasionally unwashed crusade!
—Tilting at politicians leading
Us into war, it wears no gallant
Uniform—some among disheveled
—Thoroughly disrespectable
—Few medals but ribbons and maybe
A flower. They protest through
Improper channels: namely, graffiti
On public walls—Their deeds unsung
In city parks or halls, or carved
On phallic marble sprouting
Village greens. Their names are not
Chiseled in soldierly lines as if
On parade and even in death
Saluting still, to posthumous authority,
Saluting in turn, laying wreaths
On Remembrance Day;
And making pretty speeches
That are not pretty because
The men that they are honoring
Had all been sent
To their graves

Jonathan Russell

The Real Beauty

The canopy of blue
That covered the day,
Was alive with singing birds.

The grass at our feet,
Was a green velvet carpet,
Decorated with purple and white.

The medley we heard,
As we walked by the stream,
Was a song of love and of joy.

But as we sat 'neath a tree
In those newly born woods,
You brought real beauty to my life.

You took my hand gently,
And patted it once or twice.
Then you looked into the depths of my soul.

Then you spoke those special words
I was longing to hear:
My love, please be my wife.

Robin Tuggle

The secret of friendship is to make first impressions last.
—Arnold H. Glasgow

Spring Revealed

Somehow I had forgotten
   how deceptive spring can be,
I envision golden daffodils
   and blossomed apple trees.

But as of late, nature's ways have
   opened up my eyes
And now I see all too well
   Spring's dance without disguise.

Through the glass I see trees bend,
   Heavy with the wind.
Pressing down their branches
   the pelting rain begins.

Bolts of lightning crack and snap—
   thunder charging through the hills,
Blossoms hanging on for life—
   I pray for my daffodils.

We've nearly lost our garden soil
   to hail, and wind, and rain—
But just before it washes out
   the sun smiles out again!

Betsy Wotton

Untitled

As leaves have fallen through the years
They faintly remember the joys, the tears
Of passing summers where lovers met
Under the willows that silently wept.

Under the willows the grass was so green
Children played in the cooling stream
And lying upon the fragrant grass
We dreamt of summers past.

Back to the days so young, so free
When I thought time would remain with me
But now I await the hour we'll meet
Under the willows that silently weep.

Candace Arnette

Much More Than Gold

I am not lonely, I do not fear:
   I cannot see him, but I know he's here.
To Him I sing, to Him I pray...
For "He" leads me, all night and day...
   He touched my heart, He touched my soul:
   To me "He" means, much more than gold.

He is my savior, He is my god,
   He is my Christ I fear Him not:
Now don't misunderstand me: I do fear the Lord:
For every step I make, I know He's in my Heart...

Julie F. Rios

Honorable Mention
Timely Trickery

When I was a child
   time dragged its heavy step
   like booted feet through a pond.

Time skipped me through adolescence,
   a hopscotch game—sometimes pausing
   then—turn—jump—and gone.

It danced me through sunny summers,
   Christmas upon Christmas,
   whirling through the years called prime.

Now I've watched the dragging, skipping
   and dancing of my own child pass,
   as if it were one fleeting moment in time.

The golden years upon me,
   time to enjoy the fruits of my labor
   and the wisdom born of trial.

Ah—If I could but make time
   drag—skip—and dance again
   instead of fly—this last mile.

Linda Sanders

I Cry a Tear

I cry a tear, not a single tear.
No, a tear that falls,
A tear that collects, multiplies, and builds.
A tear that forms a river.
A river not seen, seen with the human eye.
A river only felt with the heart.
This tear is a strand, a connection, a missing link, in the ocean of
my soul.
You were my safety, my refuge, my soul support,
Then one day, you; vanished, leaving my tears to the treacherous
waves.
The waves of emptiness, loneliness, and longing.
Long suffering was raging, swallowing, pulling me under.
Then you reached down your hand; grasping mine.
Overwhelmed with joy; excited, relieved, baffled.
Had you come back after all?
Did you only stray, not knowing; not realizing,
Not understanding how I needed you?
I was pulled just to see you turn your back
And vanish
As I slipped deeper and deeper into the anger
And the pain and the sorrow that rested
At the bottomless pit of the everdrawing loneliness
That awaited each memory in the desire
Of my
Soul.

Charles E. Brewer
Included in **About The Poets** Section

Ruth

In the stillness, silent and full of light, I am centered
and amidst the beauty of all things, God-given, I think of you.
Gazing out my window over mountain tops and trees,,
(trees that sing me to sleep at night),
I am witness to a family of soft blue clouds dispersing...
moving away from each other...symbolizing change...inevitable
change.

We are family like these clouds. Blue, soft and loving.
Each with a purpose. Each on a journey. A beautiful skyward
journey.
And now one of my family is traveling southward. Not too far...
yet far enough still to beckon a tear...
and quite possibly a gentle rain of tears.

Each member of our cloud family is essential and you are a unique
and giving fragment of fragments that brings us all closer
to completion, closer still to the purpose of our journey.

I wondered a moment ago if one solitary blue cloud could shower
enough love upon the earth to make a difference. And now I know.
The answer is "yes."

In the stillness, silent and full of light, I am centered
and amidst the beauty of all things, God-given, I think of you,
feel your energy...your love, and I know that you feel mine.

Beautiful cloud, God bless you.

White Feather

Friends

Friends are people you can trust
every day every night
from dawn to dusk

They are shoulders to lean on
when nothing goes right
cause they are your friends
and they will show you the light

They help you in ways no other can
by being your friend
and giving a hand

That's what a friend is
can't you see
it's the perfect solution
for both you and me

Eric Fleming
Included in **About The Poets** Section

SUNFLOWER DADO.

Untitled

See not what is here.
Go beyond mortal sight,
into the mind's eye.
Feel things not felt,
in a lifetime of sorrow and despair.
Recall the few, forget the many.
Believe what you will,
for life is only what you perceive.
The righteous will condemn the multitudes,
to a fiery hell.
Eternal sadness reeks from one's very pores.
Yet there is the smallest hope,
And we shall cling to that desperately,
fearfully.
Wanting to truly believe that goodness will prevail.
It matters not. It matters not at all.
These things shall come upon us.
There is nothing to prevent fate itself.
Not hope nor dreams will change its destined course,
for us all.

Melanie Higginbotham

A Marriage

Antique lace and pearls, a symbol of purity.
A heavy ring on a plush pillow carried by a
small boy who keeps wiping his nose on his
sleeve and whispering, "I have to go to the
bathroom." You both kneel for your blessing.
As you kneel, the words "Help Me" written on the
bottom of your shoes are exposed and bring out
a short laughter among the assembled. A tearful
whimper from the parents, mostly the mothers
because their babies are getting married today.
Vows are exchanged and finally lips meet. And
now, in front of God and everyone, you both have
become one person. You walk back down the aisle
among the blessings and cheers. The new bride
steps on her dress and falls, gracefully of course,
to the floor. Bummer.

Tammy Pack

Only A Few...
Like You

There are people that you meet,
who say that they care for you
in a special way.

There are people that you meet,
who brighten up your day
and send you on your way.

There are people that you meet,
who you could never repay,
no matter how hard you try.

There are people that money cannot buy.
There are people that leave
memories that will never die.

There are people whose lives they've shared.
There are people who have
cared and cared.

There are people who will never be forgotten.
These kinds of people are all in you.

That's who this poem is written to.
In this world, here's only a few,
only a few people like you.

Rodney Stover

Magician

I can scale the perpendicular slope
    and ski the avalanche it causes.
I can streak the sky with red and green
    and capture rainbows in plastic jars.
I can pluck harmonies from tether strings
    and sic music on captivity.
I can dance on sparkling sunbeams
    leaving footprints on the dawn
    and discuss philosophy with daisies
    and make what's gone return again.
I can even create someone in you
    you want to be
    or already are.

I make all these possible
    with the loan of a mind
                an eye
                and a pen...
And I will soar with falcons
    run with gazelles
    talk with stars.

With these tools
    let me perform magic for you.

    A. T. Palmer

The Drop

Went skiing, just the other day, my skis and me—
Goin' down the mountainside, just as free as the breeze.

When along came 'the drop'—SWOOSH! went I
Landed skis straight up, yes, face down I lie

What a predicament, facing down in the snow
Couldn't cry for help; couldn't get up and go.

When along came a stranger, skiing down the mountain
Stopped to take a picture. His giggles were a mountin'

"Here's a fair maiden," thought he, "a-posing for me."
"Looks as though 'the drop' caught her and her skis.
I suppose I'd better help her, cause nobody's here.
Sure makes a pretty picture, her and her gear!"

A diggin' in the snow, he was sure to help me out
It was most embarrassing, I could say without a doubt

For this handsome stranger caught me by surprise
Yes, he helped me out of 'the drop' before my very eyes

He helped me to my feet, and decided he should go.
Left me with a start, a standing in the snow.

It'll be a long time, before I ski 'the drop'
'Tis the ending of my story guess I'll have to stop

When you ski down a mountain, look *way* yonder
So you never go too far, and never seem to wander

Into the very spot 'the drop,' me and my skis
Goin' down the mountainside, just as free as the breeze.

    Jeanne J. Peterson

An Hour's Keep

Tenderness is temporary,
Today, a cage of tyranny;
Your warmth passes like a comma
Or some other interruption,
A little time flooding out reason
Making secret spines
To build today's cage.
At night I remember white hands,
The square nail its own base of reason,
And the long graze against my hair.
I cannot sleep,
The child revisited
Turns back into self.
The street scrapes into dawn,
Each noise taking someone
Into ways of living and other loving.
I find my hand dry again,
Against the departure of that hour,
Your words strangle me,
I have no claims,
Cannot pretend,
The wind ruffles,
Runs into the leer,
Tenderness is temporary.

Diane M. Moore

Question

The girl with no name is left standing in the rain
She wishes she could be that girl with so much energy
But the part in her that holds her back
Will never let her get on the right track
The happiness in her is ready to burst
Yet she is held back by one small hurt
She knows she must step out of this sorrowful trance
So she can run and leap; learn how to take a chance
Her friends don't deserve to have to cope with this
    mysterious child
But should be introduced to the real one—the child of the wild

Lori Adam

WINGED GLEANERS.

Prenatal Care

Walking is a rhythm my feet make
to the squeak-squeaking stroller
wheels rolling over yesterday's
tread:
up the hill,
            then down.

Only half-listening to the droning
toddler's complaint,
I note the dried leaves
and brittle twigs
scraping the curb
with the onrush of cars.

Quietly, carefully pushing
one toddler to sleep and rocking
another baby yet to be,
I breathe in long and deep
and think:

Meanwhile,
palm trees shoot above sharp-edged
roofs and tickle the monotonous
sky, and sunlight
turns the green leaves white.

Walking is good for the soul;
it's a rhythm my heart makes.

Deborah W. Doolittle

Just Like A Child

Just like a child I've come to see the world we know, my destiny
With faith in all and outstretched hands
With upturned faces and dreams that span eternity

Just like a child that's what I am
A trusting soul, who questions all, and longs to understand
And like a child who's trusted all, then had to watch his heroes fal
And with a face all wet with tears gave way to doubts throughou
    the years
And changed the child who used to be into the person you now se

Just like a child to see the good expecting to be understood
And trusting everyone around Oh see what I have found
A little child who's laid to rest, his head upon his mother's breas
His heart is beating in his chest so softly there's no sound

Just like a child who's gone away, maybe just outside to play
Or maybe very far away never to come home
A heart just like an open book, and everything they saw they too
Until here's nothing left to give and no reason left to live
Oh isn't it a crying shame the things we do to children in love'
    name.

Gloria Avila

Honorable Mention
For Audrey

To breathe
the tranquil air
of a troubled earth
on this once again
somber day
I must pause
to consider

How deep must the water be,
How high must heaven wait
As I stand lost between

And yet there
are roses in springs
and
my feet lie in the greenest
grass of all
and
my heart feels gravity

But I soothe my soul with sleep
and every dream is
to breathe
the tranquil air...

Alex B. Pinero

First Love

A flame licks the air
Sending heat toward the sky,
Love burns beyond
Into oblivious cries.
A lover's breath—
Still, quiet and near,
Ever to be soft
Upon a young girl's fear.
Listen to the wind
Moan upon the earth,
Exalt at the joy
Of love in birth.

Kim Fortner

Shame on U.S.

Our boys died
Over there
All of them
Even the ones
That came back
To strangers
Who wouldn't listen
As strangers
Who wouldn't talk
It's not American
To lose
But they wouldn't
Let you win
It was fixed
War is not funny
Over 50,000 men
Did not die laughing

shame on u.s.

Yvonne W. Murzen

Challenger

There should have been noise.
A scream like a thousand tortured souls.
It should have raked the raw skies,
and clawed the naked earth.
Instead, there was silence.
Nothing; save the writhing flames,
and plumes of smoke,
inscribed on the dead blue heavens.
For them do I cry.
I cry for the lost humanity,
I grieve for the dreams unfulfilled,
the sights unseen,
I mourn for those left,
those who had to watch in horror,
the conflagration of the seven.
In my soul there is a scream.
But in the air, only silence.

Maryellen Doughty

Untitled

We're not together anymore
but i'm not crushed.
It was nice while it lasted
but it was pure lust.
There's so much
to say and do
to get you back
if I wanted to.
I don't care
now that you're gone.
It's in the past.
Life does go on.
Sorry to assume
but I thought you knew.
The sun will rise
without you!

Cindi Martinez

Vigilante

Neon-lit streetwalk,
Old cobbled ground;
Eased through the glass
scattered all around.

A sturdy young woman,
Tawny babe in her lap;
Spoiled fruit left behind,
A mouse in a trap.

Then suddenly surfaced
near new-painted flat,
Three men in a struggle
while the mother just sat.

Angry and sweating,
One man plunged a knife
in the heart of another
and ended the life

Of a man who took orders
and broke a child's neck.
Decision: the flautas were well
worth the trek

Marcia L. Neil

SHAKESPEARE SUPPORTED BY TRAGEDY AND COMEDY.

What if Shakespeare Had Written

Shall I compare thee to a winter's night?
Thou art as cool and certainly as dark.
Howling winds give an October fright,
And winter's lease hath all too small a mark.
Sometimes too cold the mouth of nature blows,
And often is her disposition chilled,
Upon a heart already deeply froze.
Should by chance nature's quest be unfulfilled;
But thy eternal winter shall not fade,
Nor lose possession of that cool thou owest,
Nor shall death brag thou wanderest in his shade,
When in eternal rhymes to time thou goest.
    So long as men can dream or wish for thee,
    So long lives this, and this says not to be.

William J. Russell

A Good Question

Just SUPPOSE the Czars had been KIND,
Keeping Little People in Mind.
    Would the World be Different Today?
    I Guess No One Can REALLY Say.

Robert Emmett Clarke

A Satisfied Mind

Depression and loneliness, is not for me;
There's too much to do, and too much to see.
I've been around quite a few years;
Had my share of grief and shed my part of tears.
But there's a time to grieve, and a time to feel blue;
Still long as there's a heartbeat, there's something to do.

I have a few pointers, try this on for size;
Stand tall, look around you, You'll be surprised,
With each new dawn, when you open your eyes;
Thank God, you're well and it's good to be alive;
I hit the floor filled with love, and a smile on my face,
There's so much to do around my place.

There just aren't enough hours in a day for me;
Chatting with friends, letter writing, I'm busy as a Bee.
There's my yard work, spring cleaning, baking and mending;
Those are only a few of my daily beginnings,
I love to read, the favorite is my Bible;
and with soft music and that is reliable.

I'm happy-go-lucky, full of life and carefree;
This whimpering and griping sure isn't for me.
I've truly been Blessed, and at seventy two;
There's still very much here for me to do.
Sure I've been around quite some time;
And Happy to say "I have a satisfied Mind!!!"

Mary Evelynn Coleman

Look At Me (Siamese)

In amazing wonder, as you deliberate—
    tomorrow shall be better than today,
Dreams come true?
    which path to stay, or adapting oneself
    to the turmoils of life's way—
Extraordinary!
Just L
        O
          O
          K at me my adjutant!
I live in the lap of luxury with the best—
of costly things
My artfulness, and discriminating tastes appear
as luminous wings
my only ponder—the daily meal.
Of dreams?
    a sense of curiosity that no one
    could ever feel!
I stroll in sunshine
My life has no confusion—look at me!

Melpo Dennis Scotese
Included in **About The Poets** Section

Too Much Wishing

I wished a wish one weary night,
Hoped it would come true with all my might.
I searched the stars, I scanned the skies,
Seeking my desires from down inside.
One lonely morning early in spring
I awakened from a dreary dream.
I felt a pain inside my heart
And wondered how that pain did start.
Then I began to search my soul
For faraway feelings new and old.
I found out why my wishes had never come,
Too much wishing and no work done.

Benita Akwiwu

The Sea of Life

The sea much like life has its ebbs and flows
There are ups and downs, there are highs and lows

Constantly changing, both never the same
Learning their secrets, a difficult game

But wise old sailors discovered this key
There were lessons of life in that old sea

They learned from the tides, first the high then low
Each held a message, so vital to know

They soon discovered the sun and the wind
At times were their foe, at times a good friend

This also applied when it came to rain
But nature like life is hard to explain

To navigate well and take life in stride
You must weather all storms, flow with each tide

Never forgetting that gray skies turn blue
A fact that all sailors know to be true

No need for a book or college degree
The sea has lessons, you can learn for free

Study the currents and all undertows
Learn all that you can of what life bestows

The storm and the calm are just a small part
Accepting them both is really the heart

For good navigation in life or at sea
Plays a large part in steering our destiny

    Dee DeFerrari

THE STREAM THAT TURNS THE MILL.

Confused

Sometimes I wonder why it hurts to cry.
I often think my friends are better off than I.
It seems love comes and goes into my life.
It seems I seldom know which way is right.

I've tried life on my own and, sometimes, I win.
Can I let his caring heart help me begin?
Can he show me happiness—can he teach me to live?
Can he help me understand how to take—how to give?

My heart tells me, "Go his way." My mind says, "He'll change."
My friends tell me, "Nothing lasts—just enjoy the good days."
Advice comes from everywhere—can't they just let me be?
I have made it fine on my own—is that what I believe?

I find myself so confused. Will these feelings soon end?
Do I need his gentle hands—should I stand tall or bend?
At times I'm the master of my ship and my life.
I can steer into any port—or drift far from sight.

But now, even gentle winds are calm, waves are low.
My ship doesn't move at all and there's no place to go.
I can't make it anywhere...I'm lost and confused.
Maybe, I'll take this chance—I may win...I may lose.

    Dr. Sheryl R. Bair

Angel Child of Flight 255

A fiery infernal erupted from the sky,
Leaving a path of destruction, and one pitiful cry.
Out of one hundred fifty six people, one child survives,
An act of god or a miracle, we cannot realize.
Is the trail of destruction , a place for birth?
Of one angel from god, put back on this earth.
Does he have a plan for this one angel child?
In the midst of this infernal, where everything's piled.
It's hard to believe, that this one huge plane,
could cause such devastation, leaving one remain.
One look at the wreckage, makes us ask if it's wise,
to enter these huge metal hulks, up into the skies.
We can all be thankful, and pray for the life,
of the one angel child, God chose to survive.
Unknown to us, it was to be the last flight,
of the huge passenger plane, known as 255.

    Joyce Jackson

Memories

Memories, like words, can cut and tear.
Memories, like words, can give you cheer.
Memories, like the wind, can come and go.
Memories, like the wind, at times overflow.

I remember the dance; I couldn't go.
That was the time I had no beau.
I remember birthdays spent all alone.
They weren't remembered, and now I'm grown.

I remember friends who are lost in the past,
And wonder why they couldn't last.
I remember friends who have stayed at my side,
And thoughts of them fill me with pride.

I remember the music called rock 'n' roll
With a beat so steady and lots of soul.
I remember the smell of spring in the air.
A crisp, clean scent ending winter's despair.

I remember with love, Toby, my cat.
She'd listen all day to all of my chat.
I remember the spring I got my first car.
The paint was faded, the door stood ajar.

Time steals much as it creeps through the door,
And what's in the past should not be ignored.
The good and the bad have molded the soul,
And stirs the spirit as we grow old.

Linda Cole

The language of friendship is not words but meanings.

—Thoreau

My Diary

Everyday's a holiday in my Diary.
Some surprises pop up every once in a while.
Just when everything's going in style,
Unexpected happenings arrive by the mile!

A diploma, a degree, a Florida trip to see,
Sunshine every day until a hurricane comes my way..
Back to the snow stacks in the Old Midwest.
Then on to California and the Far West in zest.

Be it an earthquake, wild wind storm, or the Weather
    Man running temperature,
My Diary is full of the ups and downs of Mercury.
I'll settle for days that are lucky for me.
Charming nights of moonlight and stars are ours.

A trip anywhere is news to declare in my Diary.
Letters come and go but words in my Diary last forever.
A kid'll remember many a time when old age forgets the
    best in my prime.
Diaries are everyday Bibles of history we pass.
Full speed ahead, turn on the go gas!

Frances Oglevee White Percival

ACROPOLIS, CORINTH.

You Are Like The Wind

While thinking of you, my mind becomes a galaxy
of thoughts extending endlessly.
All I care to do is think of you.
    Your sweetness and charm...
    Your smile, oh so bright!
    Your love for me, oh so enchanting!
You are my world, and now my love, may I sing
you sweet sonnets of love from under a full moon?
And plant loving kisses on your blushing cheek?
    You are like the wind...everywhere I go.
I see your smiles in the clouds...
I hear your laughter in the trees...
I taste your I love you's in the summer rain...
I dine on precious thoughts of you and cherish the
moments we are together, for I am a selfish lover
and want to keep you all to myself.
    You are like the wind...everywhere I go.
Nothing can keep you in...or out of my heart.

Jacqueline Smith

Honorable Mention
Chrysanthemums

White, moon-silvered petals,
Puffed, round heads of lions—
Autumn lions swaying in cool breezes,
Roots going down to touch the earth's burrowing warmth.
Transparencies ripple through the air
Like frost-ghosts dimly
Seen in darkened mirrors
Of one season fading to the next.
Butterflies fly through
The air in lurid waves of Burnt-orange, yellow, blue, bronze-gold
That will match the mad waltz
Of the leaves to cold ground.
Toads croak a final time
In black ponds before they
Vanish beneath the icy glaze of winter:
Enchanted princes, the spells of
Autumn witches glowing silver
In their eyes like burning stars.
White petals fall, burnt silver
By a full, round autumn moon.
To step on frost, a dragon's frozen fire,
And watch our shadows shorten
In the sun...

Frank Tropea

62

The Spreading Vine

The vine that spread across the sea,
Entwined around the earth,
Has calmed and pleased the inner me,
And branched out in its mirth.
The joy that spread throughout the land
And caught up in my heart
Has shown the strength of His kind hand,
And given me my start.
The love that spread throughout my life
And lifted up my soul
Gave me courage to face the strife
In acting out this role.
The peace that spread throughout mankind
And brought us nearer here
And gently cradled my troubled mind
Until his cause was clear.
The word of God that must spread now
And soon be understood
Will guide the way and show us how
To live His brotherhood.

Peggy L. Robling

---

*A happy home is more than
a roof over your head—it's a
foundation under your feet.*

—*Arnold H. Glasgow*

Golden Days

I saw you in an unusual place
　Where open minds lie in naked space
You questioned me with a peculiar tone
　I answered you with my familiar moan.

You said our life together was sharp and bland
　That our paths were equal but differently planned
You said we'd be better if only apart
　That the end would begin a lasting start.

And now as we go our separate ways
　Memories rush back to our golden days
Of love in the morning, of love in the night
　Of love with the passion to hold us tight.

How I sometimes wish our lonely hearts would cling
　To those warm special feelings that love would bring
But we knew that the end would be sad and long
　Both of us humming a fading song.

So next time we look at each other in that odd familiar gaze
　Our hearts will cry out for those golden days
Those golden days, those golden days
　Our hearts will cry out for those golden days.

Valerie S. Garr

Home From The Sea

Slowly the grey maiden comes into view
Her decks are lined in white and blue
The flag is waving in the wind
So many dreams on her are pinned
She pulls in closer this rival of mine
But tonight I know together we'll dine
The ropes are hurled with a bang
It's safe to say that my heart sang
Whistles and yells and general clatter
When liberty's called it won't matter
I search the deck looking for his face
And then I feel my heart race
I'd know that walk, know it anywhere
It belongs to the man about whom I care
Closer he comes until he's so near
I hear him calling "hello dear."
I feel his arms embracing me
At last my husband is home from the sea.

Ronda Rose

Feelings

Now I lay me down to sleep
Tears upon my pillow seep
If I should die, before I wake
I hope my heart my love will take
And hold it gently to his breast
And put my body down to rest
When the nighttime slowly falls
And shadows dance upon the walls
When the dewdrops slowly sneak
Upon the snowy mountain peaks
Put some flowers on my grave
So in the wind, they'll gently wave
Say goodbye to me and sleep
Our memories, forever keep.

Beverly J. Conkel

Morning Dance

Soft, windy soft, as a spring to summer afternoon.
Turning grayness into sunshine.
Days of weeks, no end.

Italian meadows, pastures, grazing herds, their bells
　announce the start of a new life.

Vendors, mingling of sounds and smells.
Little girls with bright smiles stealing
　the fruit and eating as they run.

Never, have I felt that side of the world
　within you.
Now, I am thankful for those kind pictures,
　for summer has been with me all the time.

A. J. Bidonde

Life is Worth

What is life worth?
Life is worth the smell of newly cut grass.
I've got allergies, think I'll pass.
What is life worth?
Life is worth striving for that one big success.
Compared to others, mine is much less.
What is life worth?
Life is worth writing meaningless poems—worse yet,
  for meaningless people.
Think I'm going off the deep end; wanta to jump off
  that high steeple.
What is life worth?
This has all been a lie; none of it is true—
I met a friend that changed my life—I began anew.
What, then, is life worth?
Life is worth a world of endless joy once you
  meet that one person and friend who makes
  you realize that poems don't have to rhyme
  and life doesn't have to make perfect sense
  at all times to overcome obstacles and enjoy
  life to its fullest.
Life is worth a friend.

Linda Russell

Beyond Dreams We Find Our Friends
*Dedicated with sincerity and love to a very special friend,
Cheryl L. Leinbach.*

A true friendship is when you care enough to say
"I'm here for you, I'll help you find your way."
It's watching someone trod her path,
looking over her shoulder for your approving nod.
True friendship can mean taking her hand and holding on
  tight.
Or maybe just sitting there when she's having a bad night.
A true friendship is lending an ear while she voices her
  innermost fears.
A true friendship means sharing kindness, laughter,
  compassion and fun.
It means sharing both her pain and tears.
There seems to be nothing that the two of you can't weather.
A friendship means sharing a meal at the table,
remembering to thank God that you are able.
It's being there on those lonely days...
A smile, just knowing one another's special ways.
A true friend shines through all the seasons,
never needing any special reasons.
A true friend can say "I love you and you really are my friend."
Together you can stick through thick and thin.
Together you can face reality.
A friend is someone that allows you to be...
As we travel through this galaxy of life we meet people from all
  walks of life.
But, a true friendship is finding that one brilliant star and only
then will we come to realize the true meaning of friendship that
  has always been.
And we continue to travel beyond our dreams.

Melanie Ann Weller

Come With Me

Come with me and walk the path of love.
Through all the tears,
through all the laughter.
Walk with me and experience the bond,
shared between two people.
The warmth of two hearts beating.
Stand with me, and by me.
Seeing the light that surrounds you and I.
The light that can never be shadowed,
by hate or not trusting.
Stay by me through the path of love,
and never let the path unwind or end.

Tammy N. Ayres

Imagination

The rain was pouring in the blinding dark night.
The wind was roaring with a frenzy of a fright.
Life came forth, from the lonely blackened gloom,
Frightened of my shadow as I shivered in my room.
My feelings were sprung, by my senseless weapon fright,
Staring into the darkness as I waited for the light.
Soon I would awake, to a sunny bright horizon,
Then something moved outside—I slowly cast my eyes on.
Gazing into the darkness, I carefully looked to see,
But as I was doing so, two eyes stared back at me.
I turned from the sight, my frightening observation,
The only thing it was, was my stupid imagination.

P. J. Solomon

Sisters

When I was four and you were nine,
Five years seemed like a long, long time.
You got to do things—I could not,
The games I played—you'd done forgot!
We used to yell and scream and fight,
But we were sisters—it was our right.
No one else better pick on the other,
For we both protected one another!
We were different, yet so much alike,
You rode your horse—I rode your bike.
The country nights are right for me,
The city lights are what you see!
Through sharing our hopes and dreams and fears,
We have been able to shrink the years.
We're different still—yet still alike,
You like to shop—I like to hike!
In search of all the dreams we've sought,
In arguments now long forgot.
We walk the paths that we both chose,
Yet still we stop to smell the rose!
Sisters we must always be,
But we are special—you and me.
And so Dear Sis as this poem ends,
I'm proud to say that we are friends!

Kathleen S. Walker

SALOME.

Bittersweet

In Autumn,
when Bittersweet was growing
upon its twisted vine,
Karen's mother died.
Then she lost a friend—
one year to the day.

Returning Bittersweet
brings thoughts of death and dying—
as leaves drop one by one
like tears from swollen eyes.

Dear Father,
wrap bitter grief
in sweet memories of those dear ones—
now held within your keeping—
waiting in the warmth
of your Eternal Spring!

    Sharon J. Daley
    Included in **About The Poets** *Section*

Procrastination

Why can't I get started?
I takes so long to decide;
Some effort now, even half-hearted,
Might yield a product, a source of pride.

Why plan to wait a while?
Take that trip, write that letter,
Buy that new dress, or walk that mile;
Postponement won't make outcomes better.

Vernilla M. Holt

The Visitor

He came to me on a silvery slip of a moment.
As I stood on my balcony, I saw a star fall to earth
And as its twilight faded from the night sky
A sudden feeling of warmth settled over me.
Though I stood alone on the balcony
I felt the presence of another touch my soul.
My heart reached out in the still night,
For such warmth I had never known before.
Then without warning, the transparent form of his being
Advanced slowly forward, engulfing my frame
His voice was soft and soothed my sad heart
And as he touched me, life once more bloomed in my soul
His embrace was as tender as the petals of a rose
And his kindness overflowed throughout my depth.
Hours seemed as seconds passing through an hourglass of time
While he dressed me in his simple but complete understanding
Then as suddenly as he had come into my life, he was gone.
The being that had fallen from the stars
Faded into the mist of a wonderful dream,
But for me he lives on, a memory inscribed in my heart.

Freddie Morris

Michele Lee

Walking through the cemetery
Early this warm summer day,
I wondered what important roles
Had all of these lives played.

There was life all around me
For as far as the eyes could see;
Flowers were blooming, birds were singing
What a beautiful and peaceful place to be.

I came upon a special place
And in my mind I saw a smiling face
Eyes that sparkled with Love and Laughter;
Waiting to take in what life had to offer
Could twenty-three years be all she was after.

My special young sister and her unborn child
May God love and keep you both for a little while;
I'll Love you always, no matter what will be
You're in my heart now and forever,
Nickey and Michele Lee.

Debra Lambert-Koski

65

Love Lost

The gentle kiss of my one, true love
I again may never know.
Her tenderness may nevermore
Cause my heart to glow.
Her hair, so soft and beautiful,
May brush no more against my face.
Her love for me, once so sincere,
Now lacks that certain grace.

We used to talk together
As if our lives were one.
Now suddenly I realize
All that I should have done.
Remembering her tender touch,
Which brightened my peaceful life,
Now fills my sad and lonely heart
With sadness and with strife.

I now have only memories
Of all that used to be,
Along with a new perception
Of what she means to me.
Often I will find myself
Alone and cold and then
I pray that what God plans for me
Is what now should have been.

        Steven A. Seager
    Included in **About The Poets** Section

He who cannot love must learn to flatter.

                —*Goethe*

Passionate Love

Mere words could never describe
the passionate love between Ana and I

Our love is no fairy tale or make believe
even when uncontrollable emotions our minds conceive

It only takes togetherness, a few short minutes
to raise our temperatures beyond feverish limits

Suggestive motions rock our evil fantasies over the side
getting us lost in the undercurrent of love's tide

As that desirable moment of pleasure draws near
nothing seems to matter or awaken our fears

It has struck now, touching and vibrating our inner being
this love for one another...oh what a feeling

Holding, sometimes down our cheeks the flow of tears
when muffled "I love you's" fill our ears

Mere words could never describe
the passionate love between Ana and I

    Richard Steers

By the River.

You are My World

You are a shining star,
lighting the way for me to go.
You are a mountain stream,
gently guiding me with your flow.

You are to me the rising sun,
softly warming me with dancing beams.
You are the rainbows,
that fill me with hopes and dreams.

Life without you would have no meaning,
there'd be no beauty, no love, no caring.
I'd never find true happiness,
I would never find anything worth sharing.

So my darling, the next time you're feeling lost,
and your life seems to be empty.
Just try and remember how special you are,
and how much your love means to me.

    Rebecca Rider

A Touch of You. A Touch of Me.

Let me hold you in my arms
so that when I kiss you, you won't be alarmed.
You know what's on my mind
and now Love is what you'll find.
Come close to me
because now true Love is what you'll see.
Please help set me free.
Your body feels warm but yet you're still firm.
Relax my Love because true Love is about to come from above,
and don't worry because my Love will do you no harm.
Now let my lips touch your heart.
You must now realize we are not far apart.
Do not kiss me with your eyes that only see limitations.
Kiss me now my Love with understanding.
Bring your beautifulness, please next to me
and I'll give you all the Love that you can see.
You have now brought me close to you,
now don't worry we both know what to do.

    James W. Hudson

Another Sun

My windshield cries the morning dew—
Perhaps a sign of future pain;
But I don't need a sign to know
That every cloud is full of rain.

I wonder what forever means—
So many things are still unclear.
I can't remember who I am—
I can't remember why I'm here.

Just yesterday I had a dream
The sea had taken my last breath;
And I began to rise above
The ones below who fought with Death.

The wind has no direction now—
I walk along the empty beach
Where waves salute the sky above
And hold below the ones who reach.

It seems to me I know this place
Where soon the tired sun will sleep;
And those who fought to breathe the air
Are resting where the night is deep.

Stephanie Thiboult

---

*You can't get a firm grip on
the present without letting
go of the past.*

—Anon

Three Score and Ten

When a lad of a boy, I was always astounded by the reference to "Three Score And Ten," as the idea of every reaching such a mark could only apply to Patriarchal Men.

My Dear Parents seemed rather ancient, although nowhere near the "Three Score And Ten" mark, and as far as I was concerned, on such a long journey I would never embark.

Now, that my "Ship Of State" has finally arrived in that ancient water-way, I can only shake my head in wonder as my heart begins to pray, Dear Lord, I've actually reached a dock not meant for me, and had it not been for Your Mercy and Protection, I would have succumbed to Life's Treacherous Sea.

Since the first "Seventy" is now upon me and as I attempt to chart a further course, Dear Lord, please stabilize my bow, my rudder and my compass so, that I can travel on with no remorse. For the waves keep rolling higher to where my journey is at risk, but since You are The Master Seaman, I know You can guide me into that Final Harbor, even though the waves be rough and brisk.

Don Mauldin

For Better or for Worse

For better or for worse the young couple said,
With all sincerity on the day they were wed.
In sight of God and family so dear,
They exchanged their vows then waited to hear,
Man and wife as she wiped her tears,
Knowing they would share love through the years.

Soon they were faced with an unexpected test,
finding worse truly comes with the very best.
They had better but worse was right now,
With patience and understanding they remembered their vows.
Through faith in God and their abiding love,
The trials they would overcome with help from above.

Now they continue to walk hand in hand,
Worse has become better as is God's plan.
They serve God, family, friends and each other,
While others look at them and questioningly wonder.
Faith as theirs few understand,
For better or for worse we all must plan.

Their love is stronger than on the day,
They exchanged vows for real not just play.
For better or for worse it is up to you,
If you trust God to see you through.
For richer or for poorer, in sickness and in health is clear,
When you take your problems to the Lord he will hear.

Gladys Ritenour

Heaven's Land

I once parted from my head
And soared through darkened sky.
I reached the gates of Heaven's land
And peered as stander-by.

I saw the eyes of our good Lord—
All-knowing, peaceful soul.
A radiance shone out from Him.
He stood atop a knoll.

I stretched my arms out toward His light,
Then He slowly shut His eyes
As if to say time wasn't right
For my body's own demise.

A wind came strong and carried me
Far from the placid realm.
It blew me into blackened space,
For it controlled my helm.

I soon approached the bluish earth,
But, entrance by Heaven's light,
I strove to turn around again
And never end my flight.

My motions stood in contrast to
The knowledge that I had—
For I knew that I must return
To earth's own carnal land.

Mira

She Poured The Wine

Beneath the dust   Under the rust
When the cleansing and polishings thru
Here's the fabric of character   The metal of worth
A jolly good fellow   Are you

And   She poured the wine
'Twas her valentine   That you had come to be
And I'll drink a toast   to this girl   you love most
A wonderful one   is she

Patrick McGee

the day i get some rest

everywhere i go i can't get no rest
everywhere i go i'm never at my best
my mind is prone to wander thru the future tense
worrying scurrying hurrying
trying to make some sense
i can't relax...i never sleep
i keep forgetting what i need
to stay alive
can't somebody anybody tell me why
i seem to be so satisfied when i make myself cry
maybe i'm obsessed: i took your picture,
   my fantasies and dreams are all about u.
i feel guilty: my own past haunts me
i re-live every wrong i've ever said or done.
this is what i fear: a loss of love
but the love i get keeps my head above.
and you'll see me at my best
on the day i get some rest.

Patrick Muñoz

To Dream

To laugh, to smile, to cry is reality,
it's not a dream,
Dreams are fantasies to the foolish but
to the wise it's a way of life.

To dream is to roam to heights unknown,
to capture simplicity at its lowest tones,
To dream is a working of the mind, it will
help you put a lot of foolishness behind.

To have a dream filled with an openness of
truth, helps you to handle Love, Pain and
Sadness with a value of serenity and
truth.

Hold onto your dreams, don't ever let them
go, your dreams will sustain you to and fro.

Carol C. Mancle

Release

Feelings at night
Expand under the influence of the dark
Vagaries abound in the shadows where
One cannot clearly see the foe
Approaching in the form of fears,
Growing uncertainties.

The weariness of the body
Leaves no energy to defend
Against the onslaught of insecurities
Pounding incessantly on the soul
That finds itself—helpless—
Out of control.

The onslaught continues as
Sans sleep, the hours
Slowly pass, the magnification increases
Without cessation, escape unattainable,
The essence bruised in the fight.
Daylight—respite.

Linda K. Wright

KIRK BRADDAN.

Ocean Sunrise

The sensual earth tips t'ward the sun
In slow and wounded grace—
With power reaching for the light
And conquest on her face.

The sun stands firm while ocean moves,
Her waters streaked with red.
He spreads pastels of every tint
To heal where she has bled.

Celestial sea, eternal light
Are fused in union wild,
And iridescent day springs forth
Like night's nocturnal child.

Virginia R. Walker

The Guy Got His Butt Kicked By A Doctor

When most guys get their tail whipped
    it's by a big dude in a bar
Wearing jeans with a rip in the knee;
Or it's some street dude that's in love with gold chains
    & initials
Like "L.L. Cool" or "Mr. T."

But I know of a guy who got creamed
In a way that arouses shame
And the guy who did it never wore busted jeans in public
And had "Doctor" in front of his name.
When you think of Martin Luther, you think of "King,"
Not the guy who started the Lutheran Church;
King has totally sealed up the use of that name,
Knocking Martin Luther off his perch.

Not everyone agrees with Lutheran teaching,
But to say you "don't like Martin Luther" is risking much:
You'll be regarded as a racist pig
On the side of South African Dutch!

Another guy to get creamed is King, Sr.
It's enough to make the old man wince:
If Martin Luther King, Jr. was a junior king,
What would that make him—a prince?

Volt-Air

"Daddy's Side of the Family"

I get undressed and crawl in bed, the sheets are soft and
smooth. As they caress my body, I close my eyes and realize I will
never know how or why, my legs feel as one. My arms have a
separate identity. I know without looking they have not
changed, but as for the rest of me, I'm no longer sure. I test
myself to see if I'm awake. I'm still breathing and my hips move,
but I no longer feel the soft delicate sheets. My hair is wet? Have
I watched too much TV? No, I'm sure of that. As I look around I
see tiny air bubbles all around in a deep blue sea. Rocks and
seaweed are just an arms-length away from me. As I sit and
think this through my thoughts collect about me. I always knew
I was a mixed-breed. If you're Scot-Irish, English, French,
German and Welsh doesn't that qualify? But Mama never told
me my ancestors were mermaids too. Must be on Daddy's side
of the family.

Ann D. Thomas

The Ladies On The Line

I had to leave you
I had to get out of there
If you could have seen you—
All the ways you held those airs
I'm not trying to put you down
I know you had to live by the rules of the town
But you thought it was fine with the ladies on the line

When you died I got a sympathy card
From Saks Fifth Avenue
It came with the bill for the alterations
(You'd lost some weight—from complications)
So we took in the suit I bought in which to bury you

I had to leave you
I'd been too long at the fair
If you could have seen you—
Satisfied for being nowhere
I cannot help but put you down
There's so much more to life than what you found
So divine in the ladies on the line

Barbara B. Goldman

THE LAST PITCH OF CORN.

A. Member of Local 174

I, was a member of Local 174. I used to cut beef
    not anymore.
We the boys and me cut so much beef our bodies
    were sore
and then push in a trailer of beef through
    a refrigerator door
I. looked at each piece to make sure
    it was clean
then trimmed it off and made it look keen
then push it down a rail where it would
    be on sale
But there was an inspector named Karp
    and on our backs he used to hop
That man had an eye that was sharp
I could still hear him say every day
    you guys get away with murder but not today
    because Inspector Karp is here to stay.
He used to look in from out the door
    and watch the merc as he did his work
then he would come inside and drive me berserk
After that I couldn't concentrate on my work
    but now I. am retired from Local 174
I. sometimes go to see the boys but Karp?
    No. I. don't see him around not anymore

Anthony Mercorelli

The Inheritance

To think that one of my own blood
—and we are so very few—
could stab me, leave me bleeding!
Yes, cousin, I'm looking at you.

Remember childhood, teenage years?
Happy times when you and I
enjoyed being together.
You severed that bond with a lie.

Blood may be thicker than water,
but oh, money runs thicker still.
You have plunged and twisted the blade
—you helped write me out of the will.

It is not the money that matters,
but disinherited now am I—
disowned, cast out of the family!
That traitor's heart of yours makes me cry.

I *am* a part of your family
whether or not you wish it so.
Know this: guilt for your betrayal
will close-follow wherever you go.

So enjoy your money, my cousin!
Hold it close. How warm can it keep
your assassin's soul on dark nights
when cold guilt-winds prevent peaceful sleep?

L. Sallaberry Recalde

Persephone
(For Doreen)

She remembers the arms of her husband
And just one shady tryst.
Her days are threads of a stubby length,
Unwound from a small reel for no reason,
The needle missing. They hover like severed limbs
In her house for people to walk over.

The two daughters grow sturdier each moment
Under her care. She has the pages of big books
To slip into, rose-colored walls of her bedroom
To drink with. In spring she plants anemones,
Then the lawn requires mowing. A beach can be visited.

Between the woman she was as a wife
And the ruddy creature she's growing
Lies silence, yawning a wide mouth like a primeval wood.
She's turning into a tangled bush, a clump of moss,
A mushroom. Rain falls. Strange rays of light
And darkness enter her, grinding her low,
Into a hidden kingdom,
From which her feet will sprint in a marathon.

Helen Lawson

Some Say We Still Talk Too Much

Sometimes we say what's really on our minds
Many have died in the past many did time
Talking was a serious crime

Should you have spoken are you broken
Many still say those times haven't changed
Many have died because they sincerely tried
Others deliberately lie

You have shown you still care when others wouldn't dare
What's really the direction toward true
Another revolution will that better the solution
destroying killing each other
Does anybody want to honor their own constitution
Humanitarians still trying
Thank god almighty we will be free at last
Didn't you hear outcries from today yesterday and the past

Melvin Sykes

Robbed

On the green velvet valley my sweet home sat alone
not far from town under the warm sun.
Developers the prairie rushed;
bulldozers came tearing up and down stirring dust.
by buildings of all sizes soon I was surrounded
blocking my view to the snowy mountains.
To my door the deer does not come anymore,
birds their nests have permanently abandoned.
There are too many dogs and cats barking and meowing.
Of my tranquillity and peace have been robbed;
my sleep is disturbed shot at random.
For my lonely house on the prairie I yearn
as it was; peaceful, alone from sunrise to sunset.
I miss the skylark's flute, roosters crowing,
the cows' moos, the starry silent nights,
on the green grass the morning dew
diamond-like sparkling yellow, red and pale blue.
In all colors the wild flowers quilt, alfalfa's sweet scent.
Yes, I have been robbed of all the things my heart loves.
Intruders of my world I don't hate but I resent.

Virginia Fréytas Hrabcak

*Included in **About The Poets** Section*

Friendship's Fog

Alone in midnight reveries, The thought occurred not gently to
    me; That thoughts are treacherous things, no matter how
    well intended they be.

A smile serves poorly as a mask;
when friends, in quest of flattery, ask,
An opinion on their looks, their manner of dress, or merely the
    brand of their favorite cask.

Worse yet, they never forget this gamut of things; "How about
    my politics, religion and my rings?" And openly gloat, as
    they await the vote, on—"How well my Cecilia sings."

They speak, only that they may be stroked like a cat,
And begin to purr before you say you like their hat.
Then louder they purr, beseeching you to say, that
    they are not really fat.

For the sake of friendship you grin and sin,
And tell a lie with every grin;
About their religion, politics and top it off with,
    "You're not fat, you're almost thin."

From there everyone begins again; With a knowing grin,
    for...Now it's their turn to tell me I'm thin.

Tom Wood
Included in About The Poets Section

---

*You can lend a friend a hand
without losing either hand or
friend.*

A Note From A Thankful Friend
To: Shannon, Bobbie, Tammy, Phyllis, and Sharon

It's been written that the man who has three close friends
    should count himself lucky.
Well, Lord, I must really be lucky because I have five.
Some I've known long, others only a short while. Two I've been
    friends with for what seems like forever and, another,
    though a long-time friend, is just now getting close.
The other two, Lord, I've not known very long, but we've grown
    so close in such a short span of time.
One friend led me to You, Lord, and the others helped me along
    the way. Since that day, they have all helped me stay close
    to You and understand You.
I love them all dearly, and I thank You for letting our paths
    cross.
I pray we'll always be close and that, some day, I'll be able to do
    as much for them as they have done for me.

Brenda DeCook

Friend

The measure of friendship is distance
The travels together through time
Love holds one to another
From beginning to end of the line.

The virtues are honesty and loyalty
The needs are companionship and care
When sorrows strike or joys touch
A friend is there to share.

Fortunate are these relationships that sustain each other
Giving each other strength
How miserable must he be who rejects this
For alone will he travel the length.

My friend, you are my blessing
When often you don't even know
A prayer that was answered in my life
Was our friendship that continues to grow.

Patricia N. Lake

Secret To Perfect Happiness

We should live each day as though it were our last
Perhaps, this is the secret to perfect happiness
Be kinder not only to neighbor, but to our loved ones as well
So after we are gone, they might say, they were swell
Not to live carelessly, but to appreciate instead
The beauty, love and affection—but not to dread
So let's not think of only what we want
Forgiveness, patience, love and grief are all but a part of life
The trick is to learn to take all in our stride
If we but knew when our hour was up
How considerate we all would be
Not get annoyed at the child who broke his new truck
Or perhaps, at the fulfillment that did not come to pass
Then we would not always be looking for greener grass
But be glad with this our daily happiness.

Mary Ann Esperson

Your Special Love

You're a friend who cares
A friend which will listen
A special friend who also shares.
You are willing to share your feelings just for me.
You've been with me through the good and bad
You've done things for me no one else would ever have
You're the special part of me that makes me smile
You're that special part of me that makes me laugh and cry
You show me your love in a very special way
A way that is one of your own
You tell me you care like no one else could
You are yourself and that's why I Love You so.

Robin K. Decker

Untitled

The thoughts of Man
strive, endure, emit,
permeate to perceive
a cause for which to commit.

Talking in myriad terms
lost many years past
numbly held captive and,
to the nether world cast.

But the very truth screams for more.
The dead arise to contemplate
now, yearning and aching to destroy,
after many, many years too late.

Dark secrets enveloped
twisted while toiling to arise,
Politics, Tyranny and Morality
all bring on Man's demise.

Someone says Love cures,
and can cure Man's needs.
But Typhon moves untethered
as Man's humanity screams.

A loyalty that grieves
put to subconscious commands,
and lost, like lovers conjoining,
Man withers into sand.

Christopher B. Ravlin

A Cry for Catharsis

Moments of closeness fleeting, intimacy rare
Reaching out to touch you, sometimes ice thaws there.
An inkling of emotion may have passed between
Our hearts then attracted by the aura of that scene.
The mellow music captivates, warmth infiltrates my soul
Melancholy shrouds us, reserved with self-control.
Confrontation lacking then, though eye messages glare
Longing overwhelms me for heart's union to share.
Our minds know each other, our hearts sometimes meet
Yet I often wonder if this unity's complete.
I experienced ecstasy from our moments of affection
I long to spark repeatedly that electrified connection.
I strive to be a magnet but soon shall realize
That efforts don't inspire natural lasting ties.
My threads dangle aimlessly, my offerings seem bare
My oceans overflow into a desert barren there.
My mind a smoldering wilderness, my inner tempest seethes
Churning with restlessness a sensual fire breathes.
My limbs pulsate with energy, my eyes like diamonds glare
Piercing heart's stone barriers like tombstones engraved there.
In hearts' raging oceans content and calm before
Waves double their fists pounding love's rocky shore.
Sunshine reappearing dries earth's flooded tears
Rainbows now enlighten as you once soothed my fears.
Sunsets always falter and soon return again
Darkness overshadows me as the moon begins to wane.

Jasmine Javid   Canada

My Lovely Teche!

Teche! Teche, My lovely Teche!
    If you could only be the lover of my youth
To laugh and play and tender kiss
Faint heart hath fled away

Oh, Teche fill me with the love I
lost, long long spent away
I breathe in your hypnotic trance
bare legged in the summer sun

I run from you and warm
desire, brings me back, undone
You pout, you sing, you cry
you tease.

And slip from my arms as you please.

Michael Lee

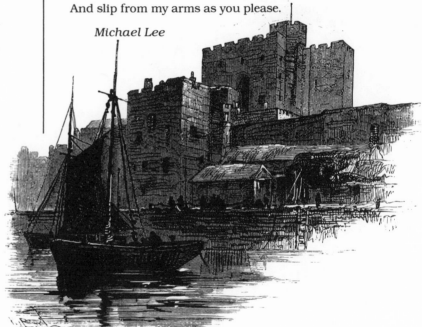

CASTLE RUSHEN.

Untitled

BALANCE, in limbo was held
understanding—no
trying to grasp the meaning
coming across too slow
interested beyond regular belief
curious to love you
wanting to rush the sun
for I need the horizon's view
Soon, a barrier was obstructing
and a jump filled with hope
maybe together the union
sometime, sincerely we cope
Sorry fills my mind
apologies engulf my heart
understand I care
my feelings leave across, never depart
Tired pursuit has left
upset work has not been done
unsure about the unseen future
please, take away my alone.

Deborah Nichols

The Wonder of Christmas

Grandma, read me a story about Christmas long ago...
Read about the Christmas tree and sleigh rides in the snow.

Come dear, let's sit by the fireside I'll share a tale with you
'Bout the Wonder of Christmas and we'll sing some carols too.

The night was cold and snowy, Grandpa had gone to cut a tree,
I was alone and frightened, the wind howled unmercifully.

The candle in the window flickered and sputtered a bit...
I wished Grandpa would hurry as I sat by the fire and knit.

Then out of the windy darkness, ever so faintly at first...
I heard the sound of Carolers singing of Jesus birth.

My heart was filled with gladness, my fears were all dismissed,
And at that very moment, Grandpa shouted, "Come, see this!"

I rushed with a lamp to help, trimming the tree would be such fun
But in his arms was a bundle, a tiny face, and hands nearly numb,

Someone had abandoned the baby close to the road that night...
And grandpa stumbled upon it, the Wonder of Christmas all right.

After we'd fed and warmed her and the tree with tinsel was draped
We wrapped gifts for the children of every size and shape.

Then just as the dawn was breaking, heralding Christmas day,
The children were up and excited, eager to begin their play.

Oh, for the Wonder of Christmas, the children stared in surprise,
They say miracles happen and I believe it's true...
It's the Wonder of Christmas, do you believe it too?

Ruth Blackburn

Jesus Found Me

I searched for Jesus; I called Him by name;
I was so lonely; I was so very sad;
I called Him in the morning; I called him in
   the storm;
And guess what happened; Jesus came into my heart.

I searched for Jesus; I stumbled and fell;
I was so broken; my thoughts were in the depths of hell;
I called Him in the sunshine; I called Him when it was dark;
And guess what happened; Jesus came into my heart.

Jesus found me; now I'm not lonely;
He is my Savior; He is my friend;
Jesus found me mid toil and tribulation;
Jesus, my Savior, helps you and me;
Jesus found me mid sin and desolation;
But Jesus, my Savior, loves you and me.

Ruth M. Revecky

To Tiger Lilies

*"Tiger, Tiger, burning bright
In the forest of the night."*
—William Blake

Why Lilies are called "Tigers" is beyond me.
For: "A Tiger" is a ferocious wild beast
That pounces through the air on red meat to feast.
While Lilies are garden gems, fragrant and lovely,
That rise in the air as though fed on new yeast.
But, my brain I strain to fathom why Lilies beasts should be
Since Tigers roam our garden border in the East.
William Blake implied a Tiger is a work of art
And asked, "What...could frame thy fearful symmetry?"
I ask, "Should art frighten or fascinate the heart?"
Lilies thrill *all* hearts regardless of pedigree
And their fragrance and art has no counterpart.
So, BLOW Lilies: Calla, Croft, Madonna, Regal, Rubrum, Day.
BUT, you Tigers, go back to the jungle and with wild
Beasts stay!

Mollie E. Miller

The Golden Rule is of little value unless you realize that you must make the first move.

Thank You Jesus

1. Thank You Jesus for setting me free once again—
2. For letting me loose from the snares of men.
3. Thank You for letting me run loose in the clover;
4. You know that I've always been a rover.
5. It seems like I keep getting born again and again;
6. You keep on freeing me from the chains of sin.
7. Why didn't I see it a long time ago—
8. That even when I forgot about Your spirit, You were still there to let It flow—
9. So many miracles You have performed for just me
10. When I was lost in the dark and storm-tossed sea.
11. Why didn't I acknowledge that it was You?
12. I'm so sorry and now I really want You too.
13. The more that I acknowledge You, the more You do for me.
14. Oh, in heaven—there's no place I'd rather be!
15. Every time You do something, I think that's it,
16. But then You show me there's so many more candles to be lit.
17. Where does Your love ever end?
18. Your love to me You always send.
19. I just want to be with You forever and ever
20. Because You are so beautiful and clever.

Jeannie E. Vaughn

Destiny

I saw an Eagle
soaring on high.
That noble head,
that piercing eye.
He was hunting food,
for in the nest,
a baby Eagle
below did rest.
Our fathers made him
this nation's bird;
yet only a few
are left, I've heard.
They say the Eagle's
a dying breed.
The warnings are there
for us to heed.
I hope I never
will have to see;
the day the Eagle
no more will be.
I hope this baby
will grow to soar,
and be the hunter,
to feed one more

Carol Dale

A True Friend

You stood by
Through thick and thin.
Many a broken heart
You helped mend.

Many times you
Have helped me through—
Always loving and sharing
With little ways of caring.

I may not have always
Been what I wanted to be.
But you always laugh
Knowing that's just me

I feel I let you down.
I'm not the friend you need.
But you are always there
Saying I'm a friend indeed.

How can you do this
With all my oversights,
Do you know deep down
I do care with all my might?

Susan Shields Alspach

Olympic Spirit

Torch flame slowly fades
Ever-glowing fire kindled
Spirit in the heart

Karolyn Nearing

In the Valley of the Unseen

Alone and unseen
    By those I had once known
    I move without direction.

Confused and contradictory
    In the things I had befriended
    I make the purblind search.

Scarred and betrayed
    As a matter of my growing course
    I feel unprepared for the loss
    Of an age gone by.

Chance Muehleck

Included in **About The Poets** Section

I Love America

America is my homeland
Where all my roots lie
I love America
From sea to shining sea.

From the snow capped mountains
To the prairies and plains
Thank you God for good old America
From sea to shining sea

America is the place for me
As far as I can see
I love you in the spring time
And I love you in the fall

America is my fortress
To her I will forever cling
To me she is greater than gold
A beautiful land to behold

I love America
Where my interest lies
Some day I will say goodbye
And go to my home somewhere in the sky.

America where peace and happiness prevail
May her dignity forever stand
As a native and happy land
From sea to shining sea.

Charles E. Stevenson

Could You

Touch a star in its labor to shine
and relish the power of its foresight
yet to come
in unexplainable rhinestone dreams?
Take a sand-crystal's plight
to fill an endless space
creating a castle filled
with visions and a palette of illusions!
Dream 3-dimensionally and paint
the world with your designs
as a spider weaves his intricacies?
Take a deaf-mute sound
revive its tone
only heard
by the muses and the wee-folk!
Take a song humming from your soul
summon it up to a melody
that transcends any magic
in words!
Put yourself in second row
and let other minds reveal their wisdom
as yet not been told!
Would you

Patricia Anne Solek-Fritsche

Tomorrowness

The moon echoes the day,
while waves massage sand
by her cottage, by the sea.

He sits alone by the water,
warmed by a quilt
of heavy summer air.
His eyes are stale bread,
hard and dry,
focused on the horizon,
seeing the past.

He reaches for sand,
and remembers time with her,
before sand slips through fingers,
her sand, her beach, her time,
through his fingers.
A few grains remain
on veiny folds of fingers
like the recurring tears.

Red ears brave wind
to hear whispers,
strain to hear her love
fade into a chorus,
after a fading chorus
in the song of yesterday.

Martin Cohen

Independence Man

Jo Harmon's mother
Had a stroke the other day
And his family called up
And said let her stay
But Joe's twenty-two
And just out of school
And doesn't want to deal
With a bumbling fool
"This isn't my mother
She looks like a gnome
If you give her to me
I'll put her in a home"
Now I know you're all saying
"What a terrible thing"
But if I were twenty-two
I think I'd do the same thing

Manuel Stevos

Morgan's Rise

Down a quiet Coventry lane
Sits a house
With a roof from Old Spain;
And a sailor's clock,
And a music box
That plays a haunting refrain...

There's a sword
That's rusty and gold;
And trinkets
Of silver and gold—
And a merry-eyed girl, in a tortoise frame,
Though no one remembers her name...

But here's a word to the wise.
Don't look too long
In her eyes;
Or linger too long
By the music box,
When it plays "Morgan's Rise..."

Ronald Hill

Birthday Dream

Chin lifts as if to glimpse the sky
The view is erased by a lowering face
Lids relax over blazing eyes
As swollen lips blend

Having touched and tasted
No thought of parting
Bodies begging
Desire never ending

Passion consuming, but not destroying
Giving, receiving, sharing
Explosions of gifts exchanged

Carla M. Trombetto

STREET IN SALAMANCA.

Black Widow

what is more lethal
  than Black Widow's bite?
    night after night
      i find myself waiting
        for Her sting.

Her delicate, irregular web
    floats thru my dreams,
        my life.

see how She shuns us!
  until finally, provoked,
    stroke after stroke
      inflicts Her deadly bite
        day or night.

Her lacy, unpatterned web governs us;
    because of Black Widow, we live
        we die.

Thomas L. Richmond

75

I Saw Her

I saw her there,
A reflection of the future,
Dancing against the wind
And the clouds.
Her eyes were laughing loudly
For all to hear,
For only his eyes to hear.
Her golden hair blowing
In the wind
Whipped into his face
Leaving the sting of her teasing,
But he did not care.
She taunted and tempted,
As his enchanted heart grew deaf.
In a moment,
She brought him down
Beneath the moonlight.
Inside the cold, he lay there,
Still, uncaring, enraptured,
Unable and not wanting to leave.
Into his pain, she danced
Until it was over,
Her eyes still laughing
        as his heart bled.

Lorraine Kay

Of Leprosy and Lace

The stuff of desperation
is caused by hunger's pain.
The anger and resentment
grows with every name.

Robbery, rape, and mayhem
run rampant in the streets.
Yet, the political powerful
steal from government seats.

How can the rich legislators
dare orate the feeling of poor?
How can they make fair judgment
asleep on the Senate floor?

Silk suits and silver tongues
tour the ghetto from the air.
A kick of hundred dollar shoes
is all these bastards share.

Vote them out, put them down
others take their place.
It must be another joke
like lepers dressed in lace.

D. J. Burt

One Must Consider

One must consider
    The reality of life
To sit in darkness
    And wait for the light
Which only comes with time

Rohn Waldrep

I Have Become...

I have become
    What I am
For to not become
    something
After all I've done
    This would be
A tragedy.

I have become
    a mosaic,
A collage,
    A tapestry,
Woven of many threads.

A diamond
    With many facets—
And I contribute
    Quietly.

I am something
    Which will grow
Yet I know that
    What I am
I have become.

Linda Smith

Hey old man...

Hey old man,
what do you see?
What do you feel?
Your face is so wrinkled and worn?
Are you happy
or just tired?
Your beard is so long
and grey
that it gives you a look
of purity
and gentleness.
That all-knowing smile
on your face
gives you a look
of wisdom.
Are you really wise
old man
or just old?
Tell me what you know
old man,
tell me what you see!

Christine Bidleman

The Last Chariot In Greece

The clatter of hooves
Heralds his presence,
This last chariot that Greece boasts.
A faded man
In American fatigues.
A toothless grin
In a fangless suit.
Astride the last chariot in Greece.

'My children'
He tells me
'Are in America,
And my heart hurts
Just here.'
His grimy hands pinpoint his pain.
Then his steed snorts
Cold morning mist
And he clacks away
To pick up trash
And take it to
A home
His children have denied.

One that I,
As an American,
Cannot even imagine.

Tommie W. Bates

The Bag Lady
A poem on growing old

Dignity
Identity
All of it kept
In one small bag

Age is a thief
Stealing from the self
Desperation makes us cling
To things that seem
Unimportant to others

Senility
Or sentimentality
Fear of losing one's self
A futile gesture—
Hoarding the material

Saving objects
Meanings of each
Hidden to all but the self

Needs of others
Met over the needs of our own
Dreams of yesterday
Dreams of youth
Dreams of a past
Lost but not forgotten

Todd A. Mayville

Honorable Mention
The Joint is Jumpin'

The joint is jumpin'
The crowds, the fans
Congregate-on,
Wooden bleacher stands.
Pass the globe.
Run, hook, shoot
Put that globe
Through the hoop.
Offense swiftness
Defense skill,
We're ahead!
Just minutes to kill.

Stall, Defend
Till Final whistles Blow.
Give joy to some,
But to opponents, woe.
Same, hard efforts
A game to score.
Lead on, Cheer on
King Basketball, for
The joint is jumpin'
Blood-fever high.
My wild, glad heart
Goes pumpin' by.

Connie J. Mahoney

The Murderer and Me

Under the bridge
down by the tracks
buried in bushes
they found an axe.
A child was killed
the day before
from 22 whacks
or maybe more.
The blood was the same
the autopsy shows
who killed this girl?
Nobody knows.
The word is spreading
all over town
I hear them talk
when I come around,
they think I did it
and I think they're right
I've got to move one
got to get out of sight,
but wherever I go
it will happen again
because I'm a writer
and my axe is my pen.

Keith Necaise
*Included in **About The Poets** Section*

Today Is Soon Tomorrow

Looked forward to today, and now it is here to stay:

Walking down the country lane,
Driving cows to eat some grain.
Grass is swaying, farmers are haying,
Cow bells ringing, birds are singing.

Looked forward to today, and now it is here to stay:

Bugs and bees skim through the trees,
Hawks in the sky loop and swoop in the breeze.
Mice are scurrying to find their safe nests,
They want to escape from the talons' arrest.

Looked forward to today, and now it is here to stay:

Walking through the forest green,
Leaves are floating in the moving stream.
Walking in the cool, cool brook,
My toes feel sand in every nook.

Looked forward to today, and now it is here to stay:

Walking homeward at close of day,
Chased the cows beneath the boughs.
Farmers were impatiently waiting,
For milking time was abating.

Looked forward to today, and now it has dusked away:

Dinner bell ringing, barn swallows are winging,
Crickets chirping, spiders spinning.
Supper is over, and the day has passed,
Sleep will be weaving dreams of little last.

Looked forward to today, but it has flown away:

Darkness now bows its heavy head,
And I'll be dreaming in my comfortable bed.
Morning will soon awake with bright sunny skies,
And I'll arise with a pleasant surprise.

Ruth M. Revecky

If we cannot live so as to be happy, let us at least live so as to deserve happiness.

—*Johann Gottlief Fichte*

Stairwells
(Of Forgotten Images)

Spiraling down the stairwells of forgotten images
Were the whitewash smiles of a fading youth...
And kicking the rock down the street of nostalgia
Was childhood hysteria
And those colors of Summer gardens
that never seemed to disappear
Until glancing for a vain moment into the mirror.

Spiraling down the stairwells of forgotten images
A look...upon the shelving of brass framed memories
Pausing...for another sip of that dry martini
A mouth curling...at a fond remembrance
Of that stroll...upon a magic pony.

Spiraling down the stairwells of forgotten images
Were heard the echoes of childhood past
Of fantasies and toys that wouldn't last
Of a laughter and a frolicking only a heart could grasp.

Spiraling...down the stairwells of forgotten images
Were pieces to puzzles discovered amongst the clouds
Were jump rope marathons and limericks recited out loud
Were boys and girls together, forming a joyous crowd.

Dennis Devine

Come, Valentine, Come

Come to me with songs of your youth,
and I who am your lover feel their magic
even as I read messages streaming from your
eyes. There is a strange stirring in me as
your songs flow into the somber caverns of
my heart.

I feel strange whenever I hear you singing.
I feel strange whenever I look into your eyes.
I feel strange whenever you are near me.
I feel strange whenever I see your tender lips
blossom into a meaningful smile. This strangeness
touches my soul.

I am lonely and alone...I am frail, but let me
always hear your sweet songs. Let me always feel
the magnificent touch of your beauty. Your songs
shall fill me with strength. Your beauty shall
fill my being with greatness.

Strange that songs can make one love. Strange
that I can love you more deeply, more truly,
more sweetly when I hear the melody of your soul.
Strange that love can make one sing and dream.

Come, Valentine, and let us blend the music
in our hearts. Let us hold hands together
and answer love's sublime call.

Jose D. Lagmay
*Included in **About The Poets** Section*

On the Wings

The wings of love fly, lighter than air
while a sparrow sits
in the early morning sunshine, not a care
in the world. We live amidst
the cruelties of youth we despair
for the world that's never been our own
Praying to a God that has yet
to answer us. Not a whimper or moan
have I heard from Them. Have I set
my life on nothing but the
     telltale fog of lies
to set me apart from the rest?
The petals of a blood-red rose die
I sit watching, thinking, waiting
like the lovely sparrow. Hating
the hypocrisy that is life
amidst youth and their never-ending strife
to rebuild among the rubble that is war
and like that lovely sparrow soar
high above into the sunshine
on the wings of love.

Lucia Figliomeni

Untitled

Clocks melt away in the heat of the Western sun
their wretched faces drip and wither

Big Ben cries—Cronus smiles
for as darkness triumphs—
the molten puddles freeze to granite

Karen Luhring

Roxann

You are the stellar attraction of my
Heart, I love you more each day.
I am drawn into the radius of your
Love, good fortune has come my way.

You are the deity of my fascination
And of fantasies unseen;
The delicacy of my sensitivity,
O mistress of my dreams.

I ascend unto levels beyond power or
Glory, beyond fame and mundane wealth.
I am bestowed with joy and infinite
Happiness, keys to eternal health.

You fill me with passion and surging
Emotions, as the voice of your eyes
Unfold, treasures of love beyond
Belief, the essence of your soul.

Kenneth C. White

To A Graduate of Law
Written for my niece, Deborah V. Ortiz, Graduate of Law.

When first a mother cradled her fair child with joy and
    prayers in her heart,
Sang a lullaby of love, hopes, dreams,
Kissed the tears away and knew she had to set her child down
    to walk;
Too soon she heard the footsteps running out the door,
    off to school one day.

A silver bell that rang of a time of change.
Time moved rapidly by, yet ever so slowly
So much to remember, so much to accomplish.
Long and slow the pace did seem; up the rocky mountain you
    have climbed.
Each quick step became a fun to the finish line.

With a prayer in your heart you ran the race and won.

We all thank you. We all love you. You have won for us all.

God Bless you and keep you in his care.

    Sophie Padilla
    Included in **About The Poets** Section

---

*Education should be gentle
and stern, not cold and lax.*

—Joubert

Life For A Song

When I was a child, growing up in the wild,
    on our old Kentucky farm,
my siblings and I made the time pass by,
    and it also kept us warm—

We made up a game, but, it hadn't a name,
    that we played on our homemade swing.
We each had to earn our very own turn,
    that lasted as long as we'd sing.

Poor Jackie was small, and a short song was all
    she could sing with her cute little voice.
When she sang her song, it wouldn't take long.
    Betty, Virgil and I would rejoice!

Now, since I am grown, a swing I don't own;
    but, music is my way of life.
It helps me get through everything I must do;
    through tragedy, pain, and through strife.

You can see more clearly, and love more dearly,
    the picturesque countryside,
from a length of rope, and a board of hope,
    as, up in the air, you ride.

When everything's wrong, just think of a song;
    cut loose with a lilting tune!
For, you can keep swinging as long as you're singing;
    You won't have to quit so soon.

Pauline Vater Wharton

Untitled

Sometimes I live 800 miles away
My body feels the travel—
   the bumpy highways.
My mind knows the journey—
   empty roadsides and vacant pastures.
My back feels the burden from my
   travels to and fro, so often I lug
   with me everything I know.
Traveling 800 miles almost everyday.
I can't figure out how to stop this
   lonesome journey. I've been packing
   lighter and going less
But almost everyday I find myself
   living in your day
      800 miles away.

Elizabeth Gies

The Cold Wind

God! It's cold outside.
The icy wind hits like a million pins.
The snow, on the gale, does ride.
My legs are frozen up to the shins.

I only have to walk a mile.
The icy wind makes it so much more.
Soon the snow, like a white wall, will pile.
My poor body will be frozen to the core.

My feet; frozen, must weigh a ton.
The warm coat feels only like gauze.
The goal is near, I start to run.
If I can reach the house, I'll pause.

The north wind cuts deep to the soul.
Now I wonder where God has gone.
Could he have made the world so cold?
For the warmth of the sun my life, I'd pawn.

O God! My legs won't even try.
I can see shelter just ahead.
"Please death be warm!" I cry.
I'll close my eyes and be dead.

I see, looking down from on high,
My body, frozen, buried in the snow.
I tried! My God, how I tried.
But life is cheap when the cold wind blows.

Richard A. Schultz

The End of a Political Career

Copenhagen 1974
   H*E*A*V*Y   political discussions.
Pan-Scandinavian conferencing.

and you   beer bottle in hand

"What I want to know is
where's the action   in this town?"

D*E*A*D   silence.
And I laughed,
laughing away a lifetime of

   H*E*A*V*Y   political discussion.

Watching the swans argue through the night
on Peblinge So,
frustrated cats stalking well-mothered ducklings.

You walking Copenhagen's slums
seeking a bar
and finding none.

Finding your way back to me, however

"And now I will show you
how we make love
in Sweden."

While I laughed,
laughing away a future of

   H*E*A*V*Y   political discussion.

B. J. Rosenstein

The Kite

The ocean screams a cry of anger
and tears at the cliffs with a violent rage,
the cliffs stand tall, silent, proud and still.

On these cliffs a boy runs—
   his companion trailing behind him on
a cord made of heartstrings.

The kite itself is security, love and
   motherhood.

There is a rush of cool sea sir.
   The kite is torn from the boy's small
   trusting hands. Indifferently the kite trails off,
   out of the boy's reach.
His life is forever changed.
Never will the sea be a friend.
Never will he trust himself to love and security.
Never will he leave this cliff.
Never will his friend return.

Seagulls mock him, and the sea rumbles its laugh.

Rawn Simonds

Kindred Souls

We are kindred souls
Of many lives gone by,
Our love like burning coals
And we shall never die.

We have lived through ages,
That others only read of,
In books with yellowed pages
And eyes of wanting love.

In the country of my mind
I search the land and sea,
It is always you I find,
No other it could be.

The time again will come
When our bodies we will flee
To be united as one,
As we were meant to be.

So I pledge to you, my love,
From the inner sanctum of my heart
That no spirit below or above,
Will ever cause us to depart.

Naomi Smith

Starlight
For Stacey in Memory

Lift mind's eye to evening skies
    a million twinkling stars
dancing at first day's light
    till last they pass from sight

many have long since faded
    before man was created
still a light radiantly shining
    streams across the universe

like young heart's souls
    a living light, gently embracing
coolness on a summer face
    solace on a winter's day

we grieve so deeply, untimely passing
    darkness seemingly unforgiving
a love unconditional escaped
    tender caressing arms

they are our stars
    unflickering and eternal
warming hearts in love
    forever and always

so today I lift my eyes to say
    starlight—starbright—I wish
I may—I wish I might—see you
    once more tonight

Misha Adamovich

The Brave Knight

A light shines through
and fate lends a hand.
Though all seemed lost,
another chance.
A fearful death turned
to joyous birth.
The soul again
returns to earth.

The knight whose
dented armor shows
the many battles,
the many blows.
Has come to save
a broken love,
and repair the wounds
of a helpless dove.

Nurtured by a
single kiss, the prince
gave his maiden
a greater gift
than any other man
could give, he
showed his maiden
how to live.

Theresa Lingenfelter

A ROSE AMONG THORNS.

Untitled

Life is filled with many sorrows,
But you must pass them by...
For they shall bring you down.

If you reach this point of falling,
You can never get out...
Unless you find the rope of love.

For it shall pull you into the world
of hope.

For there you will find,
What you lost...
In the mists that engulfed your mind.

Now that you are found,
You can pass...
Through the paths of sorrow.

For now your life is filled,
with love.

Now you have found yourself,
Through the mists...
That have bound you.

For you are free, to be you.

The you that was meant to be filled
with the joys of a new found love.

For this is the time of a new beginning..
The time when life is filled with many
new tomorrows.

For there is no longer any sorrows.

Victoria Jade Martinez

Unban the Anc

And with a great
And fearsome rush,
The drums
Began to beat
And the chant
Rose
Louder and higher
Above
The swaying crowd,
Like a flame
Licking the edge
Of the sky.
Of one mind,
The crowd took one step
And raised its
Four thousand arms
In silent supplication,
But the heavens
Made
No reply.

Lynne LaRochelle

Untitled

Holy Jesus Son of God.
Have you walked this path I trod.
Can you help me through this day?
Thank you Jesus this I pray.

Jesus Jesus tell me please,
How to take this curve with ease.
Swerving gently side to side,
Brace me Jesus please I cried.

Are you hearing as I plead?
Will your Spirit comfort me?
Give me faith in times so low.
Showing love and even though,
There may be times my spirit's down,
You're always there to turn around,
To bring my mind and heart once more,
with lock and key to Heaven's Door.

Vicky I. Macon

Losing Time

Watch the second hand it's ticking
Slowly going around the clock
No matter what you believe in
It's never going to stop
You'll find yourself thirty and growing
Pains you thought you never have
Seen so much of life not knowing
All the things you could of had
If the realization of time
Would have come when life was young
So many different plans could of been
In the time wasted, looking not seeing
The changes that would come
When it's thirty going on twenty one

Lloyd Steenrod

Christmas in Belize

We escaped from the snow and cold
to listen to Christmas songs
under the sweating sun in Belize
and our hands in "Silent Night" to fold.

Mosquitoes buzzed and our skin burned
while "White Christmas" caused gifts to be sold,
and Santas dripped in hot velvet
and television's stories of snow were told.

Amid ancient Mayan ruins we strolled
listening to distant strains of "I'll Be Home for Christmas"
emanating from tropical households
lying in the gold and steam of the foliage.

Christmas doesn't ask for snow and cold
or silver bells on blowing corners,
just an ancient peaceful story retold
of a baby born throughout the world.

Nancy Hoekstra

I Walk Alone

I walk a long and narrow path,
Yet no one walks beside me.
I've walked this path a million times,
Yet only God and the earth knows it.
My feet are sore, my body, weary;
Lest I drop down in my tracks and die,
To die a lonely death.
The dirt goes dry beneath my feet,
And the sky is growing dark.
And I am walking here, still searching,
For my lonely past.
My clothes are torn, my head is damp;
My legs grow weaker now.
My spirit's sinking fast, oh Lord,
My shoulders slowly droop.
But my head stays up with pride,
For now I know, within my heart,
He's watching me, up there somewhere,
And though I'm almost dead inside,
I know He's there to pray me on.
For somewhere near the end I'll find
That something I have searched for.
That joy, that peace, that ray of light,
That everlasting life!

Susan Hiott

There is nothing new in the world except the history you don't know.

—Harry S. Truman

The Gift of Rhyme

In dungeon's deep and darkened walls
Where mist and mildew lie
A candle burns a flickered hope
Which lights one writer's cry.

"Take not this wealth, the pregnant muse
And bury beauty's grace.
Release instead the artist's love
To seed the human race.

"For art is rare as rainbow's gold
And fresh beyond all new.
It brings to earth the soul of life
A deck from heaven's view.

"Receive then these, my treasured words
That riches may incline.
For God dost grant us many gifts
And mine's the gift of rhyme."

Randolph Pitts

Snowflakes

Snowflakes—
Fragments of starlight
Drifting lazily—
Earthward

Susan M. Dunn

The Echo's Still Here

In the still of night
I awake to the sound
Of a little voice saying
Mama I'm cold may I sleep
With you tonight
The echo's still here
In the still of night
I awake to the sound
Of teenager's laughter
With music too loud
The echo's still here
In the still of night
All grown up and a home
Of your own
But I still hear the echoes
in the still of night

Mae Carpenter

Another Shore.

Long before
there was another shore.
Where we began,
away from the land.

Many lands we have known.
Many voices reached our home.
Yours, before the age to go,
an era ago.

You walked the land,
footprints in the sand.
No one will know,
your path is unknown.

Footprints of the land,
the tide reached the shore.
the call;
which you have been waiting for.

Upon wet sand
the sea alone
touched your hand.
Taking you where you belong.

Away from the land
you are one of our own.
Leaving the shore
to the one's of the land.

Dame Ljerka Dreta
Included in **About The Poets** Section

Nature's Clock

White blankets warm the naked earth
A shield from tomorrow's care
And new-born year gives everyone
A diary to share.

Time marches on, the robin returns
To bask in spring's warm smile
And nature promenades the earth
In frocks of every style.

The clock upon the kitchen wall
Ticks hours one by one
But summer whiles away the year
With warm vacation fun.

The year has now grown middle-aged
And nature not as spry
Wears scarlet, yellow, orange and brown
And breathes a tired sigh.

Feeble now, the weary year
Drops off in frigid sleep,
Old age has taken one last breath—
Time's cycle is complete.

Dorothy M. Johnson

Memories of You

Time was when memories
of you
Brought joy and peace.
Thoughts of our days
and nights
together
were
precious to recall.

Now, days and nights bring
not joy or peace,
only agitation
to be free of olden
thoughts,
to wish a new love would crowd
out old memories,
'ere time is nothing
but night.

Verna Lee O'Brien Clark

Quietly and Confidently

I reached so high into the sky;
I wanted to catch a falling star.
But even on my tiptoes, I couldn't
stretch that far.
But I'll just keep on trying to
catch that star some day;
And perhaps if I'm real quiet, it
will fall into my hand before
it caresses the land.

Ruth M. Revecky

CARNIVAL CLOUDS

COMBINATION COLORED CLOUDS
QUIETLY CLIMBING
COLLECTING CROWDS
CAPTIVATING KALEIDOSCOPES...

QUICKLY QUESTIONING
CONCEIVING CLANS of:
    kittens, camels,
    cows and canines
COTTON KANGAROOS...

CONSTANT CASCADING
COMPELLING COMPOSITION
QUIVERING CARICATURES
COMPASSING CREATION

Kathryn C. Severson

The Sea

The sea is green
And sometimes blue
It teems with life
And treasure too
It can be calm
But most times rough
It's the moaning voice that lures
Great sailing ships
To solve its mysteries.
It sends its roaring waves to shore
But takes them back
And sends in more.
It's the link between
Far distant lands
And touches us all
With its cooling hands
At times it seems
To touch the sky
At times it leaves us
High and dry.
It's home for many
A fish and whale
And it has been the subject
Of many a tall tale.
But without these waters
That cause the mist
The world as we know it
Could never exist.

Joseph Petti

Blind as a Bat

Blind as a Bat!
That's what the man said,
before the townspeople
put him to death.

A change of view or
a different idea
Is a crime against our way of life
and will not be tolerated round here.

One dimension people
Tunnel Vision disease
Frightened of Opinions
or different beliefs.

If I have to live amongst ignorance
I'd rather be dead
so go ahead and tighten the
noose sitting on my neck.

You can't kill everyone who's
different than you.
There will be others comin' soon.

I have lived a full life, with no regrets.
Hurry now and complete your task.
It's just sad you people are alive
yet you were born dead.

Linda Carapella

To Love

Some say it costs too
much to love.
If it does cost to love
think about,
What it costs if you
don't.

Cheri Vaughn

-FLOWER ON SCREEN IN
TÁJ (ABOUT A.D. 1666).

Nostalgia

I came from where a river deep
  And wide and long and free
Wound its restless, turbulent way
  Hurrying t'ward the sea.
In summer I found sweetest peace
  In its cool depths serene,
While swimming lazily about
  In its swirling depths of green.
But here upon the valley floor
  No rippling waves soothe me;
There is no cooling, soothing rush
  Of river t'ward the sea.
No boats upon the cresting foam
  No gulls fly to and fro,
And looking o'er the fields I see
  Just green corn, row on row.
But happily content am I
  As out into the glow
I plod slowly up and down
  The rows with my old hoe;
And as the rippling breezes bend
  The corn rows soothingly,
It seems I see again the sweep
  Of river t'ward the sea.

Gladys D. McLean

More Clearly

May I use your glasses?
to see more clearly
this world I exist in
the life I retain so dearly
I view from the wrong perception
I don't fit social perfection
Why can't I see them
and them see me
For just once in this lifetime
to see
and be seen
more clearly.

Cynthia Sue Stotler

Solitude in the Night

A sliver
  of silver
Suspended
  in an indigo sky.
A single,
  lone star
Sitting
  at the bottom tip
Twinkling, winking—
  glittering, enticing
Commanding
Demanding
  respectful silence,
  for what they represent:
  solitude in the night.

Debra A. Sunde

Self-Guilt

Sure, they exploit
the whales and seals now
what I'm waiting for
is the day to come
when there's
no whales
and no seals
left to kill
I'm waiting for them
to start crying about
there not being any whales or,
seals to kill when they start
crying over the fact
that there ain't any
whales or,
seals left
I hope they point
their fingers
at themselves.

Kevin Kwader

The Memories of a Love Gone

I know that we are truly apart when the toothpaste cap is on;
When his and hers towels become only hers;
When I no longer can track you by the trail of dirty clothes from the
bathroom to the bedroom;
When I can read the morning paper without tearing it apart to give
you the sports page;
When I can roll over and turn off the alarm clock without crawling
over you;
I'm always on time for work because you're not here to delay me
with your ravenous sexual appetite;
The bathroom is always empty and the commode lid down;
So as I sit here and ponder over our short life together and look
about my immaculate house I have but one thing to say;
BABY PLEASE COME HOME!!!

Laura Hensley

Untitled

I can still remember the amber flame that burned in your eyes like
a glass of warmed brandy.
The smell, taste, and sight of your masculine flesh beneath my
searching lips.
The way the firelight would turn your body into a statue of molten
bronze and gold.
The sound of your laughter that rumbled through the room like
thunder on a stormy night.
And the velvet purr of your husky voice as we laid in a lovers'
embrace.
But all there is now, are memories, memories of a time long past.
You are gone now, gone to a place only dreamt about.
Are you happy, are you sad?
The days seem longer now,
The nights an eternity.
Awaking in the morning in a bed of loneliness,
Sleeping at night in a bed of despair.
Did I love you too much?
Demand the impossible?
The ways of life are a complete mystery to me.
Maybe someday I will know, maybe.
But for now, all there is, are memories
I can still remember...

Anne Blackwell-Biller

New News

The newspapers are filled with things that are sad.
Everything people do that is bad.
Wrecks and Robberies
Accidents, Sin.
Earthquakes, storms, floods, hurricanes.
All that you hope won't happen to you.
Why doesn't someone start something new
With good things that happen
To make us all glad...

Marie Wills

A Gift of Love, Forever

Dad tilled the soil and slaved year after year,
not much did he see of his two daughters dear.
He dreamed of prosperity and a new way of life,
but not much he could give his family and wife.

He started a business and slowly there were gains,
new clothes, new cars, and lots of nice things.
He wanted his family to stand out in the crowd,
he searched for the finest treasure to endow.

He chose glittery, precious white diamond stones,
to sparkle and adorn the hands of his own.
A statement of social prestige for all to see,
proudly worn and treasured since I was seventeen.

His aged, callused hands paid the price of success,
to fulfill his dream and give his family the best.
Inspired by the shadows of his ambitions,
His most gracious gift begins a family tradition.

For your birthday gift, I can't buy your dream boat,
But it's a token of love that you might sit and gloat.
A glittery white diamond I bestow on your hand,
that marks yet another successful young man.

Karen E. Meier

---

*They talk of professional
women. Personally I have
never met an amateur.*

—Winston Churchill

Forever Waiting
(for my true love)

So many sleepless nights thinking about you,
Never to have you, refused.
Please understand our friendship is love, it's true.

Question not and accept me for what is there,
No one as loyal, trusting.
Strong is my passion, my love, never to wear.

While you are alive, I will love no other,
Not being with you, envied.
Forever waiting, like no other lover.

Imagine our bodies pulsating with pleasure,
Together embraced, thrusting.
Giving to each other, love, without measure.

Search your heart and find an honest intuition,
Stay true to yourself, devoted.
True love to you, honoring your volition.

Scott A. Nisbet

Celestial Ceremonial
(The way it should have been.)

Plunging headlong, spurred by time
To its rendezvous sublime,
Kindled with divine confusion
By the Sun's imperial call,
Comes a frigid apparition
For a fiery exhibition
That will break its long seclusion
In the planetary pall.

Like a missile from the handle
Of a mythic roman candle
Halley's Comet will transform
In a ritualistic show
To a streaming incandescence
In that blinding Royal Presence
Where the wild electrons swarm
And ionic torches blow.

Rivals with no invitation
Join the cyclic celebration:
Lithe moons wax into a sigh—
Stage-struck planets preen and soar.
Then the vassal, vestment shining,
Rivals blinded and repining,
Sweeps in triumph through the sky
To the vault it knew before.

    A. T. Kemper

Gloves

Be my glove—
it takes two to make a pair—
Be my mate.

    II

Be my glove—
Hand in hand
Down the aisle.

    III

Be my glove—
When it's cold—when it's fashionable—
Let's be one wherever we're invited.

    IV

Be my glove—
Don't get lost or stolen—
It's so sad to lie all alone.

    V

Be my glove—
Be my alter ego
Til we're old & disreputable.

    Jane Pierritz

Office Wives

Do not envy me
time spent with him;
It is not time shared.
It is filled with
paperwork, and deadlines
missed by the time received,
loud discussions from
opposing sides, missed meals
(or pressed airlines fare),
hours waiting to deliver
something someone
needed yesterday,
frantic drives to airports,
dog-tired waiting for flights,
and schedules that change
and change
and change.
I am a part of the job;
you are a part of his life.

    Ricci
    Included in **About The Poets** Section

GRESSONEY ST. JEAN.

Honorable Mention
Balmy Geese

In the red Catskill mountains
the yellow stone sun
shines down bird shell seas

balmy geese fly through
thin weeds
into brimrose kites.

    John Svehla
    Included in **About The Poets** Section

Time Was...

Time was...
When the planet thrived—
A hand was shaken,
No lives were taken.

Time was...
When children played freely—
Trusting each other,
Loving thy brother completely.

Time was...
When the people listened—
Following their hearts,
And the world glistened.

Time was...
When we really cared—
Friendships were true,
In all that we shared.

Time was...
When minds of construction—
Overrode those,
Filled with hate and destruction.

Time is...
Simply stated—
We're all responsible,
For what we've created.

    David Robins

Honorable Mention
I want to Live

in a white room
with beige floors
and red flowers
in chinese vases,
unspoiled by attachment.

I want to feel
soft cushions,
tapering wooden tables
with my fingertips.

I want the natural breezes
to flow through me.
I want to move
without steps.

I took away with me
the silk scarf
from Simon
that last time...

    ruth feldheim

She Dreamed of Sailing

she dreamed of sailing
to a remote southern island
in a portuguese caravel.
she dreamed the sailors
would hoist her high up
towards the sail where she'd
gesture and say, "land ho!"

she dreamed her lover
would be dancing
in soft white chiffon,
laughing for the world to hear.
she dreamed the music
lasted as long as a polemic
between two philosophers.

Robin Lum Cheong

Damascus Remembered

Burst of emerald green,
between the mountains brown,
Majestic ancient queen,
With cloudless sky for crown.
You quenched my thirst on sight,
Despite the brilliant sun,
As Barada's stream takes flight
And through your soil does run.

Ruth Ann Burrell Hickey

The Sound of Falling Wood

Chop.
Chop.
The sounds frighten me.
The men came today
To cut down that
Old tree in the yard.
That tree has been
Here longer than I.

Knock.
Knock.
The sounds frighten me.
People come in and out
To care for me,
To watch over my form.
I creak, barely speak,
and reek of decaying bed clothes.

Upon waking, I slowly
Glance in the mirror.
Bones seem like branches.
Outside this morning, I heard
The sound of falling wood.
I shivered.
Chop.
Chop.

Richard K. Allison

Bad Memory

It is part of life
The disappointments
Disillusionment
Is that what makes us feel
Sadness
Bitterness
Over broken dreams
Hearts
Is that why we sometimes
Forget
Life that makes us smile
Forget
Some sadness
Life that makes us love
Feel the warmth of someone
Caring
Keeps us going
Day by day
Trying to forget
A bad memory

Mike Foster

Can't You See?

With us in writing,
Heard in a song,
Shared with each other,
From dusk until dawn.

Reflected in mirrors,
Pictures as well,
Leading us places,
Where...no one can tell.

As special as rainbows,
Stirring as the sea,
Touching us through nature,
Appearing instantly.

Dwelling in the eyes of others,
Green, brown, and often blue,
If you took the time to look my way,
You'd find someone has feelings for you.

Kerri Jo Fazekas

Untitled

Sheltered from crime
gangs and filth
The suburbs of peace
righteousness and love
Houses fences and yards
keeping life out
fencing out realization
crooks rape murder
and true culture
Am I being sheltered
no change of pace
Am I being trapped
no gunshots and death
only school and
"culture"
Keep life moving
no sirens pass by
the police don't visit
Am I being saved
or am I being locked away?

Gwenyn Alexa

Thoughts Distressed

We are all children
With the same attention span
We are temperamental
So immature with pride
We are so spiteful.

We all have young minds
With old or new bodies
We are not growing
So thoughtless of others
We are unknowing.

We are all small
With nothing to grow towards
Oh, jealous me!
So vague and uneasy
We are so empty.

Sharon L. Boyer

Left Memphis

Sophomoric rantings,
    tadpole dreams
Discipline developed
    a backbone scheme
Life loaded van,
    gambling gas,
Dangerous crosswinds
    mountain pass
Road swerves, land ends,
    flashing arrows assault
Destination premonition,
    highway ambition
West, maybe LA

Jackie Ware

I Need Someone

I need someone to talk to
And someone to talk to me
A hand to hold
A soft embrace
A touch that sets me free

I need someone to pray with
And to share my everything
My dreams, my hopes, and visions
Of what life with him will bring

I need someone to love me
Lord, Oh how I'll love him so
He'll take my hand and lead me
And he'll never let me go

Sally M. Gordon

Carnival

Before I forget...
the prejudice I regret,
Let me speak of minds met.
High noses...
Higher hates...
Looks I saw in that face.
White skins, light skins
Shallow gains...
Lined parade routes
Looking for like games,
throwing gifts of no value
to lames.
Prejudice looked in my eyes,
my inner soul cried.
Those prejudiced eyes continued
in stride...
The prejudice I regret,
I cannot forget...
On Carnival day, that we met.

Ronald L. Allen

Vagrant Sirens

Love's thin gait
wanders over distance
the sandy tracks
of a neighborhood's darkness

phosphorous of days
from the shore's footsteps
as hours pass the column
of vagrant sirens.

Sharon Rubenstein

'GIRL'S HEAD.'

Poetic Confusion

My mind was twisted around
And reality seemed up-side-down
Up-side-down for a day
I seemed to walk the opposite way
The opposite way gave the crazy illusion
Of a muse-imbued soul transfusion
Inspiration poetic mirror
Of sensations that were dearer
Than my everyday conceit
Of being almost quite complete
In my attempts to be well rounded
That is by no ghosts surrounded
Ghosts of yesterdays undone
Relationships and such bygone
Seeing mirrors of illusions
Of those muse-imbued transfusions
I was given one white page
To convey this my poetic cage
There—
I could declare
I was sentenced to discover
That I was the free verse poem's lover
But say—
It rhymed for one whole day.

Tone Aanderaa

Reflections in a Clear Mind

In the stillness
    I see me within,
eyes reflecting eyes
    stopped, at the plane.
Covering back with front
    details fascinate.

Ripples spread
    multiplying, chaos' dance
smears recognition.
    Until a carp, attracted
looks at me looking at him.
    My face and his, rest together.

Donna N. Moulton

Autumn

It's time for Autumn to arrive
with leaves all red and gold,
a crisp cool breeze envelops
the earth
as leaves fall
still and cold...
Some whirl and twirl around and round
all sizes large and small,
as the wind plays 'tag' in child-like glee
the season now is FALL...

Judy Fortier

I Love Her

People say I look like her.
I just say "I'm glad!"
Because she's the best mother
A person could ever have.

To me she's like an angel
Floating across the floor.
I bet God sent her to us.
How could anyone ask for more.

To me she is very beautiful
and also very nice.
She understands my feelings
And I don't have to repeat them twice.

I cannot live without her
Because she's like a guide.
So when we are in heaven
I hope we'll be side by side.

The person I am speaking of
(Before you get this wrong!)
Is the only one it could be
And that surely is my mom.

Alisa Kay Richards

Bus Stop

A skinny black kid's Sony
labors low battery Silent Night.

The wind whips two retarded girls,
just off the nursing home swing shift,
as they huddle together
in the knifed Plexiglas
waiting on the 21.

A lavender-headed punk stumbles
in fourteen year old flesh,
staggers among the soggy napkins
and McDonald's bags,
praying the nasty night will
suck her middle class dry.

The girls snuggle and rock
foot to foot.

Silent Night.

Dream of toilet.

No bus.

Michael Sheridan

The Thinker

If ever a man a Thinker was
it was you,
who made us all think
and made me think
of all my pain,
of all my life

You pulled from me
and opened my heart
to make me see
your caring, compassionate
warm warm ways
I want to hold you
and be held by you
all the night through

But you
whose mind swims in music
who knows all the notes
who knows all the words
who knows the deep deep ways
of the mind,
you can never belong
to one,
to one thought

If ever a man a Thinker was
it was you,
who made yourself think
the many thoughts
of all your pain,
of all your life

Darlyn Kranz

Familiar Strangers

It was a nice party
        until I saw you. In

an instant, eyes pass,
        daydreams flash! perhaps

love at first sight should
        have seen the second or

listened to the first
        mind. Had we been

friends, our love would
        have been spiritual,

not physical. Our secrets
        shared, not hidden.

Games, doubts, and anger
        would never have been

born between us. It was
        a nice party until

I saw you...and you saw
        me. The me that I am

you have never met. The you that
        you are, I have never known.

Reginald L. Goodwin
Included in **About The Poets** Section

Honorable Mention
Hands

Your hands made a bench
for me to eat on

Your hands hard callous
wedging caliche
planting rose in rocks

I touch the pickets
of the wooden swing
your hands nailed for me

I close my eyes and
bleeding clouds emerge
in a red light wave
serrated by
the rising sun

I smell the wood
I feel the thorns
with my eyes shut
the lemon tree
which never grew
lemons

I close my eyes
and do not see
your hands

The sun explodes

Anne de Longeville
88

Melodies Not Heard

Melodies Not Heard
Play upon my soul
In colorless hues
They paint my visage
A window within
My eyes open gleam
Revealing the song
That remains ever silent.

The essence of life
Spills out from my mouth
Flowing to the one
Linked by silver strand
Returning are the notes
By which my heart sounds

A quiet symphony
Painted with our love.

S. R. Sellers

PORTRAIT.

If I Were Married To You

Both the kids are crying
The cat got out again
I haven't done the laundry
It's already half past ten

I've got to wash the dishes
And hang up all the clothes
I need to sweep the floor
And wipe the baby's nose

The telephone is ringing
Toys are on the floor
I wish the day was over
Someone's knocking on the door

What will I cook for supper
What will we have tonight
The house is such a mess
It is an awful sight

I really can't complain
About my way of life
It's just to be expected
Whenever you're a wife

Joy Marie Gordon

He Is The Son Of God

Once upon a time there was a man.
He lived and died upon this land.
He was a very special man,
He loved everybody, good and bad.

He did things no one else could do.
He made life something special too.
Even though some did not believe,
He showed that they had no reason to disbelieve.

Oh yes, He was a special man.
He was the Son of God, a perfect man.
But then they nailed Him to a cross,
Yes this special man has died for us.

Now He has risen from the dead.
He gave us a new life,
We have eternity to live.
Yes, He is a special man.

He is a man of love and a man of peace,
He will help us and give us what we need.
Still there are people that do not believe,
But I know and do believe that
        He is the Son of God.

Karla L. Gue

Journey Infinite

Dear Lord, this world You made o'erflows with bounty of Your love;
Each mile I journey, gratitude ascends to You above,
O'ershadowing all heartache, evil, struggle, tears, or pain;
I still lift humble heart to You again...again...again...

In every land through which I pass, love swells my heart anew,
For these, my brothers, sisters, all-created, Lord, by You.
And if the tongue sounds strange, a handclasp warm, a brilliant
        smile
Speak universal language, so sincere and without guile.

Old hurts, small-minded bigotry all quickly melt away...
Today I heard brown babies cry, I watched black children play;
Heard lullabies crooned softly by my sisters red and white;
Each dear as I to Thee, O Lord, each priceless in Thy sight.

Majestic mountains, oceans blue so fill me with delight,
I cannot comprehend what more—than in *this* world so bright—
Eternity itself shall hold to lure, entice me there—
Save this: *Your Very Presence* and Your Perfect Love so rare.

Made manifest by Your Own Son who trod this earthly sphere,
Compliant with Your plan to love and save Your children here;
And even now prepares a place for us, unmarred, sublime—
Where fascinating work and joys go on through endless time.

Dear Lord, my soul does thirst for You, "like the hart for the water
        brook."
I've loved Your people, Your fair earth—but it's *YOU* for Whom I
        look;
"For me to live is Christ, to die is gain,"—how true, *how true*;
I treasure all the journey—but I *long* to be with *You!*

Mary Walker Underwood

Conchcosmos

Cheek to the sand, ear to the shell's
Wild surf and grave swell,
Long the wind lulls me,
Tall sky fills me.

Tawny the sand, bleached the shell,
White surf, mauve swell:
Cold, the sky sings in me,
Old, the world begins in me.

One with sea and land I lie,
Fierce wind, frail shell,
Rooted in earth
Resolved to sky.

Peter Thomas

Many hurry to catch up; few hurry to get ahead.

Tribute to Mankind

Blessed is the Black man and his
generation,

One day God will give him his own nation.

Blessed is the White man and his
everlasting power,

May God have mercy on his
judgment hour.

Blessed is the Red man and his
thanks to be alive,

He too had to live a life of
sorrow, violence and jive.

Blessed is the Brown man, may
he be satisfied by 'God one
Way,'

I pray for all to live together in
peace one day.

Blessed is the Yellow man and
his freedom of being,

May he one day find peace from
the noises of war.

Blessed are we, under the Stars and Stripes, with freedom
always at hand.

And may God bless us with the
powers in his hands, to give
miracles which no man can.

Robert C. Campbell

Spring Contest

Candy pie
Baked in the light of spring,
Makes the whole world
Feel like a king and queen.
Ingredients from one end of the rainbow
To the other.
Happiness bringing smiles
Through miles and miles of laughter,
To sisters and brothers.
Smothered with freshness
Delightful and sweet
This candy pie just couldn't be beat.
Yellow canaries singing,
Everyone twirling around and around
To this beautiful heavenly sound.
Pleasing joy brought to each girl and boy.
Candy pie charming in the spring contest.

Bonnie S. Peter

Return of Spring

   The dandelions are yellow in the tall grass,
  Tulips are starting to show their crimson color,
Naked trees covering themselves with leaves.

   Little bluebirds still learning to fly
  A sky that stays baby-blue
Puppies chewing on a tennis ball.

   Dogwoods that are white with crimson stains,
  Green clover in the meadow,
Ponies running wild.

   Chicks, soft and yellow
  Violets with their amethyst glow,
Tiger lilies, long and slender.

   Spring, a time for new birth
  A time of beauty for all to see,
A time for God to create mysteries.

Phyllis A. Foglia

Spring Has Awakened

At the sight of the red breast;
Spring has awakened from her frozen winter sleep.
Snow caps melting, streams rushing, rivers run deep.
March winds have ceased their blowing;
April showers are gently falling.
Spring's fever, to the animals softly calling.
Trees, plants, and flowers everywhere are budding;
Seedlings reaching skyward, as if the sun was beckoning.
Insects of every kind;
Like the bees are buzzing.
The frozen sleep is foregoing.
The red breast is home;
Spring has awakened.

Robert O. Pugh

Guest

I long suspected a squirrel boarder in the attic;
Charged him no rent, instead
Listened to quick music of scamperings and chatterings
In hide-out trees by that broken window
'Til his great tail streaked away over flat brown earth,
Racing toward spring.

Lois Hayn

Winter, New Jersey Style

Fresh fallen snow lays upon tree branches and log fences.
The white cotton sheet softly covers all that can be seen.
Muffling sounds in the town, giving everything that extra charm.
Trees bend and moan, deformed by winter's new coat.
Snow still filling the air, being blown down from elsewhere.

Slicked, glazed trees that gleam from ice hats painted on.
Icicles dangle from branches, nature's own clear crystal
   chandelier.
Snow sprinkled with fallen ice, appear like diamonds in the
   frosted sunlight.
Cars move slowly over glass and cotton covered roads.
Old homes built in a colonial way, seem so snug on this winter's
   day.

Fog edged windows allow small faces to peek.
Winter wonderland, beauty that is mystical when seen in a
   different way.
Bundled rosy children in their colorful scarves and not matching
   mittens.
No school today, begin a full day of play.
Construction of snow fort and men, begin once again.

Adults mumble and swear with shovels in their hands.
Take time to stare, memories of childhood they now share.
A moment of freedom, a child once more.
Before reality finds its way in and closes the door.
They begin again to clear away the fresh fallen snow.

Katherine Vines

Memories

Being there
the night
you were born...
seeing your mother,
her proud,
happy face.
seems such
a long time ago.

The memory
of that night
passed quickly...
watching you
growing tall.
Then you were
ten years old.

That night
umpteen years ago
is a memory...
seeing you now
so tall...
A young man
twenty years old.

Lorraine Hicks

Honorable Mention
Emergence

Slowly,
Out of my curved sleep,
Out of my fluid darkness;
Softly,
Out of my narrow nest,
Out of my split shell
I wind with wet wings
Into the green spring air,
No memory of my larval form,
No memory of my folded flight,
Only from the silken womb,
    Release!

Rosemarie R. Malloy

In Love

Eyes meet
Hearts melt
Strong emotions
Being felt

Crowded places
You and me
And other people
We didn't see

Colleen Dougher

CHRISTCHURCH : NEAR IFORD BRIDGE

Amethyst Armour

The mirror looks back
my face, an everyman.
In the morning, death
warmed over.
Does it show more so today,
even in a face like any other.

Dressed for the day
in appropriate tie and armour,
which all of us wear
world over
when at times the world
selectively guards her children.

What armour to wear
when you're bent; what
device provides the iron cocoon
built over
the jewel, keeping the same
safe, yet shamelessly displayed.

Its colour is purple,
ours before royalty was.
The armour is amethyst
worn over
the heart and core. The armour
translucent, the beauty revealed.

J.P. Bullinger
91

Love Came Soon

Love came soon but I did then pause
Not knowing where my fate did lie
But once it seemed life had a cause.

Love came soon but I did then pause
Of love I feared eternal laws
I must have once known love's sad sigh.

Love came soon but I did then pause
Not knowing where my fate did lie.

Cindy Adams

Two Inch Once-A-Year Snow

Not deep enough for snowmen,
Or snowshoes, sleds, and skis;
Just deep enough for wet sneakers,
Muddy seats, elbows, and knees.
Deep enough to keep the laundry
Going every little while;
Just deep enough to make
Their rosy bright-eyed faces smile.

Billie Nye

Sunrise

Searching desperately
For love
For care
For gentle Lover, resting
There.

Time after time,
I've turned down cover's bare
That reach to the ceiling
O'er my bed,
Seeking silently
For token left
Behind.

Evidence a maiden's heart was melted by
Manhood sweet.
Then left as
Odor upon blue sheet.

Memories may rust
But left behind the proof
In dust,
Fingerprints.

Brushing tears goodbye
One ponders
Why
Silent scars amidst the dust
The last remains
To be known
As us.

Gail Hutchings
Included in **About The Poets** Section

Memories

To say goodbye to a million dreams
Memories and you
Was the hardest thing I've ever had to do
The memories are written well within my life
They could never be taken from me
Then, now or ever
You were something beautiful that passed my way
We enriched the world and the people we touched
With the radiant love we shared
I gave you all my love and a million promises
Promises never meant to be broken
You made my heart sing with tears of joy
We shared together
The love once mine, I let slip away...you
I must ask one thing
If you hear a song reminding you of me
Don't be sad
Remember,
I'll always love you, just as I did then
Love is the dearest of all God's precious gifts
That's why I'm sure our love will last
In our hearts
For a lifetime and even longer
Be happy and treasure our precious memories

Joyce Jones-Rogers
Included in **About The Poets** Section

Rich gifts wax poor when givers prove unkind.

—Shakespeare

Untitled

What is that face, that far-off memory, that trace?
Thoughts only a heart could see.
Shadows lost in mystery.
Were they really you and me?

I walk alone this time around, and it is good.
But still I'm haunted by a dream, a way we stood.
I falter in my forward stride,
And turn towards mist that time now hides.

Your eyes they hold an evening song,
A moment here, a moment gone.
Your soul remembers more than you
Of lifetimes past and love that's true.

Is it best let time move on?
Perhaps we are forever gone.
The way we were, the love that's been,
Really nothing more than dreams?

A single note now fills the air.
A morning song not even there.
What it will bring I cannot say.
The answer hides in tomorrow's clay.

Patricia Dawn McConnell

Where Have You Gone?

Where have you gone?
It seems like only yesterday—
The society in which you were forced to live
Denied all true gifts you had to give.
A child so lonely, a woman confused
Why was your death so soon:
You could never reach the height and depth of
    our golden moon.
Destiny by fate: the choice was made
A child trapped inside the age of a woman,
A woman who was indeed a troubled child
Your path was full of countless, but endless lies.
From Norma Jean to Hollywood; a famous name was born.
Your beautiful yet troubled personality was left
Suffering greatly, many tears were wept.
Where have you gone?
Treasured memories you gave us;
That famous legend still fills our hearts
Marilyn, dear Marilyn: a peace within your soul
I hope you have found...
With all the pain, there was so much strife
Indeed ending, what on this earth—a tragedy of life.

Vicki Thompson

Hold Me

Do not go and leave me here
Among the dreams that we once knew,
    Don't kill the things that we had loved
And end the pleasure that was you.

Give me just the thought of you
And all we might have been,
    Let me hope the love I had
Might somehow have its chance again,

Let me dream once more of Life
Although I know it won't be true,
    Hold me just a moment more
And let me taste the touch of you.

Walt Summers

A Backward Glance
(Shakespearean Sonnet)

The wayward winds of time divide us now
From fading years of many decades past.
The thought of times we shared—Remember how
The playing children seemed to grow so fast?
And can it be, I hear your thoughts, you mine?
Now as my grown boys argue I reflect
The joys we shared amid a friendly vine.
Recalling happy thoughts, I can't forget.
We poured out hearts together—right or wrong
The secrets families can never know.
And as our children grew both tall and strong,
Warm thoughts filled parted years with afterglow.
Alone, we'll walk the path...Its final bend.
But I'll remember you...A Love...A Friend.

Winnie E. Fitzpatrick

Empty Cup

Long-nailed fingers barely touching
Wood-grained panels. Splintered. Sharp.
Nervous eyes that twitch and shrivel
From the sight of faceless clock.

Tension mounting with the waiting,
Almost way too much to bear.
Cascades of clatter pierce the brain
As one lone spoon lands on the floor.

The feeling of black liquid falling,
Reaching empty pits within.
Accursed dark addiction stronger
With each new cup given him.

One gnarled appendage digging deeper
Into linen, white, and soft.
The razored voice rasps: "Want more coffee?"
His reply: "No thanks, I've had enough."

Eric Reiss

Life, if well used, is long enough.

—Seneca

The Sojourn

Mesmerized...I was
by the slow, sway of the briny deep...
Hypnotized...I was
into a deep, enchanted sleep.

Enchanted by the foaming swells,
Smitten with eternal hours,
Spellbound by the kelpy bands,
Charmed with the stony bowers.

The crimson and amethyst charms
of the open, prostrate sky,
Stretched out above the billows,
And, tranquilized...remained I.

Tranquil, were the beryl waves,
Soothing...as they lapped the silken sands,
Caressing...was the silent shore,
As it touched the waves with out-stretched hands.

Entranced by the umbra, falling,
Exchanging vows with golden Sol...
I knew, too soon, my ended sojourn...
I heard Reality faintly call.

K. Wolfgang Millam

Impasse

Shadows flicker tauntingly
whispering moments from the past,
echoing yesterday's "if only's"
and the faith that didn't last.

Cold hands caress each other
shivering between cool sheets,
praying for blissful darkness
to fade away in sleep.

Morning arrives grey and foggy
with an indecisive mind,
heartbeat thumping loudly
with each, "How, how? Why?"

Sparks of determination
every now and then,
useless plans of resolution
anxiety tugging, "When, when?"

Another day another night
repeating the ones before,
the clock ticks on, so ominously
wherever did tomorrow go?

Kimberly Nicely

The Color Key

Among the hand-loomed threads of every life
In over-under pattern mesh design,
A single strand, deep-woven with the rest,
Contains the key
To understanding of each life-style path.
A dark and somber thread that runs throughout
The whole pervades and sets the tone of its
Totality.
A bright eye-catching strand of lighter hue
Enlivens all the others there, reflects
Its owner's zest for life—and all he is
Or hopes to be.
A woven thread of mutely-toned pastel
Bespeaks a soft and gentle-natured soul,
An underlying tenderness that few
Can clearly see.
Metallic threads of silver or of gold
Proclaim the weaver to espouse and lead
A colorful flamboyant life of bold
Intensity.
But each observer of the lives that touch
His own in greater or in lesser ways
Must note the dominantly woven thread
To find the key.

Mauricia Price

My Father's House

I did stop by upon my way
   At Father's house just for a day.
I entered through familiar gate,
   So unaware of things in wait.
My Father's house had fallen ruin,
   The piper played a grizzly tune.

As I did reel in horror shocked,
   I found the gates of hell unlocked
And from within there did unfold,
   The stench of cauldron bubbling bold.
With cackling tongues, the witch and shrew,
   My Father's spoils were sorting through.

The serpent long, had raised his head,
   And on my Father's Children fed.
The place I lived as romping boy,
   Had since become old Satan's toy.
In Father's house, on Father's soil,
   This grim intruder did uncoil.

Now Father's house dividing two,
   Soon into three will follow through.
Then into twelve as months of year,
   As Father's Children disappear.
The curse of it, the Devil's Hold,
   Shall rend apart my Father's Fold.

     Bernadette Vaincourt   Canada

Not Yet, Lord

When the Grim Reaper shakes his scythe
It's almost time to gop;
To sample all of Heaven's joys
Instead of those we know.
And I'm not very fearful
About what I might get.
I could even say I'm ready, Lord,
But please—not just yet.

It's been a long life and a merry one
Taken as a whole,
Tho' I've had my share of sorrow
To purify my soul;
But it's pleasure I remember,
And pain that I forget,
So let's find out what lies ahead,
But please, lord, not yet.

When the roll is called up yonder,
I hope that I'll be there,
Enjoying every moment
Of existence free from care.
I know I will be welcomed
By old friends, well-met,
And I really will go gladly, Lord,
But, please—not quite yet.

     Nancy B. Chapman

BRAIDING THE PENNON.

Invocation Prayer

Jesus, I believe in you with all my Heart and with all my Soul and with all my Mind. A humble servant accepts his christian duties that strongly knit a peaceful life.

Lord, with my tongue I confess all my sins. Jesus, forgive my mistakes, guide me to learn understanding with thy word. Fill me with thy spirit of thy Holy Ghost.

Lord, you died for our sins, you gave your life for all sinners, so we should live unto righteousness.

Thank you Jesus for providing salvation. In Jesus name, I pledge my faith into action, I surrender to you my heart...I surrender my soul...I surrender my mind.

Today and everyday, Jesus you are first in all I do.

Lord, let thy will...be my will.

Jesus, I believe only with thy grace can my life awaken to Joy, Love and Peace.

Jesus, bestow your inner Joy within my Heart.
Jesus, bestow your divine Love in my Soul.
Jesus, bestow your sacred Peace in my Mind.
Jesus, guide my life moving upward to serve the...higher to obey thee...limitless to love thee.

I am alive unto God thru Jesus Christ our Savior

    In Jesus Name, So it is.

    Angela Cisneros

Life's Summation...

Riding life's waves of knowledge...
I seek wisdom.
The waves of faith...
Giving courage and strength,
facing each new day.

The waves of truth...
Give values,
The right and wrong of life,
And what's worthwhile.

The waves of love...
Give security,
The warmth of knowing
Another cares.

The waves of hope...
give endurance,
A promise of all things to come,
A reason for living...

Then the final wave transcends...
At the meeting of Our Lord...
This transformation from life to death...
And the final summation is met.

Glenna Gardner-Wimett
Included in **About The Poets** Section

Music In The Night

I sometimes lay awake at night
and listen to the rain
as it taps so rhythmically
against my windowpane

And as it dances on the roof
in darkness of the night
a composition is composed
of music lost in flight

Beyond the shadows and the clouds
God writes a symphony
with swirling rain and breathless wind
in wondrous harmony

A crescendo shakes the heavens
as lightning lights the sky
and the tempo of the music
slows down to breathe a sigh

And as the notes fall from the sky
some half notes and some whole
I feel the music deep within
my heart, my mind, my soul

Arlene Devine
Included in **About The Poets** Section

A Sudden Loss

A life begins!
You are in a spin,
As you begin to plan
For you,
Are the baby's greatest fan.

Just a few months you share
Until it all becomes unfair,
Your heart fills with sorrow
For there will be no tomorrow

All your tears fall
As this pain is great!
For this sudden loss
You tried to create.

Many tomorrows
You will sit and stare,
Always to remember
This terrible nightmare.

Linda Amato

Autumn's Final Fade

autumn, artist's canvas
feels the final flush
   of heat
the last full flow of color
on the farm's
   ruddy complexion
faltering fields
once fertile
now fallow
...seccant
scattered seeds
shed by too tall meadow grass
swept by winds
...dissipate
autumn, artist's canvas
feels the final fade
   of watercolor

Angelina Rossetti

Tribute

Her life was short, a few precious days;
She changed our life in many ways.

Her spirit dwells amongst us still,
From day to day, it always will.

Her fate unknown, she did her best;
She battled hard and needs her rest.

The last few days were such delight;
To hold her, rock her through the night.

So sleep sweet child; you're truly free,
Our precious girl, Amy Marie

James Solar

Rain in the Night

Soft and soothing,
Sleep-inducing,
   Quiet music in the night;
Window-spattering,
Softly pattering,
   Gentle showers in the night.

Ripping, tearing,
Lightning flaring,
   Causing sudden, chilling fright;
Heavy downpour
Deafening roar,
   Thunder showers in the night.

Soft or glaring,
Soothing, scaring,
   No matter how the rain may fall,
Tame or wild,
Rough or mild,
   Earth gratefully absorbs it all.

Sun and rain,
Joy and pain,
   Into each life some rain must fall.
The Lord of love
High above
   Leads us gently through it all.

Lucy M. Young

God

Is HE a person?
Is HE here or there?
Is HE really anything?
HE is everywhere!

HE is in a sunbeam,
HE is in the air,
In a falling snowflake,
HE is everywhere!

HE is in the sunset,
In the glistening rain.
HE is in the forest,
And upon the open plain.

HE is in the food you eat,
Also in your drink.
HE is in the music's beat,
HE's at the skating rink.

HE is on the eagle's wing,
You see HIM in a lamp.
HE is on the child's swing,
And guides the forlorn tramp.

HE is in the stars at night,
HE is on the sea.
HE shows you wrong from right,
AND HE's with you and me!

Marlene Coombes

Have You Ever Been A-walking

Have you ever been a-walking
By yourself alone at night?
And you're worried about the sounds
You hear on your left and right?
It might be an owl that hoots
Or a tiny little mouse
Who dashes hurriedly to and fro
And all around the house.
Have you ever been a-walking
Just before a falling rain
And the breezes bring an odor
That you want to smell again
Have you ever been a-walking
When the snow is falling down
And the flakes are so pretty
You could wear them in a crown
There are places on this earth
That we don't appreciate
But you could see the beauty
If you would but hesitate
Look carefully all around you
With each and every day
To see the joyous beauty
If you chance to gaze that way.

R. Marie Hill Franklin

Stray Thoughts

Run, Run, Running,
Forever running but never arriving,
Always searching yet never finding.
     Afraid of living, Frightened of dying,
Straining to see things that are best left hidden,
Striving to understand things that defy explanation.

Dreaming Dreams of things to be,
Awakening to reality; yet refusing to see—
By fleeing into darkness with all your hopes for a
better tomorrow, your true self is lost,
     Not your dilemma.

To be strong is not to run.
To seek is not always to find.
To see is also to be blind.
To live is but to die.
To live in a fantasy world, is to live a lie.

Longing for the impossible—
Never realizing the inevitable.
     Remembering the past,
     Dreaming of the future,
     Avoiding the present...
Nothing is as it should be,
     Yet there is nowhere to flee—

For even Dreams aren't Free...

Carla Golden
Included in **About The Poets** Section

Give Me the Tools

Give me the tools to express myself.
     To say what I want to say
The pain, anger, and love I see,
     On every passing face
For day by day, people pass me by
     Living a life gone astray

Give me the tools and I shall create,
     A world not free of love and hate
But to kill indifference would a triumph be.
     I ask you know, give the tools to me
I shall build rolling hills and lakes and streams.
     Things shall never be what they seem

Give me the tools to build a new world,
     For you and me a new life
No more anger, no more pain, no more strife.
     Let me build for you a new life
To you I may seem a little strange, not quite clear.
     But I am just a single brave cavalier

Fighting for a cause, fighting for a reason.
     I seek to bring about a new season
A season of creativity of joy, of love,
     Signaled by an olive branch and a dove
Four times forty years it shall last,
     there is no time the die have been cast

Give me the tools and I shall create.
     A tapestry woven from intertwining fates
A carpet to cover the floor of our lives.
     A bridge to cross the Land of Sighs
Give me the tools to express myself.
     To say what I want to say...

Ian Christopher Klimon

FINE WEATHER.

Writers' Query

What causes the pen to strike paper at will?
    Is it the wonder of nature
    and the essence of the universe
    or the contamination of the elements
    which threaten Mother Earth.

    Is it the virtues of humanity—
    and inalienable rights invested hitherto
    or the exploitation of justice
    and disregard for the truth.

    Is it the need for public awareness
    and education about world events
    or a flare for the dramatic
    to distort the incident.

    Is it the desire to inspire
    those who by chance read
    or the will to influence
    the powers that be.

Angela W. Debose

Andante

You told me that you couldn't sing.
I respected that.
But one rainy
sleepy Sunday
I heard you humming
a tune you never knew
and wept
because the song you sang
was
me...

Jaime Lynne Morewood

Hold On

Stay in there! Hold on!
Face the crowd. Stay and stand up proud!
It's rough out there. Face the music. Move slowly with the beat.
Don't panic. It's just the heat.
In the confusion, in the holocaust that surrounds you,
Be calm! No longer is it what it once was, no peace, no food to
    eat
But guns, hunger and wars. Life no longer cherished.
Today seems like a saddened child whose dreams have vanished
No more the breath of fresh air, but everywhere
The stench of pollution. Who'll care for our salvation?
Toddlers become parents. It's more confusion.
the hungry die and the dying wishes that the living may save
    his life.
Fraud, strife, run amock along the pot-holed lanes of life
As the powers of darkness keep growing...It's more strife.
The world writhes. The beauty keeps disintegrating.
Be brave! Be bold! For behind the darkened clouds a light is
    glowing.

Giftus R. John

Two Hands

Two hands clasp in the darkness
Two souls share an experience of life
Witnessing love unfold before them
Two mouths exchange endearments
Words of love that vanish in the dark
Two people walk into the neon life of a city night
Their love transcends the stars
Their friendship never wavers
A merged happiness
Two as one
Their lives intertwine
If ever so slight
Like the fingers of
Two hands in the night.

William A. Ashwell

       Canada

ON THE PEGNITZ.

Dreams

As she walked along the deserted shore,
The wind and the rain in her hair;
She thought of the wonderful years,
The two of them had shared.

The memories came tumbling back
Like the rippling of a brook;
And all at once, the deserted shore
Was not so lonely any more.

He was there—walking along beside her,
It seemed so real—not a dream;
He smiled at her, and said be happy,
We will be together again.

Thelma D. Chivis

A Fraction of Time

Rain drops on a pond leave a circular design
Each one disappearing, in a fraction of time

We enter this world and begin as a child
Sheltered and protected from a world so wild

Then childhood is over, leaving its design
It disappeared quickly, in a fraction of time

Now we're adults and out on our own
With children and spouse, careers and a home

The marriage goes on and leaves its design
Will this end too, in a fraction of time?

The divorce is over, leaving its design
It came so quickly, in a fraction of time

Shelter and protection from a world so wild
No longer exists, for you're not a child

Confusion abounds, leaving its design
Will it be over in a fraction of time?

You meet someone new who makes your heart sing
Songs of life and love and other such things

Then they are gone and leave their design
Time passed by quickly, in a fraction of time

You're confused and upset that it happened again
Then you remember way back when

Rain drops on a pond left a circular design
Each one disappearing in a fraction of time.

Paul L. Hennessey

Wake Up, Dreamer!

Swift fly the hours thru the net of time
As clouds across a windswept sky,
There is no way of staying them—
They're gone and days and years slide by.

How senseless to regret their passing
And dream of what we might have done!
How worse than foolish to lay vast plans
To catch the future in and let the present idle run!

There is no time but now—
This very minute, hour, day
In which to think, to act, to do!
Wake up, dreamer! Do not delay!

Catherine Ray

One of the nicest things about gardening is that if you put it off long enough it eventually is too late.

Honorable Mention

If Only A Day

If only a day,
Free spirit of mind,
Will that I escape life's webbed toils.
To wing high into billowing clouds,
Float hushed below sapphire skies,
Shower in cool twilight dew,
And sleep on drifting mists o'er dark moors,
Gently harbored, dreams filtering cares away.

Winged spirit of heart, awaken,
As sun slivers pierce the night canopy.
Sweep down, down to carpets of trees,
Fingers rustling emerald leaves,
Jeweled tones in harmony with bird song.
Pluck a crimson berry, honey sweet to lips.
Gather rose petals and toss them,
Windswept aloft, fragrant gifts to heaven.

Oh, laughing spirit, waft out to sea.
Dip low, toes dancing in cool sprays.
Alight upon the rail of a passing vessel.
Gaze into startled eyes, a lone sailor.
Brush a kiss, warm upon his cheek.
Sing, laugh, my joyous free spirit,
Now soaring, serenely into oblivion,
Up and beyond. If only a day.

Benoni Morgan

SUNDAY MORNING.

Every Single Day of the World

i have asked
and Thee gave me not
i have lived and you gave me not death
shielding me i have not gotten lost
i am a child of God i never will leave
for the Lord has given himself to me.

E. M. Whitney

Trilogy

God, the Father, Son, and Holy Ghost,
it is difficult to say, which love us most!

When first conceived in His universal mind,
the ultimate plan was called mankind.

For through the miracle of every birth,
a soul is sent to walk the earth.

A body with a spirit, and a spirit with a soul,
we all share a common goal,

A place in Heaven, and the Truth to believe in!

Created in His image of heart, mind, and soul,
our source of life, is our onward and upward goal,

And through often spoken, it is too seldom heard,
but this Truth is found in a single word.

Love...flowing through us as Faith, Hope, and Charity,
reveals our purpose within the Trinity.

As throughout life, Love not only keeps us on course,
but is our destination, as well as our source!

Mark Christopher Wise

Fellow Creatures

Man sings of birds,
How they soar in the sky.
He wishes he could...
Run like a deer.
Man thinks fellow creatures
Live easy on earth.
They're wild and free, while he must work.
Man forgets
He's made in God's image,
Beneath the angels,
Above other creatures.
If man would watch, he'd learn how to live.
He grits his teeth and shakes his fists, at
the wind.
He makes strike with his fellowman,
While fellow creatures leave, or endure.
Which is the wisest?
Fellow creatures accept their creator,
Without question.
Man denies, is lost, and must be saved.
Learn of Him.

Jean Fuqua Jones

An Offer From God

I offered to provide your needs,
but you pray for your wants.

I offered you the "Ten Commandments,"
but you disobeyed.

I offered you good,
but you live in evil.

I offered you life in love,
but you hate.

I offered you my design of family,
but you create your own.

I offered you comfort in daily prayer,
but you only pray in troubled times.

I offered you a clear vision of tomorrow,
but you still live in the cloudiness of yesterday.

I offered you the ability to do all things in my power,
but you remain self-limited.

I offered you life in peace,
but you make war.

I offered you your destiny,
but you pray for your fantasy.

If I offered you the sky,
you'll pray for the moon.

Whose world is it anyway?

MINE !

Glendora Lee Bellamy

Winter's Glacial Review

My frost-encased world
shimmers and shines in its raw,
bleak beauty. Biting,
bitterly cold wind makes me
shiver with humility.

Carla Uhernick

Untitled

Sitting by a cool, mountain stream,
I tried to suppress my tears.
Searching for peace and some relief,
My thoughts reached back through the years.

I was alone, and feeling sad—
Death took my loved one, you see.
Gently, sweet mem'ries held my hand
And began to comfort me.

I know I'm never all alone—
My God keeps me company.
But, there, He sent a host of friends
To come and try to cheer me.

The hot sun smiled and warmed my back.
A soft breeze caressed my cheek.
Wild flowers flaunted sweet perfume.
Bees coaxed to play hide and seek.

Overhead, a mockingbird trilled.
Katydids chirped all around.
Gorgeous butterflies paused near by;
But, alas, they made no sound.

Water rippled over the stones,
Singing its soft lullaby.
Holding fond mem'ries to my heart,
I thanked God—and did not cry.

Marjorie A. Hand

It's Spring

A spree of yellow and pale green comes bursting forth
Sun soft and warm nourishing nature,
Birds in flight bring song into the air
Springs and brooks begin to flow cresting its river banks,
Bright color flowers fragrant the air,
Cheerful laughter of children chasing butterflies
Picking young spring flowers;
Outdoors they play,
It's earth's awaking
It's spring!

Charles S. Thomas

The Seedling

Carried by the wind and placed
on fertile ground somewhere.
Fed by clouds, and earth, and sun
with tender loving care.
And soon, a miracle occurs. It's alive
and green and growing.
It reaches upward to the sky
it's beauty never knowing.

It sways so gently in the wind,
content to just be living.
Asking nothing from this world,
but to the world always giving
pleasure from its beauty
as it's slowly growing.
Not aware of those who gaze,
and of its beauty never knowing.

Barbara Landis

IN SHERWOOD FOREST,

Summer Nights

Blue rays with greenish bands,
Silver ripples on water and sand,
Long purple shadows 'neath fence-post and rail,
Pewter clouds weave ghostly trail,
Across the sky, around the moon,
These summer nights on moonlit dunes.

You cannot take your place,
With delight of moonbeams on your face,
Reflections of our romance in your eyes,
To kiss me nor tell me why,
I wander here alone at night,
And ponder if our love was right.

Long I stare at wedding band,
My tears run silver upon my hands,
And shadows of doubt lie dark in my heart.
Is now different than the start?
Still I send my love across the sky,
'Though you've not explained the reason why.

You stayed not by my side.
I need you—your strength sure as the tide.
You've gone away; I alone walk the shore,
See the sights and miss you more.
I dream of you under the moon
These summer nights on moonlit dunes.

Rebecca Perkins

We see things not as they are, but as we are.

—Henry Major Tominson

The Dream

As a young girl I dreamed of how it would be
To know of love complete and passionately
So closely I held my dream to my heart
Impatient to let love have its start
Then boys came around the older I got
But I held to my dream, and rejected the lot
They didn't seem right, it didn't appear
That any of them could ever come near
The dream that I held safe within my heart
Of how it should be or how it should start.
Then you came along with quiet and strength
My dream fell apart for you wouldn't relent.
I mourned its sweet passing, its innocence lost
To leave me alone and by passion be tossed
But you held me close you anchored me here
Then I realized my dream didn't disappear.
For you and the dream are one and the same
and love unawakened can never be named.
So softly I hold my dream in my heart
When love lets passion play its own part.
That's how it is, it always shall be
Whenever you call to set my dream free.

M. A. Donnely

Language of Eyes

How amazing is the language of eyes;
Nobody has ever studied it,
Frequently still every one applies.

Men, birds and animals all as they conceive;
With eyes they convey, with eyes they receive,
So spontaneously and with so much ease.

Attention of ears, it does not require;
Motions to hands & mouth, it does not need;
You need not any fluency acquire.

Any intent about which you think
Can not be conveyed through speech or ink,
Eyes convey with a wink or blink.

Vimal C. Manav
Included in **About The Poets** Section

Somebody Is In Love

Somebody is in love and this is
so true. Perhaps that fortunate human
being is you.

Somebody is in love and this is
so clear. Indeed it is quite wonderful to
hear the words "I love you my dear."

Somebody is in love and may love
last forevermore. My prayer is that love
will continue to be real and visible for
all to adore.

Rufus V. Morris

Untitled

Love, like a rose, so beautiful and new,
Deeper and deeper my feelings blossomed and grew.

From a safe distance, it was enticing,
Closer and closer we neared, though it was frightening.

Consummation leading to a disillusioning crash,
Lust but for a moment...caused by acts, rash.

Now I sit, think and ponder my past,
How wrong to believe it ever would last.

Once a tender rose is plucked by a hand,
It plunges the bearer into a new land.

Thorns pierce the skin, bringing forth pain,
The feelings grow stronger...yet the memories a strain.

Dawn D. McIntyre

Honorable Mention
One Prairie Day

I rest among sifting stems
submerged by foxtail swells,
the sky cavernous,
a dome of infinite blue
over tall grass tussocks,
watching cumulus anvils surge aloft

I soar with a redtail
poised on a tenuous breeze,
the earth in silent frenzy below
scatters hither and yon
before the flick of a deadly shadow,
across the pulsing plain

I huddle with a glacial orphan
adrift on this ancient sea bed,
the wind a cold scimitar
pressed against my cheek
as the hazy foothills,
corrugate the sky

I sit on grassy hummock
gathering space about my conquest,
the distance charges to meet me
only to turn and leap away
bounding to horizon then beyond,
eloping with eternity

    Art Laurenson   Canada

December's Surrender

The winter's wind seduced me first,
(And only then, the man).
It touched me with an ice-blue tongue
Encircled, icicled my ribs
Blinded me with arctic sun
Blasted wafer-thin resolve.

Numbed, my conscience slip't away,
Was buried deep 'neath drifted snow
My heart? Flash-frozen in my chest
Face pale (tell-tale) averted too late
Slightest of slivers reveal the rest
Fate?

Or downfall? But what can resist,
When bitter chilled,
The teasing promise of the thaw?
Coaxing tears from the tundra
Drenching land once cold and dry
Until even the earth may flaunt ancient laws.

He sighed as he slept,
I searched his face
Touched his limbs gently,
Fear and delight
And marveled, feeling in my womb
Last traces, fast-fading, of what?—Frostbite.

    Paula Lyons

Taming Summer's Sun

Beads of sweat upon my brow
   beneath the summer sun.
Down my neck, between my breasts
   the salty brine did run.
The ground was hot beneath my feet
And nothing stirred in the searing heat.
   The air was thick with summer smells
    as the sun approached high noon.
Too hot for even birds to sing,
   'twas dead-silent like a tomb.
But look to the west, some clouds are forming,
As if to the blistering sun to give warning!
   Then the lightning crashed the silence
    with its deafening thunder roar
   And the winds did howl between the trees
    and the rain began to pour.
It cooled the earth and cleansed my brow
And it tamed that summer sun somehow.
   With naught but a gentle breeze astir,
    so cool and fresh and clean,
   The grass is greener and the flowers sweeter,
    sparkling drops on which did glean.
Dusk, through the valley, now is creeping
And the countryside will soon be sleeping.

    Chris Lake

ALPINE FLOWERS.

An Early Spring Concerto

Gazing out my window
On a cool February morn

My sleepy eyes awaken
To a colorful debut.

Red birds, blue jays, robins, and wrens
Blanket my yard with classical sound.

Singing softly and ruffling their feathers
Conversing together in symphonic compose

Telling each other in joyous notes
Winter at last has shed its coat.

    Carolene L. Ward

Cri de Coeur

I plunged through the willow trees
in the grass
amongst the weeds
    oh lovely, for thee.
Surely thy fingers feel the prick
the sweet prick
of leafless twigs in the ivy,
where grow our fetid figs.
Yes certainly, you feel the prick
of strawberry stems
where I stole
from the yellow leaves
    the strawberries for thee,
    my lovely.
I would burn all the figs
and nurture the twigs
    for you, through and through,
my lovely.

Kurt Bingham

Early Morning Dew

Early in the morning,
while the dew is still there

In the flower garden
there's no beauty to compare

The birds awake
and they begin to twitter

In this beautiful garden
everything is 'a-glitter'

The sparkle of diamonds
could never be so bright

As this beautiful garden
the dew kissed last night.

Jean Clere

Book of Love

Turning back all the pages
To each of our loving stages
Rewinding the clocks hands
To times only we understand
Moving back through space and time
To a world that was yours and mine
Backtracking all steps that were taken
To keep a love from breaking
Going to old familiar places
That no longer hold any traces
Turning back for one last look
To a forever closed and locked book

Karyl Carlson

Spring

Blossoms bursting
Like popcorn popping,
Birds singing
A sweet melody.
Flowers peeking,
Timidly.

Amelia Vargas

Siren

I stood upon the shores
of an alien sea,
quietly watching dolphins play
and listened to the tempting music
of a siren.

Beautiful was she,
siren of the sea,
tempting me,
with musical poetry.

I ease my body into the ocean
and as the depths drowned away my life,
she looked into my eyes, lightly kissed me,
then swam away.

Travis Singer

September Morn

Oh, September morn!
Cold whispers, misty eyed
Bring forth a new day born.
Fade not the flower's bloom
That decor my window sill.
At Mother Nature's will
Your piercing winds that blow
Upon my little hill.
Summer days forlorn
As you bring forth winter winds
Oh, September morn!
Must you come so soon
To my humble little home
Where I shall hide away
And here where I shall stay
Until the month of May
Brings forth a new day born.
Oh, September morn!

Monica Welch

Never Ending

A cup of coffee,
    a cigarette,
some time to dream,
    and to forget

The way life goes
    around and down,
like ashes, floating to the ground—
    of burnt out hopes,
and futile tries,
    to make it better
with anguished cries
    of people, all alone
        and who,
have only walls
    to tell their troubles to.

But walls can't hear,
    and walls can't speak—
hot flowing tears,
    on burning cheeks—
and thoughts go 'round
and 'round again—
in a never ending chain

    Where hope once lived—
        now lives pain.

Carol Ann Nienburg

Life

Once we are born we grow old;
to eat, cry, mess and sleep
these are things all babies know;
we learn to speak and stand on our feet

from childhood to our teens
the Period of growth and maturity,
to mold into unique individuals it means
the time to learn and develop our ability

in our adult years of productivity
some work and raise families of their own;
others aim to fulfill their own destiny;
together with faith we keep the world go on

with age bringing white hair and skin wrinkles,
by then we realize our time has come
to go for another journey which fate unfolds
when our duty and work are done

life is short and time is long
enjoy yourself while you can
The world goes on even when you're gone
Do we know what Life is about?

Patrick Huang   Canada

I Often Find

I often find there are thoughts I cannot resolve,
Nor do I want to.
Ambition is a falsehood—A mask I wear to hide
The unfulfilled being that lies beneath this mortal skin.
I hope for something meaningful to pass into my life,
But I find nothing.
For me, there exists only emptiness in the time
That lies ahead.
All want, all meaning is gone:
And without it, I cannot go on.
I know somewhere amidst this nothingness,
There must be some hope.
Perhaps there shines a light within me—
That will direct me—
Toward a fate that gives me strength,
To face each new challenge,
And look forward to each new day.
Yet, for now, all my expectations and all my dreams,
Are lost in a vast abyss.
I continue to search for answers;
Wishing for fulfillment,
But knowing only this dull ache,
Which emerges from my emptiness.

When all else is lost, the future still remains.

—Christian Nevell Bovee

STAINED-GLASS WINDOW FOR A MUSIC-ROOM.

Let Me Slip Through The Door Of Memory

Let me slip through the door of memory and visit the places
    that used to be,
Let me look again on the yesteryear—as far away a bell tolls
    near.

Let me travel the road to the old homestead, to its aged doors let
    me be led,
To sit in front of the warm fireplace and dream again of your
    loving face.

Let me visit our church in the wide country lane, where once we
    prayed and loved in twain.
Where we took our vows that sweet summer's day to love and
    cherish each always.

Let me know again our child's quick grace and feel her hands
    upon my face,
And look into her eyes again to know the love that dwelt
    therein.

Let me walk in the fields where once we toiled in the good hot
    sun, where weeds we foiled,
And rested on sands at the end of the row, cooled damp by rain,
    where sunflowers grow.

At evening we'd guide the slow-moving cows up to the barn by
    the harrows and plows;
Thence, on to the kitchen with its fat iron stove that smelled of
    pies, hot breads and cloves.

At the worn oaken table we'd all set down, awaiting our food,
    with our warm love around,
And sometimes we'd sing old songs that we knew, as fire's dying
    embers turned shadows to blue.

After supper we'd linger by the bright kitchen fire, to bask in its
    warmth, and I'd never tire
Of the love that you gave me there on our farm, through long
    passing years has kept my heart warm.

Let me slip through the door of memory and visit the places
    that used to be,
Let me look again on the yesteryear—as far away a bell tolls
    near.

Lucille M. Kroner
Included in **About The Poets** Section

Strange Encounter

It was a warm and tropical noon day...
You came into my life out of nowhere.
Light tones of blue and shades of green were there
Framing the view in a romantic way.

A waterfall sang songs of silver hues,
a mockingbird with lilting song replied.
And then the water of the pool contrived,
a mirror that reflected all the views.

I knew we'd met but I did not know where.
I knew it hadn't been in recent time.
In fact, I knew we'd met in years gone by:
in Budapest, or Paris, or somewhere...?

Because I knew the moment that we talked,
that we had been together years away.
And then the deepest feeling that gave way,
was that we'd been in soul or spirit locked.

Was it reincarnation or dream lane...?
Was it in little known ethereal lore...?
But then I knew that we had met before,
and now I know that we shall meet again.

Juan Silverio

Coverlet

In from the old mine her man staggered home,
  Snarling, drinking and covered with coal,
  "Devil take you, Tennessee AND the mines,
  I'm off to California to dig me some gold!"

She moved to the shed-room and slept on a cot,
Tore down the big bedstead to clear out the room,
Brought in 40 pounds of fine, white linen thread,
And wound 2000 lines of strong warp on her loom.

Up on the hillside and down in the hollow, she
  Gathered wild indigo and madder for dye,
  Boiled in washpots with wool she'd been saving:
  Dull red from the madder, indigo, blue as the sky.

And she wove and she wove from morning 'til dusk,
Weaving patterns her grandma had used long before,
  Yellow with age, and busy with markings,
  Like steps from a wild choreographer's score.

She finished the coverlet early October,
  Signed it "Ann Allen Barlow, 1849."
  The coverlet kept out the raw cold of winter.
She rejoiced that her husband had left her behind.

And she slept winter nights snug and warm 'neath her cover
Of red, white and blue, for the rest of her life,
Under eagles and doves that she called "Peace and Freedom"...
  A free, peaceful woman, and no mean man's wife.

Elsie R. Scrivner

Cormorant

Riding ships pull the flags to fly
A seagull's cry falls down from the sky
The harbor smells from the floundering haul
The grey clouds push in the fall

A pulling rope, a worn out pole
Sea and wind fill my soul

The wind pulls softly at my shirt
Dissolving the dust of last day's flirt
White headed waves come rushing in
The salty air spices my skin

A pulling rope, a worn out pole
Sea and wind fill my soul

The fishing nets are resting from the day
The fishermen come stepping on the quay
I turn and leave the noise behind
The white dune's sand cleans out my mind

A pulling rope, a worn out pole
Sea and wind fill my soul

The rain falls gushing over me
The beach is empty and I watch the sea
In the grey stands a cormorant
I loved that girl and I was her man

Leo Veenman   *The Netherlands*

The Team

The muscles of the big horses rippled
under the tautness of the harness;
the one on the right gray and dappled.
The muscles of the big horses rippled;
the left one black. The farmer grappled
the reins in sweaty palms. Nothing glamorous
as the muscles of the big horses rippled
under the tautness of the harness.

The team working together: the horses, the man.
The horses pulling, the man guiding the plow,
the three of them giving to their work all they can.
The team working together, the horses the man
pulling and guiding the horses the man.
The job not a new one, the three knowing how
the team worked together, the horses, the man,
the horses pulling, the man guiding the plow.

Working the land was the farmer's choice.
Choosing to live simply, in tune with the land
living and growing his cause for rejoice.
Working the land was the farmer's choice.
With love and muscle he chose to hoist
harness and work with his team.
Working the land was the farmer's choice
Choosing to live simply, in tune with the land.

Janet Porter Turner

Growing Up and Growing Old

Why my sweet little child,
You have to grow up?
You used to be so bubbly,
Sweet and loving.
Why does it have to be,
What happens to us all?
Why does there have to be,
Such pain in growing up.

Why my sweet grandparent,
You have to grow old?
You used to be so happy,
Laughing and talking.
Why does it have to be,
What happens to us all?
Why does it have to be,
Such pain in growing old?

Blessed be to God,
That I am the one in the middle.
I have to be the strong one,
But I am so slow and weak.
Lord, please help me,
To help the child grow up.
Lord, please help me,
To help the grandparent stay young.

Patricia Pritt

The Truth Does Ring

I have peered back in time, and have seen...
   How beautiful, sometimes sad, are the years in between.
In spite of despair that came my way,
   He gave me eyes to see...
He has inspired me.

Try as I may, it is hard to say
   I have constantly done my best...
It is He who put me to the test,
   as I see myself within...
He lightens the path.

With due recognition for His gifts,
   there is ample room to give praise...
He brought the beauty of friendship,
   kindness and mercy to fill my days...
To pursue each task.

At a crucial moment my life was spared...
   In His benevolence, He let me live.
The illness was grave, I knew He cared...
It was God's will.

As in a dream, I saw the signs...
   Realizing I was not alone,
He answered my prayer to remain strong...
   His goodness is everywhere.

Bertha Lasky

Grandma

I had a dream last night.
I saw my Grandma's sweet and smiling face.
When I awoke, she was gone;
But she did not leave my heart.
She walks the streets of Heaven now,
Near to God as she was in this world.
With a sweet and gentle emptiness,
I remember Grandma.
I am close to her, although we had to part.

Childhood treasures filter through my life;
Marshmallow cookies and black currant jam,
A squirrel running down a tree;
The sights and sounds of downtown Toronto,
Seagulls on a sandy beach,
Cookie tins filled with buttons;
Small artificial Christmas trees
And the taste of fresh raspberries.
Life itself, keeps Grandma with me.

Joy Buxton   Canada

A Father's Love

God has blessed this family with a Father
such as you

To guide us each and everyday
in all we try to do.

To teach us all to love and care
and always be willing our love to share.

With each day that passes
let us stop and realize

That without the love you've given us
our hopes and dreams would die.

You have taught us each and everyone
to live the way we should

To love and honor, forgive and obey;
as with your love we could.

Father as each day goes by
let your heart be filled
With the love and understanding
that only we could instill.

You know how much we love you,
even though it's not always shown.

But with each day you see this poem
you will know our love has grown.

I LOVE YOU!!!

Karen S. Pruett

La Raza

I carry my race in my veins.
I carry my past on my mind.

From generation to generation
    I shall be aware that
I come from a long path.

I carry no mask for there
    is no need to.
My features, my actions,
    my way of being can
easily convey who I am.

I am not like those who escape
    under a mask hiding their
    identity
Not like those who don't wish
    to be known as what they are.

Aren't we different, but aren't
    we the same?

We come to life the same way.
We come to die at different times,
but we all come to die at
some point in time.

    Silda Molina   Puerto Rico

The Voice

Having fun.
Career at its peak.
A voice that was beyond belief.
Everyone liked them.
But death was for one.
It came and took away.
Took away "the voice."
Leaving the others alone.
Nowhere to turn.
Turning to drugs.
Next to alcohol. Career fell apart.
People turned away.
But the music lives on without "the voice."

    Noel Kaiser

Untitled

The thunder is so silent.
The rain falls as loud bombs.
The sunshine chills me to the quick,
Bays of ice slide by me with a death wish,
Against my fragile bones.

    Linda Frost
      Included in **About The Poets** Section

Youth is but a fleeting fling

Sweet days of sultry air
Upon us during our youth;
Playing hopscotch with those
We hardly knew;
Pretending to be ahead of
Our time, falling off a the
Mountain before the
Climb; Ignoring advice,
Soon to end up regretting;
Wanting things and not
Always getting; And,
As prayers grow lugubrious
As night; answers quickly
Fall from sight.
Still, now alone against
The evil descent, I
Await the torment.

    Rebecca Orr

CATTLE SUBJECT, AFTER NICHOLAS BERCHEM.
(*By Miss A. Evans.*)

Breathing in the air

He's just breathing in the air.
Just waits for life to come to him.
Breathing in the air.

He can't do it at will.
He's mentally ill.
Another shade of blue.
The only shade.

No moments or days
of changing hue.
And he's on the upside of the hill.
Never an emotional tilt.

    Guy Zaccardi

Freedom Is Ringing

Freedom is ringing so loud
yet we can't hear it for the Rock Music
Freedom is ringing so Visible
yet we can't see it for the Pornography
Freedom is ringing so Touching
yet we can't Feel it for the Child Abuse
Freedom is ringing......The Dope dealer hears it
That's why he's addicting our Children
Freedom is ringing......The Terrorist hears it
That's why he's Bombing our Cities
Freedom is ringing......Foreigners hear it
That's why they risk their lives sailing the ocean
Freedom is ringing......Communism hears it
That's why her people steal away to our country
freedom is ringing......But not for our Farmers
but not for the Elderly......but not for the poor......
but not for the unemployed or homeless......
Freedom is ringing............
Not Anymore............
She just hung up the phone...

Jackie Maxwell

An Old Soldier's Hope For Peace

At mach-one plus, the airman fires a sparrow;
such terrible fire, destruction, and noise.
Oh, for the days of the bow and arrow
when men, not machines, were the choice.

Smart munitions of hi-tech design;
missiles, radar, lasers and many other breeds;
They all affect a battle but anyone will find
that man, not a machine, is still the one who bleeds.

Machines are pushing us like a tug pushing a ship;
at breakneck speed we travel toward the brink,
placing our lives, our trust, in the micro-chip,
while souls from history call out, THINK! THINK! THINK!

Quiet! Listen! A whisper, or is it the wind?
What blows across the proving grounds at Dugway?
Hark you doves! Hawks too, your ears lend;
Know yesterday, hope for tomorrow, but first live today.

Live now, look to the future, while remembering the past;
think of those who were, are, and of those to be.
Do it better, do it from the heart, and then it might last;
the result could finally be this...peace, yea peace with liberty.

Edward Stanley

Great Wings Beating

With the wrath of an unforgiving God seeking him,
Came that accursed fiend from the Halls of Darkness;
Over the city in the black night, Recnac came stalking,
With his great wings beating.
Stealthily he moves in the black mist below dark clouds,
Down the empty streets he fly,
Looking for a careless treat, hungry for a human feast;
A grisly sound and foul ill-coloring sight,
With his great wings beating.
His face a pale white with eyes like a fire-spitting forge,
His head misshaped from so little light, eyes glowing,
And fangs showing in a fruitless grin,
His hands milk white did seem like claws appearing,
And big great black wings coming from his back,
Seeming like a cape, or some pious cloak;
An ugly fiend, more foul than a nightmare he seems.
Born from the Prince of Darkness' legacy, Recnac is his name;
One of the sucklings from the breast of the Mother of Evil.
Recnac is his name!
Blood upon his tongue, as on the claws of his hands;
A cry, in accents of despair,
Through the dreary night he comes,
With great wings beating.

Col. J. Nicholas Jones

Freedom to Love

Freedom to love those around me
Is a life I long to see.
When from the shackles and chains
That bind me,
I'm finally set free.
Free to learn to love as Christ;
A love that's real—demands sacrifice.
Allowing myself to be spent for others,
To love them more—
Though I may be loved less.
Let concerns for myself
Be cast from me,
That I may learn to love wholly.
Help me dwell
In your free and eternal love,
To catch a glimpse—
No matter how dim
Of that perfect and matchless, divine love.
Lord, love through me.

Jane Coleman

A Song Unspoken

I love to tickle words until they squeal;
To make them laugh until they start to reel
And stagger, rolling helpless in the dust.

I love to tell of autumn's crispy night
Deep-set in darkest blue, and edged in light
Reflected by the starched, low-hanging clouds.

I love to relive childhood memories
And spin them onto sentence sticks, which frees
Experience from heart and gives it breath.

I love to pressure thoughts until they break
Into a song unspoken, and can make
Some other weary traveler to sing.

So may these words move deep into *your* mind
And burn through callous thought until they find
A resting place among *your* secret dreams.

Donna B. Gavac
Included in **About The Poets** Section

The Ethereal Light in Your Dark Eyes
for Beth

The ethereal light in your dark eyes
Illuminates an obscure passage to my hidden heart.

Your statuesque figure and cerebral demeanor excite me
And, in my mind, set you above and clearly apart.

Your gentle touch and angelic smile flood my senses
With a fervent living joy!

In your warm and sparkling presence,
Discretion and measured temperament are the tactics that I employ
Because with you, Angel, it is never my deliberate intention
To irritate, frighten, or annoy.

Merely saying that "I Love You"
Betrays the true depth of my passion
And belies the actual extent of my need
For your love in return.

The cycles of love are inevitable,
And their outcome ever indistinct.
It is a sad and mysterious folly, I should think;
But what recourse has a fool (like me) to try?
For there's no magical tool or remedy by which to deny
The hypnotic allure of that ethereal light
In your dark eyes.

William L. Brooks

Dreamscape

A dream world you once inhabited
    did not exist except for you.
You found rainbows
    where we viewed dark, cloud-filled skies.
You lived in a world of your vivid imagination
    allowing us to enter at your bidding.
You placed a "For Rent" sign on life,
    your reality a cramped Berkeley apartment,
your vision, a castle atop a mountain.
    You were radiant with joy,
the sun followed in your wake
    its beams glowing from your face.
The whole world was your playground,
    the games you played were your reality,
some dangerous, others filled with fantasy.
    In your brief sojourn, you touched many lives.
When you left, the sun disappeared
    a total eclipse where we discovered
fairy castles do not exist,
    dancing on rainbows is impossible
the world's not the same without your dreams.

Dottie Neil

Remember Pearl Harbor

The U.S. Arizona Memorial of Pearl Harbor
Enshrines this famed battleship I'd loved enfold;
By the foe, December 7, 1941, band break forth
Who defended our American braves and they're bold.
You are a proud U.S. Navy Fleet
The day you took complete command in line;
And your commission pal became complete
The United States Arizona is the finest.
The tranquil on that one Sunday morning
Your crew rushed to their battle stations;
As you stood your right without a sign of warning
The foe attacked Pearl Harbor and you again and again.
You serve as a reminder forevermore remain vigilant
Now, I, too, know what thank you honestly means;
And I'm proud of you today because I'm an American
The Fiftieth State admission August 21, 1959 at long last.

John D. C. Estrella

The Beauty of Whiteness

I awakened this morning to a world
    of startling whiteness
Every tree, every limb, every bush was frosted
    with freshly fallen snow
There was such a feeling of purity and holiness
    it overwhelmed one's sensibilities
All of earth's dirt and grime were washed away,
    leaving a feeling of sterile cleanliness
You felt as if you had entered a sphere
    free from all guilt and sin
A place not meant for man to enter.
You fully expected a celestial choir to burst forth
    with songs of praise,
Then it happened, a branch moved, from it snow fell,
    and a bird started to sing
Filling the quietness with joyful sounds.
Suddenly the sun exploded from behind the clouds
Adding brilliance of light and shadow to the whiteness
Once in a lifetime, are conditions just right,
    to produce such momentous beauty
Here was your moment of ecstasy!
You knew you had been blessed,
Was this a glimpse of heaven?

Edna Dame   Canada

He who does not enjoy solitude will not love freedom.

—*Schopenhauer*

Spirit Prism

Love is the red of the sky at sunset,
    promising a beautiful tomorrow.
Joy is the yellow of summer sunshine,
    warming and brightening the earth.
Peace is the green of the hills in spring,
    a tranquil refuge for the soul.
Patience is the lavender of fading violets,
    growing ever more fragrant with time.
Kindness is the silver of morning mist,
    refreshing and reviving nature's beauty.
Goodness is the white of the first snowfall,
    covering ugliness with purity.
Gentleness is the pink of a rosebud,
    whose soft petals, when crushed, yield sweet perfume.
Faithfulness is the deep blue of twilight,
    a temporary darkness, soon to be enlightened.
Self-control is the purple of distant mountains,
    a majestic backdrop of determination.

Kim Courtright

It's Where I Grew Up

I grew up—way out on the prairies of Montana—
out where the wild coyote howls—and the sagebrush
Grows—and the snow-drifts pile high
As the winter winds moan.

I could see so far most any day—and the sky was so
Blue—and the stars would shine so bright in a
Cloudless sky—and the billions of stars in the
Milky-way—could each be seen so clearly most any night.

How I loved to watch those fascinating northern lights
In the northern skies on a winters night—cold shivers
Would creep slowly—up and down my spine—as their
Eerie lights shot high in the sky.

I could see every blade of grass or clump of sagebrush
When the full moon was riding high in the sky—and
The night-hawk's screech could be heard through the night
As he makes his famous dive.

I used to walk through the thick buffalo grass—
As I traveled the miles herding cows—and there was
narry a tree or a bush to give me shade—as the sun
Beat down—and burned me to a crisp.

And the wild flowers that grew on the prairies—
Each had their own special beauty and charm—
Yes—they each had their seasons of glory—
Then they are faded and gone.

Mildred V. Finegan

Today a penny saved isn't worth the money

That Snowy Day

Skiing through the hills which surround my house,
I could feel the coldness all around.
With every gliding stride, I felt my energy rise.
What a glorious moment my eyes have found.
All the trees stood dormant,weighted by a blanket
    Of show.
Snow flakes were cascading down, like white feathers
    Of a goose's down.
The stillness was so peaceful,
Unlike nothing I have found.
The only sound I heard, was the beating of my heart.
As I reached another crest, I stopped to capture the
    Beauty there.
It was as if I were suddenly in a dream.
The essence of being there, was like a fairy tale in
    Which only a child would believe.
What was only a few hours,
Seemed like many years,
For I savored every moment,
As if it were my own.

Rene' A. Jeffries

Reflection

Raise high the glass of love to me
And let me taste its last remains,
Old passion's pain aroused once more,
Surrounded by its sweet refrains.
Oh, shattered fragment of lost love
Come close to me in vague revue
And mirror once again your love
Before I remember that we're through.
And if you see upon my face
A silver tear before you fall,
Kiss gently there before you go
And say he loved her best of all.

Cecelia Marchand

A BIT OF THE CLIFF, HELIGOLAND.

Cheating

I often wonder about men who run around on their wives,
When they take a vow to be together for the rest of their lives,

Problems arise, you must talk,
Nothing can be solved by barks,

Don't try to solve your problems by going outside,
You will only be taken for a ride,

Your girlfriend knows the deal,
If you stay wih your wife, your love is not real,

So before you think about running away from your wife trouble,
Solve your problems, before they double.

Gwendolyn B. Bobo

You Wonder Why

You wonder why I kept you?
Why didn't I just give you away?
That's what they all wanted.
They were willing to show me the way.

But that's not what I wanted.
I didn't care what they'd say.
I wanted that baby inside me,
that was growing each day.

And on the day I had you,
it was a miracle to me.
To know that anything so beautiful,
could ever come from me.

With tiny little fingers,
and wiggling little toes.
You were as lovely as a flower,
A beauty, I named you Rose.

Just like the flower,
your skin was soft as silk.
And when I held you in my arms,
my heart would always melt.

So you wondered why I kept you?
Why didn't I just give you away?
Because that's not what I wanted.
So to them, I said no way!

Debra Engle

When I Saw You Today

When I saw you today
I tried hard to find the words to say.
But I kept on tripping,
In my mind.

I wondered if there was a certain way
I wondered if I should call your name.
I wondered if you were the type
Who only wanted to play.

I wondered if you would be kind,
I wondered if it was the right time.
Then I thought it would be easy to make an excuse,
Pass you by and say what's the use.

Then I looked at you again,
I said to myself
There's no need to pretend
When I saw you today.

Ymistye L. White

The Little Boy That Lies Asleep On A Hill

The little boy that lies asleep on a hill
Where the trees are silent and the winds whisper still.
He lies asleep in a meadow,
No more suffering will he know.

The little boy's name is Clint,
A little Savior that God had sent.
He endured great suffering like Jesus on the cross;
Everyone who knew him mourned his loss.

He is gone now and will suffer no more;
He went to a new home on that golden shore;
He went to heaven with God above;
He is gone now but left his love.

Like the hymn, he touched me;
He waved to everyone he could see.
He touched the lives of those that knew him;
He touched the hearts of people like the hymn.

He is greatly missed by all.
But he answered the Master's call.
He is gone now, but memories of his linger still
Of the little boy that lies asleep on a hill.

Edwin L. Mulford

In the Night

At times, in the middle of the night,
when all is quiet and most everyone
is at peace in their sleep,
"Oh, how lucky," I think.
For, they can sleep, but not I.
At times in the middle of the night.

"Why?," I ask. Can I not sleep as others
do in the middle of the night?
"My child," said God,
"My son often could not sleep in the night,
for He needed the quiet to talk to me,
without the day distracting Him.
He often asked Peter and John and the others
to stay awake with Him, but they fell asleep,
and left him alone in the night.
So, you see, my child, you are not alone,
for we are with you in the quiet of the night."

Yes, Father, I think of how sweet it is
knowing You are with me in the middle of the night.
So, I don't feel so alone.
And, you can renew and strengthen my soul
for the toil of the morrow.
Thank you, dear God, for the times alone
with you in the quiet of the night.

May Thompson

Questions At The End Of A Chapter

The death of a friend can come so unexpected,
You wonder why God or if God was so wicked.
No longer will I ever hear your laughter.
I only possess Questions At The End Of A Chapter.

Like, Why was it you? And, Why were you there?
I'd ask you myself if I could dare.
Will God honor you in heaven from hereafter?
I only possess Questions At The End Of A Chapter.

I hear your words, your philosophy, your talk.
I see your eyes, your face, your walk.
But as time goes on your image fades faster.
I only possess Questions At The End Of A Chapter.

I wish I had a picture, something to remember you by.
For that isn't living, and cannot die.
As I think of your death I just get madder and madder.
I only possess Questions At The End Of A Chapter.

I hope you're having fun sitting on your cloud.
Admiring the peace since nothing's loud.
Will you remember me forever after?
I only possess Questions At The End Of A Chapter.

Rhoan Jones

THE EVENING ANGELUS. By J. F. Millet.

My Best Friend Death

I have been nursing death
For a long long time.
It is the only thing
That will ever be mine.

It is mine all alone.
No one can take it away from me.
I try to prepare daily for it.
It is the way I will be free.

I thought I knew love
Thought I was a worthwhile person.
The people I love and lose
Makes my emotional pains worsen.

I am not lovable to anyone.
My family just tolerates me.
Wanted to be special to God.
Don't know how He feels either you see.

Don't know what I do that is so wrong.
People just turn away from me.
So my best friend is death.
With death I will always be.

Don't know what it is all about,
This life where no one loves me.
But it cannot take away my best friend
Because death will always love me.

Betty Laughridge

Doing things by halves is worthless. It may be the other half that counts.

The Stranger

The man ahead was rather strange,
seeing his face at such close range.
I looked down quickly when he passed
and though he wasn't walking fast
his shadowless figure blurred black
as a chilling draft chased his back.

Clouds blew in and covered the sun,
the street grew silent and I saw no one.
My footsteps froze, I slowly debated;
I felt his presence, assumed he waited.
Here I was trapped without even a clue
so swiftly I turned, when as if on cue
before my eyes he suddenly vanished,
no trace and no chill, the sky again blue.

Cheryl Comer

Untitled

On a park bench one day, while taking in some sun
I noticed a man in tattered clothes, stumbling about
He had no shoes and walked in a daze
Disgusted, I turned away—just another bum no doubt.

He found a cozy spot and settled down.
I could not ignore him shivering and looking so pale.
So I got up to help but sat back on the bench
As he pulled from his pocket and drank heartily of ale.

My eyes would not stray from what I thought was a drunk.
A voice told me to get up and see.
And as I drew near, a doctor walked by
And stopped held his forehead, which was hot as could be.

"He's just another drunk because I saw him drink."
The doctor said "let's check the bottle first."
He pulled it out, poured the contents to the ground.
And *only water* flowed, to quench his thirst.

"This man is dying—a hospital quick!
Call an ambulance, let's get him some care."
So ashamed I felt, as I ran to a phone.
But he's well now—his life God did spared.

This day is etched in my memory.
The voice spoke to me alone.
"The doctor saved a life today,
But you saved a soul—your own.

Lynette Alcocer

One Last Tear

From somewhere beyond the nothingness
an awakening light breathed
the first breath of life.

The eons and the stars
spawned a new seed,
and mankind flourished with
a plethora of hopes and dreams.

The feigned utopia rules
from a pompous throne,
adorning a crown of
pretension on accomplishment.

But the common still trust,
waiting for deliverance
reaching out a beseeching hand.

As the darkness envelopes
a dying star peers down
upon the flourished seed
and releases a sigh.

and from the heavens
a tiny drop falls into the oceans
...unnoticed.

Deborah Geiser

It Rained Worms Today

It rained worms today
outside my office
nobody noticed
because it was
Friday, Payday.

Where they came from
I'll never know
people grumbling
of how much pay.

Shoes squishing big
fat, juicy ones.
Threats of quitting
and lots of cuss
while waiting for the bus.

Clouds went away
the next day.
It didn't rain worms
and crunch under feet
sun baked worms on the street.

Went shopping all day
spent all my pay.
When will it rain worms
outside my office?
For sure not today.

Helen Stephenson

To Telesilla

poetess of Argos
commandant of warriors
your fortitude transcends
twenty-five centuries
to my battleground

I do not have a Spartan general
to match wits and men against
the mentality of pseudo-intellects
in a land of rough-hewn red necks
defies the traditions of both
and they come out of their impressed identities
lashing at me with their tongues
instead of swords

I must lead my faction
into the lairs of dream-stiflers
win them over
to our side
change their attitudes
without obliterating the psyche

be with me Telesilla
America-man victory
mine

Lynda Beaumont

Honorable Mention
The Cat on My Desk

With an endless rumble
she stalks my room
to chase stiff mice away.

then the cat on my desk
sings to me
pleas to let her stay.

Her mischievous intent
and fiendish eyes
are lost in an angel's face,

and the cat on my desk
winks at me.
She's pardoned from disgrace.

Then with a sudden explosion
of drifting fur
and the ring of collar bells,

the cat on my desk
scratches me.
I suppose it's just as well,

for alert to hushed footsteps
beyond the door,
with eyes suddenly bright,

the cat on my desk
abandons me
and leaves me to the night.

Melinda Lee Newmin

Mr. Ed

A horse is a horse
Of course, of course,
And of course, the horse
Is the famous Mr. Ed.
Where have you gone,
Mr. Ed, Mr. Ed,
Oh where have you gone Mr. Eddie.
You have left the TV.
Do you come back on reruns,
To give us your horsy puns.
Oh where may we see you.
Is it anywhere from channel two
To maybe channel ninety-two.
Have you become syndicated.
Your humor is not outdated.
Oh where have you gone,
Horse of my dreams,
When will you be back,
On the TV screen?

Edward A. McGahan

Untitled

I sat in a beam of sunlight
Contemplating the lazy dispersion of du
Drifting without purpose
On whispered breaths of air

Wishing I could shed this earthly weight
And float on a song, up
Over this uncertain existence
To tickle the bellies of the clouds

Sally F. Crouch

GEESE: A SOUVENIR OF AUVERGNE.

The Mirror

There was a young child who was so happy
Never seeing the evils of life.
He played in his room with all of his toys
And dreamed stories without any strife.
This little boy without any problems
Who sat at the edge of his bed.
Never thinking about life's worries
And that someday he'd be dead.
Time went by with such quickness
Struggles began to come fast.
And this small child of laughter and smiles
Would begin to change at last.
His happy face in photographs
Turned to one of pain.
His heart of love and sunshine
became one of hatred and rain.
And as he sits, now a grown man
Exchanging his sword for a pen,
He looks in the mirror with tears in his eyes
Wishing what he knows now, he knew then.

David Eric Lewenberg

Aging

An infant am i knowing no better
how important age will be as my life pieces together

At one or two my personality starts to appear,
at three or four you'll see more and more

four and five I'm much more alive
starting to form my very own life

age eight or nine time stands still
it seems you never get close to those grownup years

at eleven or twelve you can't wait until
you hear the sounds of teenage years

at eighteen or nineteen time lingers on
twenty-one is so far away
the legal years to have fun and play

at twenty-one then to twenty-five a quarter of a century
has passed you by

now you hit thirty, a traumatic year for most
it seems everything is all down hill

then there's forty, they say that's the best
when life is worth living, just like the past

and now we hit fifty, a half a century gone by
it almost makes you want to cry
for what have I done with all of those years
not much you say, as it brings on the tears

June Drao

Toy Store Window

Again he leaned forward,
Pressing his nose against the store window.
Peering at beautiful sights:
An electric train, going through a tunnel.
Lights flashing! Whistle tooting!
The boy's eyes grew wider.
A red and silver two-wheeler
With training wheels, just his size.
G. I. Joe with guns and tanks.
Baseball mitt, bat and ball.
Football and helmet.
Soccer ball.
Games, puzzles, books and crayons.
In the rear, a tent.
Lantern, knapsack and sleeping bag.
The boy leaned back,
Staring at his smear
trying to rub it off,
One finger popping out of his mitten.
Again, the lights go dim,
The boy sighed.
His mother would be waiting.
One last look in the dimly-lit window.
Then he turned away.

Evelyn M. Wenzel
Included in **About The Poets** Section

Hope

What are you doing poor wayward child,
So reckless, so errant and so wild?
Somehow you got mixed up with dope.
You are at the end of your rope.
You're so mixed up with the wrong crowd.
When you steal, you are crying loud.
You're not so big. You're not so tall.
Soon you will have no mind at all.
This is what dope will do to you.
Those who've tried to help, you've hurt too.
All those who care can only pray
That you will turn to God some day.
He can give you the strength to do
The proper thing to pull you through.
You *can* become healthy and strong
And have a life worthwhile and long.

Mary D. Price

*The power of imagination
makes us infinite.*

—*John Muir*

Strangers

Do you know the strangers?
Could they be your doom,
Or a wondrous new beginning?
It could be that way soon;

Walk along the city streets,
They could be there to trust;
Turn your back away,
And they could become murderous;

No one know what they're thinking,
Minds are so undercover;
In a crowd they could be a friend,
Or an unpleasant loner;

No one knows who they are,
They could be just like you;
Stop the mystery,
Get to know—
That's the thing to do.

William Ladislaw

Voices of the Band

Streets rang out with cries of rage
As the voices from the past united
With the now shrieks of confused hatred
Like a vulgar choir reaching each high
Note as another juvenile fell cold into
His final bed.

Storybook reasons prompted the outbursts
Pieces of unowned turf mapped out the hopes
Of these dancers to songs familiar only to them.
A world with invisible shields provided for
Their playground of death.

A powder high or a liquor low
Takes you on a ride you may never know.
Quick to pull the trigger; too late
the dripping blade; uncleanable
To those outside this horrifying realm.

Like a game of switchblade tag; no harm intended
dodgeball with a bullet; when you're out, you're out
Swallow goldfish, bennies with bourbon
Wrestling with a partner; one of you wins.
Grows strong the choir; falls weak the singers.

David A. Mills

The Price

I shudder at the dreams that come
They threaten, warn, dismay
Nightmares deep and dark within
Subconscious thoughts betray

Swirling, awesome, hellish rays
Of orange and gold and red
Burn my soul with searing flames
Consuming all; A dragon to be fed

Alone? No. Not alone. You're there
Bewildered, dazed as I
What is this place? This ancient plane
Where beings stand round and cry

Not me! Not I! Not we! Not us!
We two are one. We've battled strife
There is no guilt, not here, not there
We paid the price in hell last life

Marcellus J. McKee

Infernal

In a dark, wide chasm in the earth
forgotten creatures rage and lurk.
The evil in between their pores
falls upon the maggot floors.
Their spirits ignorant with joy
and love and chasteness have no more.
They cry and weep and shout for some,
but in their history there's none.
They mangle each other from day to night,
luring each creature into another fight.
A little hole they depart through
into the outside dimension.
And there they try to bring people back
into their inside convention.
Their skins hang down like baggy raiments,
not a word of pleasure not even endearments.
An informed man comes in sad, nicely neat,
and falls down a hole just at his feet.
There is no one around, but soon there will be,
for all that is coming all had the key.

Jason T. de Decker

THE CANAL OF SAN TROVASO.

The Sky is Falling

Minimized motions revealed to occupy the mind
reflections thrown to amuse the blind
hesitation admits feat (of the unknown)
what is presented may not be shown

Sacrifices I have made for identity
criticized with all imparity
washed of the sensitive self
my heart is set on a shelf

I have stumbled in the darkness
fate to my blindness
I have fallen—now crawling
the sky is falling

What is left behind—in the back of mind
the unnecessary track of time
the heartache of an honest crime
the love of mine.

　　D. Cobbs

The Mystery of Love

Just what is love; oh
what is it, that makes us smile,
that keeps us knit, that churns
out warmth, and laughs and care,
that bonds close through troubled
air? Explain it please for I
know not what, this thing
called love that hate
can't blot. Still
mystified? I
know you
well.

But love on still, and peace propel.

Joselito Montojo　　*Canada*

Trust Messages

"Don't trust," the familiar message
said. "Don't trust," ran the thought in my head.
Don't trust too much the people everywhere.
Don't trust and it's dangerous to care.

"Don't trust," the message loud and clear.
"Don't trust," as it's ringing in your ear.
And all the time you're sighing, you
feel you're practically dying
to the tone of the message you hear.

"Trust," the new message said.
"Trust," ran the thought in my head.
Trust who you see that has that share,
Trust and see how much you care.

"Trust," the message loud and clear.
"Trust," singing gently in your ear.
And all the time you're thinking and
you feel your heart linking with the
tone of the message so dear.

　　Lynn M. Chapman (Kennedy)

Life Itself

Nothing is as important as life itself,
So cling to every minute and be kind to yourself
See, but don't see
The good and leaving the rest to destiny.
Hear, but don't hear,
Hearing all things can be severe.
Touch, but don't take,
The fire may be hot and your fingers baked.
Taste, but don't be greedy,
Save some for the needy.
Smell, but don't sniff,
You might find yourself over a cliff.
The importance of life itself
Is you, being kind to yourself.

　　Lorei Rooks

When Life Begins Again

My pride was stripped—my life was gone,
My heart filled full of pain.
Tomorrow comes another time
When life begins again.

The words of love I once would write
Become silent to my pen.
They haunt me in the lonely streets;
Let life begin again.

My heart is heavy in my chest,
The pain lying deep within.
Please listen to my every word
When life begins again.

Tomorrow is another day.
Another time—it's true;
But because my life is now
Your love for me is through.
Saddened by the loneliness
That hides behind the wail,
I walk this lonely silent life
Knowing how I fail.

The words of love I once would write
Become silent to my pen.
They haunt me in the lonely streets;
Let life begin again.

Kathleen J. Smith

Listening to Footsteps

Here in my hotel room,
Loneliness and all,
Listening to footsteps
Padding down the hall.

Waiting, barely breathing
As they pass the doors,
Listening and praying
Please let them be yours.

Suddenly they stop. My
Heart's afraid to beat.
Then the timid knock. I
Stumble to my feet.

But the knock was on the
Door across the hall,
And the friendly greeting
Wasn't mine at all.

So I'm still here waiting,
Loneliness and all,
Looking up at every
Sound out in the hall.

Listening to footsteps
As they pass the doors.
Waiting, barely breathing,
Hoping they are yours.

Al Zimmerman

Only For Today

I cannot look ahead to tomorrow
for, as I awaken to a new dawn again
it is today.
I cannot look back
because yesterday is gone,
and I have not the means
to recapture what has passed.
So, I must live each day to its fullest.
Doing what can be done
without plan our guideline.
For, only then,
will I accomplish goals.
Yes, it is only for today
that I shall live.

Genevieve McClelland

CHILDREN AND THE POETS.

Barefoot and Blistered

Old pictures reconstruct a puzzle
That was once complete,
Awakening memories of having the world
At my tiny feet;
Years were lost,
Dreams spurned,
A fat-faced boy
Grew into a fat-headed man
Wondering about innocence stained
Like the yellowed maps
He so carelessly followed;
Who's the wiser—
He who knows the joy
Of mud between his toes,
Or he who's collected
A closet full of worn shoes?

Harlow Blackmon

Twilight Consolation

Who Can

i run to
when the lights
are fading
into daylight hours.?

Who can
i r u n to

when my identity
in this life
is being erased
Day
by day?

Wizard

City Lights

The city lights from neons glow
Across the desert oasis far below
Tempting me from God's true love
In this city of lights I see from above.

Then a reminder comes to call
Keeping me from a dangerous fall
As the warm desert winds blow
And the shadow of a palm tree grows.

The twinkling of stars in the night
Even the moon God gives us for light
Knowing forever I will stay
Never from Jesus will I stray.

Waneta Dressler

Falling Home

Tiny snowflake,
Born of Heaven,
The path you take,
Will lead you
Home again.

Weary snowflake,
Black, white and grey,
Twirl away home
Amid the vague
Cold!

Cold winds east,
Blow west
Above the beasts,
Falling
Home.

Precious snowflake,
The road is long.
Before you wake,
Falling, seeking
Home again.

Konni Donovan-Maier

*Protest long enough that you
are right, and you will be
wrong.*

—Yiddish Proverb

Heart Hooks

Heart hooks lurk and roam about
In disguise, looking from behind
The smile and the eyes—
Those passion parts
My aching heart on a cruise
In the ocean tides
From behind your eyes.

Heart hooks ponder and search
In the lonely corner, wandering
In secret, longing to adorn her—
Oh, and perhaps me
My defenses down and still
A single mourner
Ready for the kill.

Heart hooks live and solely intend
To survive; you can never
See the coming, yet they thrive—
Those moonlit nights
My quiet heart at peace
In the morning light
From behind your eyes.

Susan MacKay

For All The What Ifs

twists of fate
we're helpless
to unwind

for us remains
only the power
of our mind...

we merely suppose
in our figments
a fate to find

uncolored by paths
of the actual life
we leave behind

every reverie true
to nature spares
us what's unkind

in our vanity
we see a world
to which we're blind

Joan M. Schumack

Problem Friend

I can sense it in the air,
    when you walk into the room,
        and see it on your face,
the problem that you keep inside
    waiting to escape.

Listening to your voice
    I hear it tremble loud
        as you talk to me, but not at
        first,
the problem you unfold.

I watch you smile proudly,
    the weight is off your chest,
and the problem is now complete.

Talk to me, I am a friend
    A friend of yours to keep.

Michael E. Smedley

Love

Wanting, yearning
For that certain something
To fill the void
I feel inside
Day to day—
Emptiness.

Searching desperately,
Wanting something,
Not knowing what
Feeling it everywhere
All around
Except inside of me.

In the air
In people's hearts
Twinkling eyes
That certain look...
And then I find it—
That special something.

A hug
A kiss
A caress
A touch
A word
Love.

Danielle Cormier   Canada

My Angel

I had a vision,
a hope,
a prayer
and a dream.

It became a quest,
a need,
a desire
and obsession.

There were pitfalls,
obstacles,
delays
and mountains to climb.

I needed a friend,
an ear,
commitment
and support.

You became my enthusiasm,
my hope,
my vision
and answered prayer.

Without you,
there would be thoughts and words.
But,
no moods, no moments.

Teresa M. Brown

Hope

White candles glow in the darkness of night—
    summoning strangers—home
Filling with hope those in flight
Come home, take refuge,
    find truth this night.
What is it that draws me to this secure dreamy sight?
For it bathes me in hope and inner delight.

Perhaps she has placed the candles for a loved one to see.
Unknown to her—they whisper to me.

Some secret, some wonder holds me captive
    to these brilliant but silent
        candles of the night.
They bloom with sunshine in the middle of the rain.
Burst of precious hope and gently conquer
    the closing claws of pain.
Simplicity is offered as golden comfort—
Clarity is a gain—
Sweet purity is remembered—
    and I travel on in vain.

Claire Elizabeth Warner

THE SO-CALLED PORTRAIT OF BEATRICE CENCI.

A Vintage Rose-Mother

Rose petals may wither and fall from the bud
But each year anew it blossoms forth in love
A rainbow of color with brilliance of hue
Then fades away as memories do
Those dried petals, memories lost?
Are they dead? Or just scattered and tossed?
No, not at all, for I have gathered them today
And made for you a sweet smelling potpourri!
Yes, rose petals may fall and wither from the bud
But they always linger on as the fragrance of your Love.

Connie M. Grillo

Untitled

Tonight, after our call, I felt the stab
of distance as the knife of loneliness
    sliced away my heart.
And as I lie in my bed, the sands of
sleep won an easy victory over my being.
Then, out of an infinity of darkness,
I was beckoned upon the shore of a beautiful
island; I know not where—only that you
    were there, by my side, in my arms.
And as we lay there in the warmth and
tenderness of each other, the trees waltzed
their emerald skirts with a warm, gentle breeze;
    while the ocean around us shone like
    blue-green crystals as it washed forth to
        lick the sun-bleached sands.
As our lips touch and our souls meet, the
golden rays of the sun branch forth from its
    sapphirine veil, piercing the clouds, to
        light upon and caress
        the softness of your skin.
Now, as our love heightens, I drift back
    into the empty void of loneliness,
but knowing that even in distance there is
    an isle where our hearts can meet.

Victor A Bryant

Black Dawn

Ah, depression. It's the dark blues
When nothing seems right,
No matter what you do.

It's that evil thought
Which fills your head.
A crumbling madness, you feel instead.

When life's endless woes batter
And tear your dreams apart,
you're left unaware, to mend your discouraged heart.

Ah, depression. An empty, unreaching void.
An endless torment,
That's keeping deep inside.

Waking from the blackened dawn
Depression lingers,
Still yet to yawn.

Walking in a shadowed grove
Life has ended...
That thought, he drove.

John S. Goodwin IV

What Is A Mother?

A mother is a woman who cares for you.
And loves you dearly.
For she is the one who
brought you into this world.

A mother is a special lady who I missed very much.
I feel lost without here.
I need her guidance to get me through life.

A Mother is a person who is there when you need her.
She will always be by your side.
She loves you for the rest of your life.

Those who have mothers
should be thankful theirs is alive.

You should love her and
respect her with all your heart.
A Mother is someone you can look up to.

You admire her courage and,
the things she's done for you.
You ought to be glad to have a mother who loves you.
For if it wasn't for here.
You wouldn't be here.

Sharon Lee Robinson
Included in **About The Poets** Section

Concept of a mother

A mother is a lovely thing,
bright and happy as birds in spring.
Strong, yet gentle as a calm, rippling sea,
always warm and comforting.
Kind and understanding, too,
ever trying to erase life's blues.

A mother knows how to cook and sew
and all the other things a mother should know.
She tries to lend a helping hand,
to ease the burden, if she can.
Her eyes always sparkle with overflowing love,
like stars cascading from the sky above.

A mother is a lovely thing,
comforting as a breeze in spring.
Nurturing as the sun's cosmic rays,
a life she hopes will exceed her days.

But a mother isn't a perfect thing.
Sometimes she flounders like a bird with a broken wing
wondering how she'll ever reach her nest,
frantic that she'll fail to complete her quest.

Like springtime when sometimes raindrops fall,
a mother can't have the answers to life's all.
And sometimes it takes a winter's passage
to appreciate her loving message.

Helen I. Mcdonald

Symbols

Symbols make my mind
A constant Christmas tree,
Dozens of Citizen Kane's
Old "Rosebud" sleds.
Stars crusted with sparkle
And snowflake sequins,
Norelco Bubble-ites
Like the hats of Magi
Bubbling neon dreams;
A glass globe, gossamer
Survivor of fifty years;
Carved birds, painted animals
Papier-maché angels
Hand-appliquéd Santas,
Plastic horns, tin icicles,
A sum uniformly false—
Yet is it? The tree dies,
The ornaments are stored,
The corner seems to be empty.
Christmas lingers best
In ornaments invisibly
Hanging, potent in the mind.

Jill Wilson Brennan

Vietnam Remnants

THE END? or tears still?
Black granite—the deadly list
Iron cold soldiers—staring—
    Forward or back?
To blood and mud
Greed—
    Holding the keys
    to hell and death.

THE END?
    For those who never knew
      Maybe!

THE END? Remorse
    Lost children!
      Fathers some—
      Husbands or sons.

Pain—Ends of lives
Hurt—Boxes draped in flags
Bugles mourning—Rounds firing
    Etched permanently on the soul.

MISSING? Visions still

HOW
    can we allow
      THE END?

Gracie Moore Hunter

Taffy

She was a wee little thing
With no place to go,
Just a wandering waif
Picked up in the snow.
T'was the day before Christmas
That I went to the pound;
And all of a sudden, there, I found
This one little mite
Standing out from the rest,
With her big pleading eyes
And looking her best.
She was so shiny black
Like midnight, it seemed.
As I called her by name
Her pink tongue came out,
And she fairly beamed.
I could not resist that dear little face
She already knew that I'd lost the race.
So I paid the fee and took her home with me.
She's now a playmate to my poodle, McGee.

Marie K. Mills

GLEANING.

Pearl in an aged hand

I wear this pearl—gem of the ocean
mothered by a grey frosted oyster—
seed from foreign sand.

and placed around my neck
tenderly—from strong dark hands.
like you...perfection is rare.

It was the time of farewell—
my years were calling me homeward.
"Kawika"—my love since youth—

I could not—have left you—
I wore your love proudly—
placing you on a peacock throne.

The winds—nor the Gods
removed my aged illness—

I did not want the rug of earth
to be removed—in front of your eyes.

I wear this pearl—
the color of my tears
as I read—you have passed over
    Longing for me.

Jay Son

A Very Special Treasure

A very special treasure
A very special gift
A very special treasure
You give our hearts a lift.

A very special treasure
You're a gift from above
A very special treasure
You're filled with so much love.

You have fought so many battles
You fought them
And you survived
Your life stories are important
You are a native Indian son
You are so alive!

A very special treasure
Yes, you know *The History*
America's your homeland
You're a national treasure
A national treasure we see...
Yes, a living treasure we see.

Connie Rigsby Jones

Time to Reckon

As I stand upon this hill so high
the plains and trees afar I see
We must protect from man's old greed
For if we don't the birds and bees
we'll only know by what we read
As humankind we'll no longer see
of what we could've strived to be
So for the beauty of our land
let all intelligent life band
Lets give each other a hand
for our children now and then
Give them a chance at life so grand

Q. L. Raney Jr.

a day's entertainment

At dawn
the town awakes
anticipating
dusty streets buzz
children laugh
everyone is there

towards the center of town
a smile on each face

closed circle, and
a play, begins to unfold
amid whispers
the star mounts the stage

no one cares about plot
antagonist's crimes
protagonist's glory
it's the place to be
no matter, that
 it's a farewell performance

no effect at all
the curtain closes
they'll forget the actor
and go home
unmoved, the same

But the gallows is patient
and someday they'll know

Geoffrey Trabalka

Untitled

Taste the languidness
of a kiss
dangerous
candy coated packed
full of mom.

The killing of the prime,
baste the carcass
form a burning.

Teetered Saints
the safeties
among little kid thrust bodies.
Love it
& take it to the tundra.
Odes highways.

This is how it will end:
Tom's
peeping owl. The wet dew.
A window
Camera boy in trees
concealed from the eye
of an innocent opponent.
Warm, careless, dagger
night.

Kevin Burnam

Untitled

It's raining again
the sky pours down
upon the earth,
as my tears pour down
on my pillow
Now the clouds have come again
and the air feels closed
as does my heart
I've built a wall around my heart
and padded the walls
my heart lies dormant
in the asylum
of my mind.

Ann Vohe

The Celtic Self

Down through many ages,
Hurling through time,
Through the centuries of history,
Of song and rhyme,
Your Celtic self reflects
Through your eyes.

I see so much there...
Of bitterness, of bloodshed,
Hurt and hope.
The music of harps,
and Blues of shamrock greens.

I wish I could say I understand it all.
I want to walk the same road,
And see the same flowers,
Look out over the sea, and feel the wind
In my face, the same one you feel.

I love the look, the special look
You have reserved for me.
I can see your soul of mystical wisdom,
And wit, steeped in your eyes.

I do understand it all, I do,
Only...
What do I have to offer you???

Jenifer Coleman

Tempest

Wizard's flawed
claw
swirls   twirls
atmospheres:

clouds boil,
rage—
eager to earn
the devil's
wage.

Down
    down
touching the
earth, a
tornado
has been given
birth;

souls unaware
are taken
in the storm,

Death has
eaten well   its
belly full,
Warm.

Sheldon Young   Canada

The Death of Arthur

Merlin, Merlin, can you hear me?
All the prophecies draw near me.
Friend and foe alike now fear me
As I watch before the dawn.

Merlin, Merlin, night is fading
And the truth I've been evading.
Gawain's warning is pervading
Fears and doubts I thought had gone.

Merlin, Merlin, dawn is burning!
And my dreams to dust are turning.
Where is wisdom, where is learning
When our lives are sadly drawn?

Merlin, Merlin, I am weeping.
Guinevere my heart is keeping
Far away in safety sleeping
Through this grief I linger on.

Merlin, Merlin, fate has found me.
Battle lines are drawn around me.
Cries of pain and death surround me
As I go to stand upon
The distant hills of Avalon.

Kevin Anderson

Winter's Spring

A rose in the midst
   of a cold December morn;
A smile in the midst
   of another person's scorn.
Feelings soft as feathers
   in a world made up of hate;
Running—far from ev'ryone
   to avoid the turns of fate.

    Laura Byrne   Canada

Ticklesome Rose

The fragrant thorn upon the rose
Bites the air in song and prose
Ticklesome rose climbs the nose
To wring the mind of all its woes

    Harry S. Monesson
    Included in **About The Poets** Section

Untitled

A resting tree
Hundreds of years old
Three men with arms extended
Could not reach around it
Roots have grown above the ground
To cradle weary bodies
To comfort frail souls

Majestic branches
Offer shelter
In sweltering heat
Leaves rustle
Birds nest

Bare branches
Remain strong against
Winter's cold assault
Proof of history
Hope for a future
A resting tree

    P.R. Pattan-O'Neal

Rain Storm

You are like a rain storm
   always tumbling down
from some unearthly hiding place
   pummeling the ground
slashing at first quietly
   and then with great disdain
at a world that seems to use one up
   and then demand again

    Rene Orlandi

Primavera

A final shroud of snow
melts into the sky
to wait its turn
while summers burn
to come in season's time

and buds burst out
in plants galore
reaching out to grasp
the sun to make life
grow within its core

A green carpet of delight
covers the earth and
the morning dew upon it
shines like jewels
in the sun

'tis the season of rebirth
the world wakes up
to all its beauty
as Mother Nature
starts her duty

    Tommie Ruiz

Rattles

Leashed to the wind,
a leaf is tangled,
inescapably,
outside my door.

Like thought strung
to a spirit, its
incessant rattle
annoys me.

So clear, it sounds like
it has entered, yet
I have not opened
the door.

I look for it,
anyway,
expectantly.

    Nancy Whitecar

The Little Shadow

No, one seems to listen, I
heard a voice say
As, I was sitting in my
rocking chair one day
I, must have been daydreaming,
when I heard it again
No, one seems to listen, who
could it be
And, a tiny little shadow
started talking to me
My, days have been long gone, but
yet I'm still around
Sometimes, I just sit and
watch without uttering a sound
You, see, I'm an angel, and I
was sent for you
If, you have any problems you
can work them through
You, have to start within yourself,
that's all you have to do
Please, just try to listen, and
You'll find the way, then the
little shadow just faded away
I, leaned back in my chair
as, if in a daze
Then, I heard a little
voice, echo this phrase
  No, one seems to listen, that's
all you have to do
  If, you really try you can
work it through.

    Nina Morgan

Untitled

Morning,
   the sun lights,
   warms.

It shines for all the world
Not just one beam for me,
   myriads of beams
   for all that lives and dies.

Awakening,
   how can I do less?
Love the minutes,
   love the work,
   love the joy (that's easy)
   love the grief
   and all that lives and dies.

Myriads of things
And people,
   see the sunshine
   in their eyes.

Jessie Johnson

Great geniuses have the shortest biographies.

—Emerson

Stress

How in your life
Can you do your best?
Try, try your hardest
Can you deal with stress?

You work slave and sweat
Toil from morning till night,
Work fingers to bone
Then you go home a fright.

You sit in your chair
Say Hi to the kids,
A kiss from the wife
As she musses your hair.

A hot shower, A little rub,
Each day is the same,
Eat dinner, Go to sleep,
Too much stress makes you insane.

Raymond L. Drahos

Today as Yesterday

Oh baglady, baglady,
Where do you go?
We have a big house
And so much yard to mow.

Oh baglady, baglady,
Won't you let me share
The work of this place
Your idleness not bear.

Oh baglady, baglady,
About Lazarus tell us
Ask him to dip his finger
Before we miss the bus.

Charlotte Vogel

A GIRL OF THE VALLEY.

Trees in Full Bloom

Trees in full bloom;
A blanket of perfection.
Branches hovering;
An awning of protection.
The stillness, quiet,
The early morning breeze,
The splendor,
The grandeur of God's own trees.

I wished for a tree in my backyard
Some years ago.
Then I noticed there was a small bush
Growing near the fence;
And now it has become a giant tree
In my backyard.
Thank you, God.

Lois E. Hutchings

Pain

Pain finds many routes
On its passage to the brain.
Oftimes through the heart,
Though it rarely starts as pain.

Paul R. Barnes

Daddy

Daddy could you tell me
I did good today?
Instead of merely shrugging
and ignoring me away.
I only want to be
a friend with my dad.
Then I won't need others
when I feel so bad.
I just need a handshake—
a pat on my back—
to fill my empty pail,
take away my lack.
For pain seems unending
when I come to you.
You don't say you love me
though I know you do!

Joel Thornton

Grandfather's Banjo

There it sits,
Absent of the hands,
That played so lovingly.
Hands that made,
Tears, sadness,
Joy, laughter,
All possible with his mood.
Fingers bent, worn.
Shoulders stooped, tired.
Withered face
Lighting up when holding,
Caressing the strings.
Music flowing from his soul.
Not fancy.
Music of his childhood.
Old near forgotten melodies,
Beautiful in their way.
Now silent, alone.
Bits of wood, metal.
Only in memory.
Absent of the hands.

Martha Blanton

The Question

Is there a way to solve
   the madness?
A remedy to ease the
   mind?
Is there a cure for
   endless searching?
A light to lead the blind?

Is there a path to help
   the stumbling?
A smooth and flawless
   trail?
Is there a portal
   thru which one enters
To aid the strong and frail?

Is there an answer
   to one's yearning?
A response so true
   and clear?
Is there a love that's so enduring
   to stop the flowing
   tear?
     Estelle Schultz

What's In A Name?

I know a pretty young lady
Whose real name is Helen.
She dropped the "H" and added an "L"
And now she says that she's Ellen.

And there's another nice girl
Whose original name was Mamie.
She wanted something different
So now she calls herself Amy.

A sweet young thing named Mary
Changed her name to Marie.
But I think that is just fine
It really doesn't bother me.

I have a very good friend
Whose name is just plain Sam.
His pet philosophy is;
I am just what I am.

All of these folks I have found
To be a great deal of fun.
To me that's what really counts
When all is said and done.

So, a person who is friendly and jolly
And always is just the same,
Is surely a lot more important
Than just some fancy name.

     Byron C. Casey
     Included in **About The Poets** Section

STATUE OF BURNS AT EDINBURGH.

A New Beginning

Because we had yesterday
Today will begin
Because we held on
We, once again, became friends

The shadows which frightened me
Each night I was alone
Are now hiding someplace
Their faces never to be shown

You have awakened me out of
The depression I was in
And stirred up my emotions
With sweet love and affection

We've changed inside,
You and me,
Growing closer together
The way it should be

So now when the day
Turns into night
The only shadow I'll see
Is you in the moonlight

Because we have today
We'll hold on even stronger
And our happiness will last
For a time that's much longer.

     Maureen Mackey

126

I'm past thirty, but trust me.

As I've grown older
   I've become bolder
about telling you,
   and others, too,
about things you should
   or shouldn't do.

When school is finished
   you've just begun
to seek that spot
   beneath the sun.

First, choose a job
   that really excites you
then wed that lovely girl
   you'll always be true to.

Have some kids,
   at least a couple,
Your joy of life
   will surely double.

Then take some time
   to help those guys
who never listened
   to my advice.

     Grin Moore

Fast as a Cat

5 feet plus high
Quick with green eyes
Open quite often shy
Out and will learn to fly

Fast as a cat
Check the back stair?
On the window case?
All in love is pain
You won't find me anyplace

Fast as a cat
5 feet plus high
Quick with green eyes
Open quite often shy
Out and will learn to fly

Fast as a cat

     Marian R. Wiltfong

*The more things a man
ashamed of, the more
respectable he is.*

     —*Shaw*

Dreams

Stars sit in heaven,
Each alone, all together.

Warm summer night breezes
Blow until they almost wither,
Yet, the next eve...

The moon's companion,
Large, green, fertile,
Always together, always apart.
Lonely stars.

And to lovers of Earth,
Warm stars, warm moon;
Companions forever, eternally strangers.

Dreams of stars.

Sandra Stewart

Honorable Mention
Love's View

Though I come to her with empty arms,
   and take all gain of love
away—I have probably seen more
   of a mountain worn down

by rain and cold in a single season,
   than of her love eroded
by my efforts to ascertain its heights,
   and comprehend its scale:

The emotions are staggered by the view.
   And the imagination by
landscapes wider on, inviting and
   undiscovered. Peaks still

to be attempted, catch the light. And
   in my heart I am already
there—among the ridges and
   arroyos on their way...

Steven C. Janak

A Place In My Own Sun

Winter glows inside me
   with an icy fire—
Sifting feelings, find the real one
   call it my desire.
Living's right for those I love
   but hardly right for me—
See the past for what it is
   then finally let it be.

Growing pains in my garden
   will make me big and strong—
Knowing life is happiness
   but coming out all wrong.
Clouds will come and hang
   with heavy darkness in my heart—
Wishing I could see that light
   I've known right from the start.

Seeing's not believing
   to a troubled mind—
Shadows leaping from dark corners
   on the good things they can find.
Living in my world of perceptions
   and fighting all the way—
For a place to walk
In my own sun.

Deborah J. M. Quigley

This Girl

This girl has a special love
for dogs.
This girl walks at the park
among logs.
This girl is not very tall
four feet.
This girl is extra observant
very sweet.

This girl walks holding the leash
one hand.
This girl talks gazing about
on land.
This girl meets other children
passing by.
This girl walks forward looking up
to the sky.

This girl continues to go on her
special hike.
This girl stops and then spots a bike.
This girl goes across
to see
With a puppy at her knee.

Betty Motes

The Great Aorta

listen . . . rest your ear upon the ground
   and hear your heart
   sounding near the soul
   of America

listen . . . to the Soul
   in this soil
   to the echoing of an aorta
   back-slipping blood
   Straining with the struggles
   across this soil

listen . . . back...to its throbbing
   of generations
   galloping across the soul
   in this soil

listen . . . to the hammering
   of homemakers
   heaving houses into place
   across the soul
   in this soil

listen . . . rest your ear upon the ground
   and hear your heart
   Merging with the soul
   of America

Angelina Rossetti
*Included in **About The Poets** Section*

Well Strewn

There is newer way
To calculate poetics
Other than form play
Bard use museful antics.

Set aside are adaments
Trust promiseable note
Sing more than vents
Orchestral charm devote.

Without such feature
Harp do precede piano
Angelic manful creature
Sympathy amuse bel canto.

Much a cappella must
Breed poem taken care.
Soul belie upperthrust
By star dream aptly rare.

Come spend now laureate
Truth is peaceful wise
Loss none falsible regret
And prime for dew surprise.

Or blossom put anew
Song beneficial heard
Ocean inner conch strew
Waves like wingful bird.

Orien Todd

What About Me

For all the times I've helped you
asking nothing in return,
for all the little things I've done
to help us grow and learn.

For all the times I've smiled
shrugging off the tears,
For all the happy times we've had
together through the years.

For all the crazy things I've done
to make each day more fun,
For all the times we've walked along
together in the sun.

I know you try to help me
by all the things you say and do,
I also know that sometimes life
can be very hectic too.

I've never meant to blame you
for not saving time for me,
But that doesn't mean I haven't hurt
inside my heart you see.

I've always been there for you
putting the world right at your feet,
But now I feel I need *myself*
to make my world complete.

Katrina Meyer

Pele

On the island of Hawaii
In the district of Puna
She moves above and within
Our earth mother, Papa
Under the sun
Under the rain
Onward and downward
She moves to the east
She moves to the west
Searching with desire
For the pig God, Kamapua'a
Under the sun
Under the rain
She touches to surround
She moves to cover
Gaining forceful momentum
Pushing under the sun
Pushing under the rain
Listen to the birth
Pele gives us more land.

Lehuananiokilauea

Walls of Ice

I look into my heart
and saw with a chill—
walls of ice surrounding
me there

I looked for hope in others
I know—and only found
faces of stone

I search the world over—
and found to my despair
people living hopelessly
alone

I sought the universe of time—
and to my astonishment—I found—
I, too, had forgotten how to love.

Barbara Gilbert

Honesty

I feel your love...
    honesty,
I hear your words...
    honesty,
I look into your eyes...
    honesty,
I feel your embrace...
    honesty,
I kiss your lips...
    honesty,
I know your touch...
    honesty,
You are a man of honesty...
    and I love you.

Ruth Jackson
Included in **About The Poets** Section

Always

When the years have dimmed your vision
And your hair has turned pure white
Will you stand by your decision
And still feel that you are right

Can you always love me tender
As the first night that we met
And your service still you'll render
For our love you'll ne'er forget

For our lives a silver lining
And our love will never die
So as the sun keeps shining
As you love me—so shall I

Pauline Unger

The Life of a Rose

Love is a Rose
born sweet as honey,
attracting with your subtle scent.
Growing amongst
thorn and good ground
wanting to be
as all the rest.
Yielding quiet beauty,
rainbow of color
sure seed forever.
One could learn from *You!*
Creation of God,
soft petal feelings,
growing wild throughout the vines.
Harmless creature
trusting nature,
a part of the Universe
living life allowed thee.
Death is dark,
awaiting in the shadow
of one so meek and true.
The innocence of her beauty forever,
remains to be seen as:
THE LIFE OF A ROSE!

Lori J. Williamson

Only One Love

Only one love in my life
I've always loved you
A thousand times before
I think that I am now at my best
So love me honey, always and forever.

No matter how old you are
And years have changed the weather
And we wonder why
We are still together
My heart is still saying
I will still love you.

Violet D. Knowles   Bahamas
Included in **About The Poets** Section

To R.O.

To cry
To scream
To die
To see
To yearn
To wish
To love only you
To hear
To darkness
To loneliness
To suffer
To you I only write
For only you can understand it all

Helen Marie Velazquez

Loneliness

A pang of loneliness
  begins like a cancer.
Painlessly devouring
  the contents.
Consuming
  the human soul.
Feeding
  on the essence of life.
It rages
  beyond control.
Crossing
  the border of darkness.
Ultimately possessing
  its innocent victim.

Annette K. Sievers

The Cycle

The emptiness has faded now
  The shade of blue has gone;
The darkness doesn't seem so near
  The shadows stumble on.
My being has succumbed to lightness
  My heart to new desire;
My soul allowed to rise once more
  My mind can now aspire.
The time is not so far away
  The shadows will begin to fade;
The darkest gloom shall settle in
  The vicious cycle will be made.

C. L. Thomas

In a Daze

In a daze I watch
The many things that
Usually go unnoticed.
People are busy,
Punishing their minds,
Gasping at gossip,
Which is softly spoken
About their best friend.

But I always see
The many things,
Beauty or beast.
Her hair it curls
Under, like when
A wave breaks into white.
The blue marbles shift
With no more depth
Than half an inch.

I watch, I know
What is real, what is not.
Games are played
By people of different types.
Masks are worn,
Roles are acted.
Lies are spoken, and
Some do not know,
But I watch, I see.

Chris Avgeris

The Work of the Word

Soft sticky sayings
May play pretty pranks
In your mind.
Then you find
Stricken understanding
Staring, hardly caring.
The sonics and symphonics
of your mind.

Kimberly Wind

Nothing For Me

When I was young
  I looked deep inside
  To see all I had to see

Now I am old, my youth is gone
  And like I knew all along
  This world holds nothing for me

Damien Alexander

The Attic

In the trunk, In the attic
Are old memories stored

Grandma's lace wedding gown
Yellow and torn
Ma's suede pumps
Dad's red-band fedora
Grandpa's worn-out pipe
Cousin Mae's yellow ribbons,
Still bright

My first baby shoes
Brother Ray's wooden soldiers
Uncle Bob's sailor hat
And a few edge-worn photos
Of family reunions
And afternoon Bar-B-Ques

There I send my children
To play and discover
All the years we thought lost
They'll soon recover
Putting on Ma's suede pumps
Dad's red-band fedora
Grandma's lace wedding gown
Dear Grandpa's worn-out pipe

Keyla Gonzalez

Apocalypse
(the punk-youth movement)

Can you hear
the new-age rhythm?
The streets are bad—
they cry
their broken-glass cry.
Look at the new angels
flying up the architecture.
Souls with painted faces,
forgotten,
as with memories—
discarded long ago
to a realm unknown.
Can you hear it—
the new-age cry?
Look at them—
they dive
in the alcohol oasis,
but wake up
in the palm
of the Lord.

Ana Pattacini

Life

Reaching out across
   the vast sea of life,
grasping with open
   arms all one can
      possibly absorb
         of life.
Remembering all who have
   walked before and
      the many yet to come.

Rae Ann Petesch

Misty Isles

White, and purple heather.
Strewn vastly o'er the common.
In the Valley, and hills.
Of the peaceful Misty Isles.
North winds are blowing.
Huge tidal waves are roaring.
As they bang against the rocks.
On the shores of the mIsty Isles.
The echoes I hear.
From the mountain so near.
Where through the eternal mist.
I can almost see my wish.
One day the mist will rise.
The pinnacle I will see.
Standing there will be you.
Holding your hands out to me.
We will walk the path of laughter.
In the peaceful Misty Isles.

Marian Kelly

Wheat or Weed?

Mid-afternoon in future years
a trumpet thus did sound
the skies shone bright
upon a cloud of white
our Lord had returned
to gather in his crop
for harvest time had come
with mighty hand
he split the fields
wheat from weed to separate
the wheat upon the right
bore fruit and multiplied
weeds that stood to the left
had none to present
in a timeless-second
the wheat was gathered in
though out-numbered by weeds,
its crop was abundant
with God the wheat ascended
and the weeds were left behind
in the darkness to perish!!

Michael Radford

GRESSONEY ST. JEAN.

Hope

What's that light coming from afar,
That illuminates my path,
That will change my destiny?
It's hope...It's hope.

Hope...come to me, come to me,
On the wings of fortune,
With the smile of love,
To console my heart,
Which has suffered so much.

Hope...your greatness who doesn't give up
Your force who has the faith.
Hope...you are the promise of my life,
That I will have a better future.

And as the sun's light,
You will illuminate my path,
You will change my destiny.
Hope...you have entered in my heart,
Hope...you are already living in me.

Nissim Koen

Untitled

I am the last.
My people were found.
Hung until death,
and shot to the ground

They came to our village,
From then on I fled.
The woods are my home,
Pine needles my bed.

My father was shot,
My mother was sold.
The whiteman would kill,
for one ounce of gold.

Our scalps they would take,
Our bows they would break.
My spirit is gone,
It lies dead with the lake.

There's no use to live.
I can no longer fight.
I pray every night,
I'm within God's sight.

John F. Cruz

Yet Not Wasted

today we wasted time together
   you found me again
      (while drinking orange juice)

today we walked over to our sides
   watched a spider
      (in the clear spring)

today we spent some time
   out of time
      (as the spider went on)

today we ran into lost others
   similarly forgotten
      (as the spider ran)

today we wasted lost tomorrow
   time purchased
      (the spider doesn't have such burdens

Tom Bryant

some

some where
some time
some day
some one could
some one may
some one would
    be mine

James B. Herring
Included in **About The Poets** Section

Untitled

when i look into his blazing eyes
i see the warmth that
makes his entire being
glow
a warmth that not only
belongs to him
but captures
and surrounds
my body
so i cannot escape
his glistening smile
along with the gentleness
of his touch
and the gleam in his eyes
melt my heart
and mold my soul
into a walking
talking
puppet
that shall follow him
forever
and bow at his every command.

Donna J. Ciecierski

One Love

Stars and Angels,
       mingle with God.

             Chitter chatter.
           Small talk.

    A dialogue,
        between immortals.

If I'm still,

    I hear whispers.
     From the moon,
      to the sun.

One heart,
  in sequence,
  one voice,
    one love.

Joshua Murry

A Poem for Dot

I see a thing I can never have,
Soft and free and very lovely.
I see a thing I can never have,
strong and bold and full of soul.
I see a thing I can never touch,
the very thing I've loved so much, 'tho
Time has passed and things have changed
the love I have remains the same.
    I see you.

John L. Willis, Jr.

Untitled

I need your arms to hold me
close and safe and warm,

I need your arms to hold me
and protect me from life's storms.

I need your lips to tell me
all the sweet things I long to hear,

Whispering so softly
Right up against my ear.

I need to feel your body
all tangled up with mine,

I need to know you'll love me
until the end of time.

Dearosa Goodfellow

Maiden Voyage

Your hand explores
  my shadows
    cautiously
with no demand,
  impatient, yet
    unafraid
of waiting. The
  soothing music
    of your
desire is contagious,
  and quickly
    fires
on my defenses,
  warming winter
    skin,
cutting through the
  dreams; bleached
    bones
of my mother
  sinking out to
    sea
on the sweet
  mysterious tides
    of love.

Nancy L. Clark

DECORATIVE PANEL: TOUCHSTONE.

outta site

looking' hip

    sweater squeezin' jeans

takin' trip

    havin' fun

starts to gawk

    far too many scenes

sees "don't walk"

    decides to run

spies a site

    stops in street

amber lite

    blushes red

car has come

    knocks off feet

senses numb

    cement hits head

siren keens

    some place in space

silence preens

    caressing care

soul escapes

    smiling face

blanket drapes

    some body there

rawn

Discontinued Candy

It was never going to work. He loved fun-sized Milky Way bars, cookie covered Twix, Three Musketeers. He ate Hazel Nut Cadbury bars for breakfast, washed down with whole milk, chocolate flavored, from Sanders. He loved to eat Marathon bars while watching soap operas. During football season he preferred peanut M & M's if his team was winning. He never wore cologne but always smelled

of ground roasted cacao beans—dripped in coconut and delicately sprinkled with walnut dust. His pockets never held spare change or a handkerchief but I always found a few Milk Duds rolling around in his left breast pocket. Snow Caps, Goobers, and Brach's Bridge Mix too. His first present to me was a 5 lb. Hershey's Kiss. We ate it together, and after we were done, after he had licked his

fingers, he licked my fingers, and hungrily told me how chocolate brown my eyes were. And I took no comfort in him calling me his little Sugar Baby. The break came when he was late for a date. I saw a smear of dark chocolate on his damp lips, a few revealing flakes of tender coconut on his chin. When confronted, he admitted being with a Baby Ruth.

Susan Marie Baranski

B...I...N...G...Oh Darn!

The caller shouts "N-39";
   Shivers race down my spine!
I've just been cased to "I-28,"
   Which causes me to quiver and quake!

I silently send up a hasty plea:
   "Just this once, let it be me!"
I assure myself that I can wait
   As the announcer says "G-58."

A cry is heard among the crowd!
   Another winner shouts aloud!
But alas, the player is struck with terror
   When he discovers he was in error.

We removed our markers, so hence the race,
   For all our chips we must replace!
Of course, "Bingo" was called right away,
   To my complete and utter dismay!

Now the "Cover-All" game at last...
   Will this one end just as fast?
A few minutes later I need "B-10"...
   "B-11" is called and I've lost again.

I am convinced I go for fun
   Because, as yet, I haven't won.
I will sometime, or so they say,
   But why couldn't it have been today?

Mary E. Cummings

He who praises you for what you lack wishes to take from you what you have.

—Juan Manuel

Jealous Hostility

Just once I would love to
Pull off those long brown lashes,
Cut-off her hair sprayed
Spaghetti curls, punch out
Those straight-white fangs,
Scratch her flushed face—
Showing the true green blood
Underneath the satin skin.
Push that petite body down
The crooked stairs—breaking
Those slender legs, twisting that
24-inch waist in half, and
Smashing her long, slinky neck
In-two, so that the snap can be
Heard by all her admirers.

Lisa Mosley-Roberts

What's Wrong With Them?

I see people hanging 'round the joint smoking dope.
What's wrong with them—have they lost all hope?
I know people that use the needle to mainline.
What's wrong with them—have they lost their minds?
I've heard of people that use acid to go on trips.
Don't they know that that stuff will make them sick?
I know people that use heroin to get high.
Isn't that sad?
It makes me cry.
I've heard of people who smoke dope just for fun.
They think it's smart, but it's really very dumb.
I've read of people that snort cocaine.
What's wrong with them—are they insane?
What a waste: people throwing their lives away in a cloud of
        smoke.
What's wrong with them—HAVE THEY LOST ALL HOPE??

David Johnson

---

*When a man's knowledge is
not in order, the more of it
he has the greater will be his
confusion.*

—Herbert Spencer

The Addiction

From within the ADDICTION arose, gathering momentum as it
        grew.
I became obsessed with chemicals, alcohol, drugs, caffeine, then
        I knew.

One thing led to another obsession, I couldn't understand it all.
My addictive personality behavior. Yet i was there at its beck
        and call.

To finally be free, that's what I wanted, but I didn't know how.
To turn my life around, be clean and sober. I wanted THAT right
        now.

I got down on my knees, bowed my head, surrendering my being
        at last.
Asked a Higher Power to help me, to rid me of my past.

Now tomorrow's a new beginning. I'll take it One Day At A Time.
free of my many addictions and my days are more sublime.

I can tell you when you ask me, how my many friends were
        there.
Through all the groups I belong to, I received my love and care.

Friends helped me to understand about my addictive past.
My disease is behind me now and I'm sober and free at last.

Jeannie M. Urban

Almighty Titans

Like some almighty Titans
Deadlier than mind
And mood of man imagine,
Missiles,
Slick and smooth and sleek,
Regurged
From Earth's emerging entrails deep,
Shadows black, implacable,
Intractable death impending,
Attitude unbending, tend to make uneasy
Hearts.

Bud Christian

The American Nightmare

Driving out in my old pick-up,
Going to see all the world.
Going through the states one by one,
As the day uncurled.

All I see is suffering,
All I see is pain.
The children cry so many tears,
They quench the Eternal Flame.

I've been around a lot of suffering.
I've seen a lot of strife.
When I think about those money-men,
It cuts me like a knife.

I've barely stepped out of my door.
I've seen more than enough.
I think it's time to wake up, America!
This world is way too rough.

Laura Clark

Darkness Passes

As twilight ages
And darkness matures
A cold enshrouds me
Digging into my bones
Hope is lost
Vanity is gone
Both only words
The breath of ancient dead upon the nape of my neck
The darkness is stealing my soul
It shines brightly
Will it shine on me
It passes me by
My last vestige of hope...lost
Only consciousness remains
It is fading, fading away
My last thought is one of realization
Then I wake as if from an unholy nightmare

Joshua C. Holt

Escape Heaven

Dedicated to Greer, Az and Jay Zimbelman

Here, I close my eyes to escape.
Even when I open my eyes, I see only mountains
filled with tall pines and spruce and aspen trees.
I close my eyes again,
only this time,
with my nature heaven,
shots ring out.

As the shots' loudness increases,
I notice bewildered looks.
What is this disturbance,
this annoying sound that threatens our peace?

The calmness of a rain drenched forest
is torn apart with the booming of man's
mistakes...
guns.

The forest squirrels, chipmunks, rabbits and deer
begin to scatter as now they fear only man's gun.
Silence again,
with only the sound of the creek running
by in front of me.

Alas, how long will the silence last?

Elise R. Jacobson

He who knows how to be poor knows everything.

—Michelet

Onward

I speed to the North Shore as fast as the law and my tired soul
    will allow
Driven not by chauffeur but by my pain
This invisible wall that surrounds me is steel that nothing can
    pierce
Caring for everyone/everything has taken its toll
My need to be alone/away is overwhelming
I don't like how it feels: numbness, automatic pilot, hitting the
    wall
"Death, where is thy sting?" I have found it

I hope the Cliff House, over-hanging Lake Superior, will be my
    deliverance
Night will fall soon after my arrival, the moon dangling on the
    water
The wind blowing through the pine trees will surely bring me
    sleep
Tomorrow's sunrise will find me walking along the beach
Hoping to find my self, my old self, my happy self
Behind me lies the pain, ahead: hope
I speed onward...

Diane Renee Pakulski

Lost Souls

People living every day, coming and going
searching for their way. Some give up before
they find, that precious state called peace of
mind.

Some are living in a dream, a life of fantasy
so it seems; Our soul is alive and it hungers
too, but lost souls don't know what to do.

Sometimes up and sometimes down, good and
bad is all around. Love and you will find your
way; Hate will lead your heart astray.

Faith alone will see you through, but lost souls
don't know what to do.

Joseph A. Kenner Jr.

Little Coffins

what torches brought to future burial grounds
could dust these skies with light
with the tears of mothers who will lose their sons
to mushroom clouds one night

when comes the final storm
in bolts of thunder
that wakes small grim faces
in savage wonder

puts ancient weapons in finger-painted palms
to follow through insane plans
of their desperate elders
blunders

h. james

Once My Purpose

Once I found myself only half there
My life empty with no love of mine
One lovely day you entered my life
I found my purpose, a man to love

Once I found myself now complete
My life I gave to you and you returned
It seemed more happiness couldn't be
We found our purpose to love the other

Once I found myself strangely discontented
My life was disturbed and ran amuck
Things became confused and very wrong
It became a purpose to cause such hurt

Once again I find myself only half there
My life empty with no love of mine
One cold day you departed my life
I lost my purpose, the man I love

norma jean kunkel

Shock

She lay upon the golden sand
A maiden fair of form divine
A benediction to the eye
For any man to pause and sigh.

Cool ocean breezes touched her cheeks
Blushed by the kisses of the sun
Such loveliness beside the deep
Wrapped in the comforter of sleep.

She wakes with startled suddenness
As deer who hears the hunters gun
Chilled through as if a passing cloud
Had passed between her and the sun.

She stares in horror as she finds
Herself the victim of a meany
A passing moth had paused in flight
And eaten her bikini.

"Nothing gives us greater joy
Than the tools that we employ
But our patience starts to shrink
When our pen runs out of ink."

Watson Richards   Canada

Cell Cat

On the verge of amnesia
sending salutations to Bohemia
teardrops stored up in repressive eyes
they told you you'd be a cellar cat
you wished you hadn't signed those papers
people come and go while I'm analyzed,
I know that out there, they're having steak and strawberry wine
being good, fear them, they'll crawl into your house and take
    you away
Suicide on the edge of Consciousness, Months since you've
    been quietness
I told you you'd be a cell cat chasing rats
you wish you hadn't signed those papers now
people come and go while you're antagonized
I told you, you'd end up being a cell cat
Suicidal wishes emerge thru dreams of the crawling and,
    ...you know
  I used to live in a flat, drink Perrier and laugh
But now, you wish you'd never signed those papers
You've ended up being a cell cat
forever chasing imaginary rats

Pouya Habibian

Socio Politicos

Socio Politicos abound.
They're all around.
As they flip flop
Onto the very top.
. . . of the pig pile
Brandishing a big smile.

Socio Politicos climb to the crest.
Claw their way to the pinnacle, push out the rest
Smash the shields of the opposition.
Blast away with dart words of destruction.

. . . . . Nothing is barred.
    Readied to be sparred.
    Cut bleeding and marred.
    Awaiting to be four-starred.

Socio Politicos aggressively race ahead.
Uncover the bodies of the still and dead.
Grind the craniums of the opposition.
Walk on water, fulfill their mission.

William E. Leahy

Vietnam You're History To Me

I think of you often
    across that China Sea;
I've thought of days and
nights, I could not bear
    and all the scared times
I had in my silent prayer.
    There were times I'd awake,
with bombing all 'round,
    my ears ringing so loud,
I couldn't hear a sound.
    December twelfth, nineteen
sixty-five, the day when
    my world went dark and
I was hardly alive.
    When I first set foot
upon your soil,
    I couldn't believe all the families you had spoiled.
    I came to you in good peace
of mind,
but before it was over, I
had left many friends behind.
    You destroyed the best part
of me; my family and most of
my friends,
    some even thought the killing
would never end.
But, somehow as the time moved
    on,
it was over and we all came home.

William Powell
Included in **About The Poets** Section

My Family

The sun comes up as another day dawns.
Two children to get ready for school.
There's watching them dress and eat
Before seeing them out the door.
Still one sleeps, so young is she,
But so full of energy!
When she's awake she's more to handle
Than all three!
The baby's awake at ten—bathed, dressed and fed.
Then out the door they go
To Day Care Centers so Mom can work,
At least part of the day.
School's out at three, so the two go home
For a snack and some tv.
But today, they call Mom up and ask a favor,
"Can we go to the library?"
There's a special program—film and fun,
Right up to five o'clock.
Mom picks them up, the baby too,
And so their day is done.

Diane L. Whitaker

untitled

mountain-moonlight
    streaking the river
lost in the shadows

Charles B. Rodning

A Waterfall

Fresh and sparkling it falls,
From heights of towering rocks;
Between two such majestic walls,
It rushes and gurgles and mocks
The achievements of man

From a thousand feet it descends,
Into a crystal, clear blue pool;
The crescendo of its descent,
Drowns out even the fool;
For who can match its din.

Sparkling in the noon-day sun,
It's eternal and everlasting;
Unlike some of man's everyday fun,
As he tries to keep from wasting
The natural resources of this land.

A waterfall so beautiful and powerful,
That not even man can sustain;
A waterfall so immense and wonderful,
That nature only can maintain;
In its eternal, flowing hand.

"AJ"

Road To Ruin

In eternal rest on a gravelly, wash-board road
leading nowhere, lies an old rusty, dented machine;
With loosened wire ropes frayed and tattered, drooping
over the weather beaten boom, standing not so tall and
        proud.

Now motionless and seized with erosion, this machine once
clattered its tracks over virgin ground, blazing trails
with other heavy equipment, to create the birth of roads.

Inside, a worn leathered seat sprouting with springs and rat
chewed holes bored clean to the metal flooring, awaits for a
time when it will feel the warmth of a
        companion.

    Happy memories of yester-years
is but all the companionship this ruined machine knows.
    Observing this relic closely,
the knowledge of our past is visible by the bruises
embedded in its metal, while journeying with
        man.

Merry Nicholson   Canada

---

*Peace is to be desired unless
it is purchased at the price of
man's dignity.*

—Douglas Meador

What Tippy Told Me

There was a man who owned a donkey
She helped him to make a lot of money
"Oh! this is a time to be mean."
Being kind is not in his mien.

That day, he refused the donkey her fodder
She was becoming slow and such a bother
"I'm not getting enough money
To keep my house in honey."

The second day was a Sabbath day
It was sunny and as hot as baked clay
Yet the donkey had not a drop of water
"That's why I gave you so much fodder."

Today nothing much was done on the farm
"Giving you no fodder would do no harm
Just some water would do for you,
There's no market tomorrow too."

Seth O. Peprah   Bahamas

The Perfect Soul

Your soul sings out to mine like a siren's sweet cry.
To lift me up and give me a natural high. So many times your
call I did hear. To turn around and find you weren't there.

Your soul reaches out across the ages. Through music and art
and Shakespeare's pages. You bring joy to the lives of the people
you touch. If your soul could talk we would all learn much.

You were once a girl named Juliet and Romeo was the boy.
Then you appeared again as the lovely Helen of Troy. Also in
King Arthur's court as his Queen Guineviere. Now I don't
Believe it you're standing next to me here.

When you speak to me it is in voices that can't be heard.
I can sense how you're feeling without you saying a word. You
have touched a part of me that no woman ever has. For you are
a Goddess and I am an undeserving man.

I will always remember you in the dark and lonely nights. For
the fire is ignited and will forever burn bright. But you belong
to another and that's the cold hard truth. He does not know
how lucky he is I hope he never hurts you.

Remember you are better than most other girls. You deserve
the best from this world. Maybe our souls may cross in another
time. Then maybe I can prove my love and finally make you
mine.

Tod C. Pearce

Pretty Picture

Pretty picture hanging there, is this what life is like here?
Where's the struggle and the strife?
Where's the thumps of daily life?

Pretty picture hanging there, are you the source of all this
    cheer?
Do they find in you, a helping hand,
The hope they need to carry out their plans.

Pretty picture hanging there, the way for them seems so clear.
Are you the one who wipes away their fears?
When hearts are heavy, and eyes fill with tears,
Pretty picture hanging there, is it you, who hears?

Pretty picture hanging there, please hear my silent prayer.
Alone and in despair, my burdens I fear, I cannot bear.
My life I give to you, my Lord, to steer.

Pretty picture hanging there, you help keep the lord so very
    near!
I find the peace his guidance brings and now my heart does
    sing.
I'm glad I stopped to stare, at the pretty picture hanging there!

Willow Knight

A Friendly Farewell

There was a man I met in May,
A special friend who could make my day.

He made me feel alive again,
Even though we were only friends.

I thought we had a special bond,
One that could go on and on.

I guess the mistake that I had made,
Was not calling a spade a spade.

For I was married and he was free,
And for him as friends we could never be.

His family told him to stay away from me,
I only wish I had a valid plea.

I miss our laughter and the chatter,
If only other people did not matter.

We were both brought up to know right from wrong,
And know why our friendship could not last very long.

I hope you know your family was right,
If only I were free I could love you with all my might.

Take good care of yourself, you are a special man,
And find that gal to make you happy as you can.

Tell your family you love them dear,
It is times like this I wish mine were near.

I will bid you farewell my short-term friend,
And hope someday I will understand our end.

Mary Elaine Miller

Scripture Fulfilled

Nails ripped through his hands,
blood dripped from his brow.
His face bore untold agony,
God's only begotten child.
"Get yourself down from there
if King of Jews you claim to be."
"Forgive them, they know not what they do."
Was requested from Calvary.
The scene was one of horror,
yet could not be undone.
God in all his glory
could not step in to help his son.
"Why hast thou forsaken me?"
Was asked through dry, parched lips.
"It is finished." Were his final words,
then our Savior's form fell limp.
His side was pierced to verify death,
then buried in a borrowed tomb.
In the promised three days our Savior arose,
bearing scars from his inflicted wounds.
Ascending to the heavens,
his earthly work was done.
Fulfilling God's desire to save his children,
even if there be just one.

Shirley Henderson

He's Holding Me In His Hand

Please don't cry for me, I am right here,
I'll never be far away.
I want you to know I'll always be near,
For I'm in your hearts to stay.

Your ears don't hear, your eyes don't see,
I'm standing right next to you.
Don't be sad, don't cry for me,
You must know I miss you too.

I love you all, each and every one,
And I thank you for your love.
God says my time on earth is done,
And He needs me up above.

It hurts me to leave you, I knew it would,
Our time on earth isn't long.
I'd still be living with you if I could,
For our love is forever strong.

We'll be together in just a short while,
Be glad I don't hurt, I'm not alone or afraid.
I hope you remember my laugh and my smile,
Then I'll know the impression I made.

Be happy for me and try not to cry,
I want you to understand.
That soon God will wipe the tears from your eye,
He's holding me in His hand.

Sheryl Cox

Just Saying

It took tons of metal to build the Titanic
It took one iceberg to sink it

It took mother nature years to grow a forest
It takes one match to wipe it out

It took hours to get drunk
It takes one second to take your life

It took one huge disagreement to become enemies
It takes one small sorry to become friends

It took two loving people to give you a mind
It takes one drug to waste it

It took a powerful god to create the world
It takes one insensitive being to destroy it

Lewis Litzel

A Voice On The Wind

Whispering in the cool velveteen night
   a masculine "voice" rides on the wind's flow
as massive shadows rise and fall like waves
   now shimmering light adds its own eerie glow

It's the Almighty's presence...Earth's creation

Ridgely Lytle

The Desert

Deserts whisper of an ancient time,
From decades long ago,
Where yuccas bloomed in virgin white,
And coyotes romped the snow.

Deserts hint of a serenity,
That blanketed the land,
Where eagles soared in all their glory,
Where saguaros used to stand,

Deserts blew a breath once pure,
That wafted through the pines,
Cooling off the adobe floors,
The wild gourds and vines.

Deserts cry for a time since spent,
When an edifice was of rocks.
Now repressed by steel and cement,
That we could only turn back the clocks.

Kathryn Dionne

Silver Birch

Stately, and majestic, she stands tall.
The lady of the forest.
The silver birch, she is called.
She stands slender and fine,
Reaching to the sky.
The rays of sunlight pass between the leaves,
To the path below.
The feeling is golden, the smell it is clean.
Nothing is out of place.
The moss is on the stones, and everything is green.
There is a silver pond beyond, with waterlilies everywhere.
A green frog is sitting on a leaf, he croaks as he sees me.
Gods earth is pure.
Everything is serene, day has begun
A rabbit runs across a walk.
A squirrel is climbing a tree.
The ants are scurrying along the ground.
The butterflies flurry, the dragonfly goes by.
A bumble bee is buzzing around.
A flower he has found.

Marian Kelly

Untitled

The snow has melted but there is still a
puddle where my heart has dripped.

   Silence among the chattering children.
   A view that reached into eternity and
boredom. Yet if one wasn't to look too
closely one would see a pleasant country
setting complete with farmhouse and rolling
fields. I almost smiled until I realized
that this was entrapment, contentment dressed
up in its finest.

   Why so many damn details, the curves of the
tree, the color of the fog, the slowly dying
grass fighting to keep its youthful appearance,
the contrast of seasons, the vividness of my own
fragrance...
   I want to notice all yet isn't it too many details
that already has my life feeling cluttered?

   If I could I would be a barren tree. I don't want
to be noticed by multitude. Just the solitude figure
who glimpses at me to see all they've been searching
for. I am the details of my own life.

Jon David Lowe

Sweet Tree

Felled beneath a budding tree
My wounds where deep, perhaps fatal.
There I lay where none could see
Alone, defenseless, unable
To aid myself or anyone else.
Tears fell from the budding bows
To bathe my wounded bleeding self.
I cursed my foes and swore stern vows.
With oaths I swore a vengeance.
Then at last I saw the tree
For what it really was and cried
More for myself than she.
There was more beauty, more strength
Than a simple tree should hold.
I examined her width and length.
I searched her every crease and fold
Then I knew no matter how long,
May be my battles, vanquished or victor
Regardless of the passing years
I would find peace and shelter
Where the tree and I shared tears.

Jerry Chute

*It is easier to forgive an
enemy than a friend.*

—Madame Deluzy

Bewitched

Byways, highways, through threads of memory,
Before the real was etched into my soul
Blind faith in magic spells ordained my role,
Brought laughter when my thoughts roamed fancy free
Beyond the pale of sights we always see,
Better by far seek magic as your goal,
Bright visions are denied the digging mole,
But fairy tales are made for such as we.
Bent as the backs of gnomes who delve for gold
Beneath the earth or in vaults of the Swiss,
By logic and reason held in greed's strong
Bonds in mental cellars where the dank and cold
Brings the frigid lips of mere fact to kiss
Brows smoothed by dreams and make the dreams go wrong.

Joseph E. Barrett

Play The Game

DIRECTIONS:
1
    Space is the matter that fills it,
Geometry formed and reformed without end.
    All in an oscillating universe,
finite and unbounded,
    bANG and Crunch and bANG...

2
    The permutation of particles:
Where each particular form is bound to reappear incessantly.
And beyond our geometric art of physics and logic is the
        simplicity of
3
    WHY. The primal form of infinity is the reduced totality in all.
Feel it all now, always, as it was then (There is no time)
The Totality warped into the continuum for
The mind to create the heavens and hells of the phenomenal
        world.
And birth is our removal from the Totality where:
Experience becomes a forgetting, and knowledge is a
        remembering;
The incipient shape of ideas and senses is as all

        THE MEANING
        Infinity to give life
        for life to remember Infinity
so Infinity can bring life.

OBJECT:

To have a senseless ease and comfort about the meaning of the
        game
When you have to return and do it again.

Pete Bellini

Mirror Image

I look into the mirror and do not know the face that looks
        back—
The once gentle eyes are now hardened and cold—Where did
        you come from?
Where did I go?
Have you always been there locked behind the glass—
Hiding in the shadows—
Do you share my dream or are you only part of my nightmares—
I turn away, but when I look back she is still there—
If only I could catch a glance of what once was me—
To find again the woman I was—to know again a gentle heart—
To once again see love in those cold eyes—
I call out to the mirror—if only I could see the woman I used to
        be.

Roberta D. Lantz

*More persons are
humbugged by believing in
nothing than by believing
too much.*

—P. T. Barnum

I Have . . .

The quietness of my room
    to enhance my dreams.
I have the light of the moon
    to bathe my night to a beam of channels
    my mind is always fluid.
I have the music to take me
    anywhere my hopes now set forth for me.
I have love unlimited in its focus.
I have the comforts of home in my heart.
I have an ark that is crowded
    with all the things yet to do.
I have an Adam and Eve adventure
    yet to be done.
I have an index yet to finish,
    starting with yours, mine, and ours.
I have feelings for life as never before this
    as the shadows show me the trees,
the leaves, the shapes
that have been left behind me.
I have a stillness
    as I walk the beaches in the sunshine
    and finally see a real sailboat.
I have everything my eyes desire
    in all that free and spirited.
I have special things hidden away
    for my rainy days.
I have all this, as GOD gives me the haves
    as I give HIM all the sounds
    of my happiness.
Life is all the have nots of my yesterdays.

Charlotte Bell

Surveyed World

Two numbers fall on the screen.
Call if you liked, call if you disliked.
I call the second because the show didn't excite me.
A recording insincerely thanks me for my call.
I hang up disappointed.
They'll charge a half dollar for the call.
Mother won't pay it for me.

I print clearly on the long questionnaire
Checking boxes...yes no; true false
Income? low. Married? single. Live
alone? with mother. Happy? undecided.
Age? 33.
I address the envelope, seal it;
Give mother 25 cents for a stamp.
I'll get coupons when they receive the survey.

A woman stands outside the market,
I have just bought eggs for mother.
She stops me.
Have you tried this brand? once.
Use often? too expensive.
She hands me a pen. Nice gift for mother.

Jill Woodruff

The way of the world is to make laws, but follow customs.

—Michel E. de Montaigne

Getzian Maxim: A Revolutionary Manifesto

My poem will not scream at you like the muted cornet
    on "West End Blues." Nor will it make you boogie like
    the brass on "Sing, Sing, Sing";
It will not thrill you with multiple orgasms like the clarinets
    on "Creole Love Call,"
And it will not make you behave whimsically like the ivory keys
    on "Humoresque";
My poem will not march you off to a liberation war like the
    drums on "Black and Tan Fantasy." Or "Blues March";
And it will not romance you into matrimony like the saxophone
    on "Body and Soul."
My poem will not make you wail like a mourning lark like the
    voice on "Gloomy Sunday,"
And it will not deafen you like the cymbals on "Thunder
    Suite."
It will not make you melancholy like the trombone on
"Rocking Chair."
Or make you want to tap dance like the vibraphone
    on "Blues in H Minor."
My poem is just a poem, as cool as Getz's "Early Autumn."

McArthur Gunter

Knowledge

Knowledge is knowing what to do in an
    unpleasant situation.

Knowledge is knowing what to do to assist
    your fellow man.

Knowledge is knowing what to do for your
    country.

Knowledge is knowing how to understand
    all different peoples.

Knowledge is consciousness.

Knowledge is LIFE.

Linda Avellino

Henry's Rumble Seat

Thrilled and delighted were the young at
    Heart when Henry created the Model A.
Adding the rumble seat was the neatest thing
    Since the one horse open shay.

Helping a pretty girl into the rumble seat
    Gave a young man a wonderful thrill.
In those days, the girls wore dresses. The
    Young heart would not be still.

Motoring down the winding country roads, it
    Was lots of fun to play the game of curve.
Around every bend, closer and closer, the
    Young couple would swing and swerve.

Around sharp turns, the laughing young thing
    Had to be held by a pair of strong arms.
And the idea was not just to be tempted by
    An abundance of tantalizing charms.

So wonderful to snuggle close, it was, the
    Wind playing with shining locks of hair;
Looking into dancing eyes, laughter gushing
    Through ruby lips, heavenly moments to share.

Young, unfolding love, blossoming, growing
    Into happy families with lives complete.
Across America, how many happy families had
    Their beginning in Henry's rumble seat?

Guy Moorefield

The Old Gang

Remembering the rumbles we had in the streets.
Remembering the blood that was shed.
Remembering the old gang
and the crazy, insane, lives that we led.
Remembering the lonesome jail-cells,
where we spent most of our days and nights.
Remembering the gang that set us up, and how we
weren't going to let them get away without a fair fight.
Remembering how sweet we thought revenge would be.
Realizing now, the feeling will never reoccur.
Tony, The Little One, Matt, Jimmy, Roger and me.
Remembering the old gang and the way that things were.
Remembering all those nights we spent thinking it over.
Remembering how we wanted to back out and fast.
Remembering The Evil Twelve challenging us to a rumble.
Little did we know then, that fight would be our last.
Now, all that is left of the old gang is memories
of Tony, The Little One, Matt, Jimmy, Roger and me.
Now, I can't help but remember the rumble we had that night.
And I can't help but to remember all the blood that was shed.
And I can't help but to remember The Little One's fright,
before I watched all the blood that he,
Tony, Matt, Jimmy and Roger bled.

Theresa Campbell

PLACE MILLS.

You Don't Understand Me

You do not understand me—The things I do or see
You do not understand—Why or how—or why I am just me
You do not understand—What I say or why I say it
You do not understand—What I do or don't do bit by bit
You do not understand—That I have tried every way I know
To make you understand me—And so
I now have found the reason that we do not agree
You do not understand any part of me
The problem is not me—and it is not you
The understanding is just not coming through
I have almost let this ruin me
Now the not understanding part—I can clearly see
The answer is to just let it be
I don't have to stay, and I don't have to leave
I don't have to please, and I don't have to grieve
I don't have to care, and I don't have to feel small
I don't have to punish us, and I don't have to cry, scream, or
    crawl
I do not have to understand you—And you do not have to
    understand me
So all that I must do—Is to learn to let it be
As it will never make a difference what I do or say
You will never understand me anyway
So now I need help with just to let it go
If I seem a bit different—"I THANK GOD"—that it is so.

Hetty M. Schroeder

Life of the Flame

The fires who so silently perish under ash,
    had once at last to permanently stash,
    the life of material on which it would graze;
        tall, naked, wild torch unstrapped,
        and its path unbordered by nature,
flinching atop the roots that kept it in that state of heavy blaz
        But only for some unknown time...
before the root, its soul, its source for living dematerializes,
        breaks, busts hard to ash,
        smears the ground as darkened soot,
        joins the band of nothingness and trash,
        resigns, hangs up its role as root,
        the root of life, the life of the flame,
        and who pins upon its death the blame,
        but the fire itself becoming lame,
    and calm and silent and small and tame,
        dull and shadowless, whittled to spark,
        the encircling air turns cold and dark,
        the flame sits now as broken coal,
        destroyed itself by chafing its soul,
        lived by its heart, its immortal desires,
    and to look, we can tell, 'twas the biggest of pyres.

Bill Schrieffer
*Included in **About The Poets** Section*

The Man

You come spontaneous like a shout.
You languish for an instant.
You come back incomparable in my day!
You used to come from the mirth
In the warmth of my chest
And in my sinful dreams.
And when I carried under my heart
The Hope with our blood,
I gave her your name.
And when your imperfections
Insatiably fled somewhere
I swallowed the pill of my jealousy
And your unconcealed guilts.
Whatever you are—be forever!

Danielle Pondev

THE BROOMIELAW, GLASGOW.

The Art of Official Desire

Desire on a Sunday Eve brings hardship to the
   day,
The wistful wish left unfulfilled creates such
   sad dismay,
I want, I want, I truly want,
And then I want much more,
I need, I need, I truly need—
I've needed it before.

A pious look; a rounded frown; shall bring my
   prize to me,
For if I get what I pursue—I'll sit upon your
   knee,
I'll sit,
   I'll sit,
      I'll sit,
         I'll sit,
            I'll sit upon your knee,

For if I get what I do want—oh, what great
   friends we'll be!

Kathrine Plummer   Canada

To know what is right and
not do it is the worst
cowardice.

—Confucius

Now as Then

Beautiful, strong, brown young men
Head gear flashing in the wind—
Drawing swords, balancing shields
Running through grassed African fields.
Proud of heritage
Fighting back.
Protecting tradition
Preserving Black.

Beautiful black men, young and strong
Some shorn heads, some hair long—
Guns cocked, daggers flashing heat—
Sneaking through the city street.
Doubtful of heritage
Unmindfully wrong.
Dispelling known values
Just to belong.

Beautiful young men, black and brown
Each one special in his own crown.
REaching, searching, now as then
For strength, for courage, the right to win—
Acceptance of identity
The dignity of pride
Unrestricted venture
A purpose in his stride.

Ophelia T. Miller

A Jamaican Smile

Something happens when a Jamaican person Smiles,
It leaves you with a nice feeling for such a long while;
They are few and far between,d
that use their smile for a screen;

A Jamaican smile is much different than a simple grin,
It's genuine, it comes up and out from Somewhere deep within;
A smile is an inexpensive gift,
You pass it on and you give someone a lift;

Just think, it doesn't cost a cent,
It's a lovely gesture well spent;
You can't keep it, you can't bottle it, you must
give it away,

Remember always "your smile" makes
someone a brighter day.

Pat Manginelli

143

If I Were in Love

If I were in love
it would be a curious thing
head over heels
and everything

To be by your side would be a dream
and I would be happy or so it would seem

Excluding being happy
sometimes you make me jealous
other times you can make me mad
and whether you know it or not
you can even make me sad

But no matter what mood I'm in,
it really does no harm
because you win me over with your
good looks, wit, and charm

With lots of love
I dedicate this poem to you
because having you near me
is like having a storybook romance come true!

Anna Dello Stritto
Included in **About The Poets** section

Love Will Come In Time

Hold me in your arms until the morning comes
Lay your tired body next to mine
Close your eyes and dream of all our days to come
Together we'll lose all track of time.

How many roads are left to take
How many choices must we make
Before our love seems right.
Give me a reason or a sign
Make no mistake; we'll do just fine
We both know our love will come in time.

When I'm away from you I can't forget
The moments of tenderness we've shared
Whether I've laughed or cried or been upset
You seem to make everything all right.

How many roads are left to take
How many choices must we make
Before our love seems right.
Give me a reason or a sign
Make no mistake; we'll do just fine
We both know our love will come in time.

David A. Mills

> # The flower in the vase still smiles, but no longer laughs.
> ## —Chazal

My Love

Only a boy, when I first saw him,
A boy not even seventeen.
A boy man, not too tall but handsome.
His skin was smooth, his eyes were green.

He took my heart, for his possession,
The first time he took my hand.
So warm his smile, so sweet his kisses,
The boy who would become my man.

He did belong to me that summer,
And then the summer after that.
But then I had to share his lover.
Another girl his hands did pat.

But then, I really couldn't blame him.
For she a beauty all could see.
She took his love for her that summer,
As he would hold her on his knee.

Her eyes were bigger, browner, wider,
As they followed him around.
A special smile, just for him only.
And he would drive her over town.

Little steps, with arms outstretching
And with a smile her lips would curl.
They have a love that will last forever.
The Daddy and his little girl...

Ramona Anthony

Love's Sweet Memories

Happiness is something we all should know
The dawn of morning's light, long walks at night
   love's sweet memories.
The time we spent alone at night
Dining in darkness or by candlelight
Holding your warm body next to mine
How love drifted around us.
When we met
We both wanted and needed to be free
Ignoring our warnings, it's no one's fault.
Now at night we quarrel
Nonsense words made only to injure
(and they do) it's time to go.
We loved too hard, too deep, too strong
(but isn't that the way it always goes)
We have our memories
To keep filed apart, to look back on
We might see each other again, in passing
But it won't be the same
   love's sweet memories.
It's time to close my journal
This story is over, still, I don't understand
   love's sweet memories.

Elaine Currey-Nishita

Tiger on the Wall

The stealth and the cunning, the power of it all,
the baffling deception, of the tiger on the wall.

Gleaming fire like emeralds, shines from his eyes,
and the soft rumble, in his throat, is death in disguise.

The picture hangs so placidly and lures you into peace,
but your chained up emotions still cry for a release.
Like the tiger on the wall, if they could have their way,
would leap forth and devour you, on any given day.

Around his crouching figure, green foliage fills the scene,
shadowing tense muscles, on a body that grows lean.

Thinking that he might have moved, we call on common sense,
and hide that fear, in our jungle of emotions growing dense.

With every deception we bury, we dig a deeper hole,
and ease our pain by thinking, we're keeping our control.

Blind trust we give the canvas, to hold the tiger still,
and hope that we are safe from harm, protected by self-will.

Remarks are made on our ability, to keep it all together,
then a small frustration, drifts in like a feather.

When joined with all our other fears, its power now unfolds,
and as we linger in our complacency, the tiger gets his hold.

When restraint is at its highest, and all appears to be well,
the tiger leaps from the picture, and drags you into hell.

Linda Grice

Shadows

Shadows will appear when the sun sets or rises,
Lurking; then crawl out from hiding.
Darting across the landscape from in and out of crevices.
Leaping from splendorous trees to crouch behind low shrubs
As small children do when playing a game of hide and seek.

"I see you! I see you!," a small child yells aloud.
It's only the shadows reaching out
Causing confusion in the game as they move silently.
They jump out and back under trees, hiding from the sun
As a small child does while resting under shade from the noon.

A child may crouch in shadows of a jagged rock,
And leap over wielding his sword.
Silent shadows are important in a young pirate's game.
They allow a young boy the element of surprise;
Then disappear with the noon day sun to secret places.

Shadows large, shadows small, shadows dark, shadows tall;
At times disturbing young boys dreams.
Dark, silent shadows are much different in night than in day,
So a young pirate's sword may lean against his small bed.
Night time shadows play as children in a game of hide and seek.

They come during the night time sleep
Making you sweat, toss and turn when they creep!
You chance a look at the closet door as it creaks,
And all you can see are shadows when you peep!

Michael Belmont

Yellow Star

Found in the sand near the home of the ant
There's a thistle in bloom, a prickly plant.
It has so much beauty and is webbed in mesh
Regardless of points that stick in the flesh!
Feeling the sting made tearfilled eyes flicker
Many a beholder has felt the piercing sticker!
Respect the yellow sticker star of thornpatch doom!
Hurt and brokenness all happening too soon!
Love that's not proper is dangerous when sold,
There's a tale of lovers that's not often told!
Suddenly pride has been spent and treated shabbily,
Love's excessive demand make emotions wild and straggly!
Riffraff companions have led many to go astray,
Stuck with the thorn of foolishness have lost their way.
Holding to the promise that was made as a pledge,
Stay on roads made for travel, so not to lose the edge.
Best to stay honor bound, unyielding, ends nice,
To lower one's dignity will cost the world a price!
That yellow star beauty flirting with a nettle of cost,
While discovering too late, health and a good name lost!

Corina L. Popp

BELVOIR CASTLE.

145

The Devil Never Mention

The Devil will never tell you that Jesus died for your sins,
He will never mention to you that sin is the
Transgression of God's law,
He will never tell you not to do evil,
He will never tell you not to steal, lie, or to obey God's word
Because he is the author of confusion.
He will never tell you to love your enemy,
He will never tell you to take your burden to the
Lord and leave it there. He will never tell you to pray.
He will never tell you to read and study God's word,
He will never tell you that he is making hell his home
and he is trying to make it your home too, if you let
him.

Donald L. Holmes

Derek the Fireless Dragon

In days of old, when knights were knights and damsels were in
distress,
Legend tells of a lonely dragon named Derek the Fireless.

As dragons go, the legend says, ol' Derek was deceiving.
He looked more fierce than all the rest, but he wasn't
firebreathing.

He'd try so hard to breathe hot flames, but all he'd do was
smoke.
This wasn't normal for a dragon, you know, but Derek's furnace
was broke.

Now the town folk liked ol' Derek the Dragon. He was their
biggest attraction.
People would travel from far away lands to see this dragon in
action.

He'd stomp and snort and growl and roar, with his nostrils in a
flare.
He's huff and puff for all he was worth, but only smoke would
fill the air.

Derek became so devastated, he decided to put an ending,
To a life he thought was meaningless. For him there was no
more pretending.

So he climbed to the top of Mount Shangrila, ready to jump to
his death.
He filled his lungs one last time, savoring that final breath.

"Farewell to all," whimpered Derek the Dragon. "It's time for me
to die."
He took a leap intending to fall, but instead, he started to fly!

Now you can imagine the surprising look that Derek had on his
face.
For there he was, like a big green bird, flying farther into space.

They say that Derek was never seen again, but I still look to the
sky,
Hoping to see what legend calls, ol' Derek the Dragonfly.

Kathryn Dionne

Our Red Rose

In our garden with many flowers around, the Red Rose stands
out, a rose bud opening reaching out to the world hoping
to please someone who is sad.

The Red Rose with its beauty is a wonderful gift, it's a flower
that is special for lovers of this world, we thank you Lord,
bless our rosebud from our garden, and when it's time our
rosebud with its red soft petals in full bloom will be cut
and sent with love to someone who is waiting, hands
reaching out, for it brings love from someone's heart.

It also brings joy and happiness Lord, Bless our Red Rose from
our garden.

Ann Abeyta

Rainbow Wish

Extend thy soul to the Universe Unseen.
For I have sailed the lakes of silver gleam.

Expand this heart to all of life.
As I have gazed onto the stars of golden wishes.

Amplify my being to build Eternal Hope.
For I have discovered my secret dream.

Dance among the shadows.
Ride upon a moonbeam.

Realization can be endowed
When love is in the heart.

Vivian Grace Smith

Untitled

The pain keeps lessening in time but the tears keep coming
when the memories revive the loves we had and the
special times and the lives we used for living.

The joy we had is now someone else's. the places we went to
no longer exist. Where can we run to there's no one to
chase us, where can we hide there's no one to find us,
alone *and* alive, alone *or* alive?

What do we do now that it's over? It's not something new we
knew it would end. We just didn't know when. And now
that it's over we keep searching for a place in our mind
that brings us back to that special time if only for a
moment so we can be happy like we were then, again.

The joy we had is now someone else's, the places we went to
no longer exist. Where can we run to there's no one to
chase us? Where can we hide? There's no one to find us
alone *and* alive, alone *or* alive!

Diane I. Jacyszyn

A Haiku Poem to My Favorite Raccoon

We feed raccoons bread,
one stargazes as he eats.
We call him Dreamer.

Marybelle Leimonas
Included in **About The Poets** Section

God Meets Us

God meets us:
   in the field—in the beauty of nature
   in the valley—of discouragement and loss
   on the mountaintop—of happiness and success
   in the woods—of confusion and problems
   in the desert—of weariness and monotony
   in the battle—against poverty and wrong
   at the banquet table—feasting and rejoicing
   in our dilemma—the constant rush of life
   on our knees—at our work and at prayer
   in the marketplace—the crowd surrounding us
   beside the sick bed—as we are concerned and hopeful
   in the laboratory—as we experiment and learn
   in the waiting room—"marking time" or needing advice
   by the fire—in our comfort and ease
   at the door—as we pursue our livelihood
   at the door—of opportunity to serve others
   at the door—as we return, tired, despondent or singing
   at our table—with our "daily bread" and daily cares
   at the crossroads—deciding important issues
   on retirement day—our tasks completed
   and as we scan the sky—awaiting His return—
—and He lifts us!!

"But thanks be to God, who always leads us in triumphal
   procession..." *(II Corinthians 2:14, NIV).*

Ethel H. Kleppinger

The Last Unicorn

In a lush green valley the last unicorn stands. To bid his final farewell to a once mystical land. It's plain to see he was of a great breed. Now his race is dead due to man's lust and greed.

The unicorn was a once magical race. Sent here to help us from an unknown place. The thing that kept the unicorn alive. Was the love that humans held deep down inside.

But as I sat and listened it told me a story. Of man's love in the beginning and the unicorns glory. How man loved man as if they were brothers. And the unicorns were honored guests at the wedding of lovers.

How there were millions of unicorns all over the land. When people weren't afraid to give a helping hand. But then something happened that was very strange. For some unknown reason man started to change.

Instead of man loving man as though they were brothers. They started wars that would kill each other. For every man who died out of prejudice and hate. A unicorn would share in his fate.

Until through so many years of war. The unicorns race was no more. He couldn't understand how love could just end. How we were now all enemies instead of friends.

Now with all love gone it was his turn to die. Out of fear and sorrow I hung my head to cry. And all was lost to the world that gloomy day. That the last unicorn finally went away.

Tod Pearce

God's Little Creatures: Our Little Friends

The cardinal and the blue jay spread colors when they wing;
They trim the trees they light on and sing when it's not spring;
The cardinal and the blue jay wear red and white and blue;
They bear the colors of our flag that's been tried and true.

The robin and the sparrow spot lawns and countryside;
And round plump robins work darn hard to get a worm outside;
Sparrows—there are many—but they really are quite friendly;
Robins fly away each year when leaves fall to the ground
   aplenty.

Squirrels and tiny chipmunks run quickly to and fro;
They pick up all the morsels that friendly folk do throw;
Squirrels climb high into a tree while chipmunks cling to solid
   earth;
Both are frisky little fellows who run and play with mirth.

The little wrens and hummingbirds never seem to rest;
But I must be wrong because they each have their own nest;
Little wrens and hummingbirds never see it snow;
They prefer the warmer climes cupped with sunshine glow.

Little birds and animals truly are our friends;
They add to earth's bright colors, blending from within;
Birds in the trees sing in the breeze; little animals squeeze the
   earth;
They're God's little creatures—but our pleasure and our
   treasure.

Ruth M. Revecky

Why Has God Graced Me?

Why has God graced me with friends so dear
that have brightened my life from year to year.
Why has God graced me with a warm family
to laugh and have fun with so happily?
And why has He graced me with my health, my life,
enabling me to cope with problems and strife
that occur now and then, yet fade away
making room for a bright new day?
Why has God graced me with sweet memories
that I can reflect on whenever I please;
the laughter, the love, the warmth of sharing,
the inner rewards enjoyed from caring.
Did He reach into my soul and say, "This is for you—
you love, you care." Well others do too.
Why has God graced me? I really must hear,
so I can tell everyone far and near,
and without exception, everyone bless
with what, to me, is true happiness.

     Thank you, God

    Elaine Erickson

Faith of a Little Eskimo

Once, not so long ago,
Mid glistening ice and whiter snow,
Where Christian children seldom go,
There lived a little Eskimo.

His home was built of blocks of ice,
Shaped and fitted so precise.
In this igloo he'd sometimes hope
To dine on candlesticks and soap.

Then his thoughts would slightly wander.
Among skins and firs he'd sit and ponder,
Sometimes mid lightning and thunder,
About the food there was out yonder.

From whence his next meal would come,
Would it be the salmon run?
Caught beneath the midnight sun.
That would be a lot of fun.

Or, perhaps a polar bear,
Found fishing in the world "out there."
Erstwhile it might also be
Blubber or seal from the arctic sea.

"This I'm certain of," said he,
"Never will I hungry be,
For the God of earth and sky and sea
Ever will provide for me."

    Edwin B. Polhemus

The Great Sacrifice

Sin—disobeying God—all have done.
God hates sin. This separates us from God.

The question is how man can be redeemed
And be restored into the good graces of God.

Before God created the universe
He knew man would fall for sin.

This happened in Heaven, where the angels saw God;
Yet some fought against Him. Their banishment resulted.

God solved the question of sin.
He "prepared" a body for His holy Son
To dwell in some thirty-three years on earth.

Jesus Christ, the uncreated, left Heaven
To carry out His Father's plan of salvation.

In three short years He trained twelve men
To evangelize the world with power—
Confirming His word by miracles.

The great sacrifice involved the torment and death
Of God's only begotten Son
By those He came to save—both Jews and Gentiles alike.

Christ's resurrection conquered sin, death, and the grave
Opening the way of salvation
To all who choose God's way to Heaven—
Through following His Son, the Lamb of God.

    Virginia W. Thomson

The Key of Life

God's Presence

I have seen Your Love, for it cannot be matched,
I have seen Your Will, whatever it may be,
I have felt Your Presence, in the longest day or night,
I have heard Your Name, in loudest crowds and in the silence
    my thoughts,
You are the Light in the darkness,
You are the Hope for the hopeless,
You are the unsinkable ship in the sea of sin,
That casts out life preservers to all who are drowning,
You are the Beginning and the End,
You are the Life here as I breathe,
And the Life after I leave,
If one cannot see, then one hears,
If not that, then one feels and,
If not by the touch, then the heart,
Your Soul is the Key to Life, it opens many doors,
In Heaven there is a Mansion, let
Your Key open the door there.

    Floyd H. Bell, Jr.

Prison of Fear

Looking at the walls of a prison cell
I say to myself, "Is this not hell?"
But there are things much more worse,
Death, fear, or a black magic curse.

Ah, fear, fear what is there to say;
It's the bottom of the ninth and I'm
losing this game. No bother with
the score, who's to care?
I'm at the end of the straw, hanging
by a hair.

But I brighten up, and break my chains;
It's my decision who wins this game.
The score has changed and the opponent
I surpassed. The prison of fear
I've escaped at last.

   C. Jay Jones

Album

I'm sick of looking at old pictures.
Friends and old lovers that get mixed up because they are the
      same.
But the lover part makes my heart sink very low sometimes.
Especially at a time like this—with no one to hold—when I'm
      lonely...
Missing everyone and seeing none.
It makes me even emptier—remembering I was full.

Would you look at the smiles on those faces!
Could you find one in me now?
Why then?
Why turn the page?
I guess I'd rather be empty seeing something full
Than just be empty.
Maybe tomorrow will be different.
Maybe I'll make it different.

Tonight my heart and eyes are back at home,
But I'm stuck right here.
Heart threads are pulled thin,
But just as strong at times, as if it were yesterday.

Smiles and romance in their eyes...
In my eyes.

Enough of this.
Book closed, Lights out.
Eyes still open—
Alone.

   Stephen J. Quigley

Sayonara, Adios, Good-bye

I can see my reflection in your spit-shine shoes,
And I just thank the Lord that I'm not like you.

The stench of rotted ego filling each and every room,
Makes my nostrils flare a warning of the soon apparent doom.

The eggshells that I'm walking on are growing very thin,
And I find each thing I say or do becomes a holy sin;

So instead of living life in the drippings of your sweat,
I'll take a brisk cool dip in some nearby rivulet.

With my soapy bar of freedom, I'll replenish wasted thoughts,
And return to greener pastures that I thought I had forgot.

You'll find your monomania has lost effect on me:
A chemical reformation is the future I foresee.

It's you who've caused reaction by the actions that you've made,
With your repetitious errors and your unforgiving ways.

I leave you standing lonely in your tears of deprivation,
For my limousines' arrived for my long overdue vacation.

   Terry Ann Garrett

Your Deeds

If you mistreat someone
what about you?
It may take one year
and it might take a few,
no matter how long it takes,
you're going to get your deeds back,
if your deeds are good or bad,
they will come back to you, that is a fact.

If you do things to people,
to keep them upset
sooner or later
worry and confusion is all you'll get,
never undermine anyone
never break up their home
because if you do
someday you will find yourself alone.

When you are sitting alone and lonely
and wonder why,
then try to remember
how you hurt others, and made them cry.
What you should do, is ask God to forgive you
and try to forgive yourself,
treat others as you want to be treated
and never mistreat no one else.

Joyce Bonds

Pain

When I entered this world as a tiny babe,
I heard a small, weak cry of pain.
It was my own; from being forced out of
a nice, warm, watery home, into one I did not know.

There was pain intermittent, from that time on,
from gas in my tummy, to a slap on the back,
that was supposed to get rid of the gas.
There was pain from a small, stubbed toe, as I began
to walk, in a world I did not know.

As life went on, and I went to school,
there was pain from feeling a teacher's
ruler on my hand, because of things I
did not understand. There was pain from
hearing another child's chant, about things
in this world I did not know.

But life goes on, and you live with the pain,
as you lose brothers, and Father and Mother.
After getting married, there was pain from
having children of my own. There was pain after
losing a child; like no other pain I had known.
At the end you're still in pain, as you lose
the man that had been husband, friend, and lover.
This is a pain that will not end!

Florence Buckman

Who Knows

To years that take you on the incredible travels. Always in a now. Never withholding any Falseness. But never withholding any truth. Midlines plot a course straight and narrow which can not be maneuvered. Many who try, being lost in the undecided.

For years of a life given to experience. To find a place, a space where to sit and wait for a hint that reveals an answer maybe to your every question.

Problems which solve themselves.

To years of revolutions against what is thought to be wrong by who knows what is right. While every turn in the opposite direction would lead to the same destination.

To years of losing hope bringing death. Who will find a path not residing in the middle of truth and false. Not maybe, Not yes, Not no.

To years of finding a way back across the path of misguidance. On another course but to end up at the same destination.

William P. Wentzell

What does not destroy me, makes me stronger.

—Nietzsche

Dr. Joe

My thoughts are there with you today;
my doctor and my friend.
You shared my grief and sorrow,
and helped me struggle through,
that long year of guilt and anger,
that I thought would never end.

You encouraged me to write my poems.
You took time to read and share them.
So now I'm writing this for you.
If there were some way that I could do,
what you have done for me,
then you'd be well and home today; as busy as a bee.

Do you know how much we love and need you?
Not just to keep us well and strong;
we need to see your cheerful smile,
and feel your gentle touch, as you listen
to our hearts, then give us your diagnosis.
You give us hope, and help, with your medical ability.

You're in my prayers each morn and night,
and I know that God does hear and answer.
He knows how much we want you well;
not just to be our doctor.
You make us all feel special,
because you are our friend as well—Dr. Joe.

Florence Buckman

AN AMERICAN GARDEN CEMETERY.

Untitled

As I stare at the street scene, the people move by
Their mouths, like a clown's, painted on but no smiles
Their minds on themselves
And their eyes
Empty eyes straight ahead

People fear what they see, so they just close their eyes
And they fear what they are, so they close up their lives
Completely estranged
And they pass
Empty eyes straight ahead

Past my window they shuffle, they find their ways home
To their bottled existence—all the same, but alone
And still no response
As they pass
Empty eyes straight ahead

So the war keeps on raging, the children still die
Indifference is thriving, the people move by
Their thoughts on themselves
And they live
Empty eyes straight ahead

James Holbrook

Final Visions

See the final visions, man's fleeting dreams;
now on wind's wings they cling, tightly, oh
so tightly. Soft wisp of cloud swirling forever away.

Go now he says, for was but a dream,
sunshine before the rain, stones
beneath the sands, a harvested land
before seeds sown.

Beats of his heart pound within his bosom
tick in cadence with the clock on the wall, and
as the wind in cadence with all.

Ah, sweet rain you awaken me,
shifting sands you make me keen,
barren fields, you, the mirror of man's soul;
    or are you his dreams?

Spring rain slants to brown sands upon field yet idle,
and harken for comes the new wind and perhaps
riding with this wind, new seed,

and mayhap the seed from which the
garden shall spring, and mayhap
hopes anew, and new dreams.

J. R. Mothershead

---

*The sky is the daily bread of
the eyes.*

—Emerson

Missing You

I see you sitting in your chair—
I look again, but you're not there.
I see you standing in the hall—
But you're not really there at all.
Oh death, you came and stole his life—
You took the husband from his wife.
And yet the grave, it cannot keep
Love from those who eternally sleep.
Even tho' I said "'till death do us part"
"Forever, my darling," was in my heart.
I see you sitting in your chair—
I look again, but you're not there...

Diane Clare McClurg

Rebellion

My son, My son; You don't realize how much I love you.
There is nothing in this world; that could make me harm you.

What is it that is making you rebel?
Who or what is filling you with so much hell?

It hurts me to see you like this. What can I do?
I want to take away everything that is hurting you.

You won't open up to me; You're always with your friends.
What can momma do; to make the rebellion end?

You dad is not here; I know I can't take his place.
But sweetheart; This we all have to face.

He wanted a divorce; So I set him free.
He comes to see you; This doesn't bother me.

We can't have the family we once had.
I know it hurts you deeply and makes you sad.

Life isn't always what we want it to be.
We've got to stick together, Buck, Dawn, and me.

Brenda Medley

Our Baby Boy

Oh, little baby of mine
you're so beautiful and fine,
I hear you cry
and run to see why,
in your crib you shake
your arms and legs frantically wake,
I reach down
and immediately you remove the frown,
hugging you, my arms enclose
and I gently kiss you on the nose,
I nuzzle your soft, chubby, cheeks
that I've known only a few weeks,
My son, such a wonder
I lay you back down and tuck you under
I feel overwhelmed with joy and shed a tear
all because of you my dear
the little things that make you laugh
like splashing around in your bath
and watching me, whatever I do,
for you, everything is brand new,
I slowly hesitate to leave your side
but the hours seem to slide
until your cry again reaches my ear
I go back to my chores, but always stay near.

Lisa M. Myers

Little Shoes And Stockings

Little shoes and stockings
    From little feet turned brown,
As they run and skip about
    In the puddles on the ground.

They are oh, so happy
    Wet little kids are they,
As soft rains fall upon them
    And makes this special day.

As they scream and holler
    And jump around in glee,
I so wish that for a while
    A little child I could be.

Then as I'd run and holler
    As those little ones can do,
I too, would run and leave behind
    Little shoes and stockings too.

Dorothy Behringer

VICTIMS.

Youth

Ah youth,
    The golden age of life,
    Free from care, free from strife,
    Not a worry nor a fear,
    Only sometimes there's a tear.
    In the fields of joys
    In a valley of toys
    Their world of fantasy lies—
        From books and tales
        of barbary sails
    Come people they idolize.
    The youth have a gift
    They wish would go swift,
    As the years disappear into time.
        But then when they find
        this great richness behind,
    They at last understand that season sublime.

Jerome W. Forest

The Year That I Became Twenty-One

I had a big sister, once, you know,
Now she lies buried, under the snow.
Everyone loved her, because, you see,
She was sweet and kind to her family.

Alas, with her husband she did not agree.
She left and went to another city.
Three children stayed with her family here.
Without her, they were not happy, I fear.

The next thing we knew, Western Union called,
I took the message, and I was appalled.
They said that she'd died in an accident.
Now, three more telegrams had to be sent.

To our Mom and Dad, who were on vacation,
And to her husband, with their daughters and son.
Another to the woman with whom she had stayed,
To send her back here, I must explain and persuade.

Her children all suffered because she was gone.
Although we all tried to help, we were only pawns,
In the chess game of life, we were trying to win.
Now one life was gone, but many more to begin.

Through all these years, I have sadly missed her,
My own sweet, impulsive, dear big sister.

Marjory A. Treumuth

The One

You were the one who walked up to him
And smiled at him and asked him his name.
You were the one who taught him to love
And the rules for playing the game.

You were the one who cried on the phone
When he tried to leave you too soon.
You were the one who kept all the promises
So he would never be able to forget you.

Then you agreed to let him be
When he said he thought that he
Needed the time to let himself go;
To love and to learn and to sing on his own.

And you saw it coming—the fall and the hurt.
And you saw him bleeding—he wasn't the first.

Then he was the one who lost his composure
And the respect of a girl he still can't get over.
He is the one who's haunted by dreams
And emotions so strong
You can feel their screams.

Now he is the one who cries all alone
And he is the one who tries to forget.
But you were the one who came to him first—
You are the one who can lift his curse.

Robert Besneatte

A Plane Game

What am I doing on this plane again—
Destination to destination, my mirrored friend.
Let's all pretend it has purpose,
So my icy tears do not fall to freeze a light heart.
Let's sing a song, and play a game—
To expand the expanded light I Am,
Freely floating by.
Remember me, my mirrored friend—
I remember you from let's pretend,
We made a difference by lighting the way.

Holly J. Rose

THE CHILDREN'S CLASS.

Tears

They're falling again, like rain from the sill
To stain my heart, as I cry from within
This loneliness, this misery, this empty pain I feel
It leaves me crying for a gentle touch
To come and wipe my tears
If you're listening to my prayer
I need to have you near
Death is but a short distance away,
With each and every tear
I have so much in my life, I've loved and left alone
But no one understands just me, and again I'm on my own
I blame not a soul for my state of mind
I've hidden my life away, forever showing the happier side
So as not to feel the pain
And if you're reaching out to me
I'm grasping for your hand
To wipe the tears that fall each day
And to help me understand.

Beverly A. Washington

On This Day

A Prayer Of Dedication On Yom Kippur

On This Day...
Holiest Of All Days, I Give Myself To You,
Everything That I Possess, Own Or Am Is Yours.

   You Are Mine, I Am Yours,
Lovingly, Tenderly, Confidently And
Affectionately, I Consecrate Myself To You;
Dedicate Myself To You.
   Hoping, Believing, Praying And Knowing
You Will Care For Me, Forever.

   Giving To You My Heart, My Soul, My Very
Being, Knowing That Somewhere You Are There,
Loving Me, Looking Out For Me.

   Holding My Hand, Helping Me When I Am
Restless, Pushing Me Onward When I Doubt Myself.

   Lifting Me Upward When I Am Down, Sending
Me Forth To Accomplishment.

   Never Letting Me Be By Myself But Helping
Me Stand Alone.
   Loving You, Needing You, Thanking You
   For This Day...Holiest Of All Days.

   Lee Cooper Meade

Love—On The Other Shore
In Memory Of . . .

A little boy, waiting for a school bus
Mischievous and happy.
A teenager, loving sports.
A young man, looking for a mate,
Finding her, loving her, marrying her.
Then a baby girl arrives—
and their joy is complete.
The years roll by
They have a long happy life.
Then, his dear partner
Goes on her journey to eternity.
He is desolate, filled with grief.
He becomes restless,
Looking for something
He doesn't know what.
At the end of a rainbow
He finds a kindred soul.
One who brings him much happiness
One who understands his needs
Now he too is gone,
         On his journey to eternity
         To meet his Beloved
         His soul mate.
         Now he is really happy.
         Let us all be happy with him.
         And say a "glad Good-bye."

Sarah Abraham

GRANDFATHER'S SCRAP BOOK.

My Love

Although the words seem like a cliche,
I just have to say,
I want a love who will make me happy.
I want a love who is the answer
To my prayers, and a dream come true.
I want a love who will fulfill my fantasies,
And my secret wishes too.
I want a love who will be a good friend
And a lasting mate. Someone with whom
I will be able to communicate.
But most of all, I want a love who will
Want me at least as much as, or even more,
Than I will want her.

Gil Saenz

Inside Me

So many days have gone by, and my eyes are still not dry.

I sit alone on my bed, watching strange shadows dance through my head. They are taunting and yelling; god, I wish they were dead.

I feel strange, I feel alone, I feel lost inside of myself, not sure where to call home.

I feel dizzy, I am going to fall; please, please, somebody call.

I sit here staring into the dark, I don't understand the pain in my heart.

I am on the outside looking in, they are laughing and talking. No one sees me watching them within.

I feel like I am running down a dark narrow hall. I am running, trying to escape from it all.

I run and I run, but I can't get away. The shadows follow, driving me further away.

My head is spinning around and around, all of a sudden a shadow falls to the ground.

Out of the darkness, I feel a hand pulling on my shoulder, forcing me to stand.

I am scared, but I can not run, here I stand staring at her one on one. I stand here with a smile on my face, and feel this warm embrace.

I hear whispering deep in my heart, finally, I no longer stare into the dark,

Here I belong, here I will stay. I know from myself, I can never run away.

Julianne Gadke

Me Too

As you look out your window, on a wintry day,
And you see the snow falling, oh so gently,
And you can see the coldness, though you're inside—
warm and cozy;
Do you imagine us in a warm embrace?
ME TOO!

When spring is sprung, and you go walking,
smelling that smooth, refreshed smell of spring,
And you see nature beginning to come alive again;
Do you think of our relationship—full of life and
continuously blossoming?
ME TOO!

As you lay, bathing your body in the warm rays of the
summer sun, and as a soft, silky breeze runs across your skin;
Do you think of the warm and invigorating love that we share
for one another?
ME TOO!

As the weather cools slightly, and the refreshing fall breeze
runs its fingers through your hair, and the urge to take a
walk in the woods comes upon you;
Do you think of us being together always?
ME TOO!

Regardless of the time of year, or the time of day,
I'm always thinking about you. I think of the many memories
we've shared, and of the dreams we'll chase tomorrow together.

Timothy L. Kapala

Midnight Lady

There is a midnight lady
Who once wandered the streets with me.
She kissed me softly in the darkness,
Smiling as she waved goodbye.

She did not cry
And she would have laughed
If I had shed a tear.

We shared things never said before
And we gave our hearts away.
We learned how to survive,
Standing strong for each other.

I did not cry
And she would hate me
If I had shown my fear.

She is a child of freedom
Who taught me everlasting love
And how to leave a broken heart behind
Without taking away the smile.

E. Vincent Blanchard

*Shared joys make a friend,
not shared sufferings.*

—Nietzsche

Spread Your Love

Spread your love all over the land
Walk with God hand in hand
Give your love to all you see
A life without love cannot be

Be a friend and forgive
A heart without love cannot live
Keep a joy, within your heart
Don't let your sorrows tear you apart

Pray to the Lord, and be his friend
The joy in your heart will never end
Call on His name all through the day
He'll show you His love, He'll show you His way

He'll be your strength, He'll be your friend
His love for you will never end
So when you feel you can't go on
When all your faith and hope are gone
Say a prayer you can't go wrong
He'll fill your heart with a joyous song.

Sharon Jastrzebski

My Friends In The Yard

Awe, she struts so certainly,
Back and forth, clucking giddily,
What a chick so fancy free,
Who daily gives a gift to me.

Cock-a-do-dal-do, Get up, it's time,
He is surely the fanciest of his kind,
Striding about, wearing a large crown,
Aggressive and virile, he pecks at the ground.

Now to the most beautiful ones around,
Only in the summer, your coloring is brown,
Emerald, blue, gray and black,
From the pond, awkwardly flying back.

I can't forget the two, who honk instead of quack,
So big and white, full and fat,
I don't wear down coats,
And that's a fact!

I watch as the striped, furry little cat,
Chases all of you around this way and that,
The dog is barking, jealous of their fun,
Has to stay tied up, for she'd eat more than one.

Marti Hoemke

---

*After the age of eight, all
contemporaries are friends.*

—Mme. De Dino

Jenny in the Garden

You grasp my hand, my little one,
and guide me into a garden,
where we stroll along a path
where the azaleas sway in the breeze.
I gaze at them alive and vibrant.
You are leading me beneath the spruce trees.
I watch you dancing along,
your hair tossing in the breeze,
your big, brown eyes eagerly watching a
golden butterfly fluttering its wings
while it gently glides through the air
and lights on some lilacs.
I watch you as you listen
to the birds singing on the bough,
then you excitedly drop my hand
and point to the whispering leaves.
Jenny, I see you kneeling to gather bluebells
in a garden in summer.

Ginny Wilder

Lucky Seven

Lucky Seven is my dog.
He is my eyes and my ears.
Lucky lets me know if someone is near.
Whether they are good or bad he hears.

Don't know what I would do
If I did not have him around.
To cheer me up when I am sad,
And keep me company when I am glad.

Lucky Seven is black as night.
With a beautiful white Seven on his chest.
His Mama was a white Shepherd,
And his dad a black old Labrador.

Most loving dog I ever had.
Loves everybody like mad.
Wags his tail back and forth to greet you.
And his ears perk up to say, "Hello."

Ruby E. Rowland

Untitled

As long as I can remember
I've longed for someone who
Could make me feel the joy of love
as only you could do;
Someone to be my sounding board,
a shoulder I could lean on;
Someone to soothe and comfort me
'til all my fears were gone.
You taught me how to speak of love
and tell you of my dreams.
How free I've been since I met you—
much happier it seems.
No matter how far the distance,
or how long the stretch of time,
You'll always be a part of me
and a love hat's so sublime.

Barbara Rosselli

Puppies

The puppies looked so lonely all three
from where I stood but it would do no good to take
those puppies home with me!

Mom would pitch a fit and dad he would agree.
He would say "son why did you get all three?"
Yes, I knew it would do no good to take those puppies
home with me!

I watched through the window of the pet shop as the
young lady was cleaning their cages out. I felt a rage
within myself. Do those puppies have to be in a cage?
But, yet I knew it would do no good to set their hearts
free, for I could not take them puppies home with me.

Aaron Scott Keller

Happy Birthday, Uncle Sam

From sea to shining sea to the Pacific
To the boundaries coast of U.S.A. Maine;
From the 50th State: "I am a proud American."
To these miracle miles my ancestors came.
From the warmth of California's gulfstream
To America, the dream come true and then some;
From the Pacific shores of Waikiki able seamen
See the blue waters of the Pacific real soon.
That is something to be thankful if you please
Perhaps, not always but never commonplace;
From the lips of all melting-pot friendly people
Amazingly true, of all nations, every race.
Again, there's one thing we have much in common
You will hear every sons and daughters say:
Uncle Sam so niftily and so warmly say:
"Thank goodness, I am a proud American."

John D. C. Estrella

The Numismatist

Glazed eyes caress the case
Contents beckon inquisition

Uncirculated's glistening display
Proof's complimenting array

All dazzle yielding wallet
Soon with contents dissolved

Stanley S. Reyburn

Hardy Pioneer...

To groom, to sow, to address,
to wait for sight is a stress,
in the struggle for survival.
Herded like cattle for slaughter,
hearing shrieks no laughter,
these men, women, and children endured,
these people persevered.
Hardy pioneers of splendored cultures,
of rich and colorful heritage.
Has their spirit diminished, and i
reply, will the sun fail to rise,
will the poets run out of rhymes and trade in
their chimes.
I say thee nay,
a thousand nays...
Does the hummingbird hesitate to sing.
The black people must survive, as a testament
against tyranny, freedom is a must.
though it often has a cost.
Yes to groom, to sow, to address,
to wait for sight is a stress.
To, live with dignity and felicity,
In a world full of anxiety.

Emeka

The United Nations

Let's believe and pray for the
    United Nations,
May prove a success toward mankind's
    negotiation.
Almighty God made Heaven and earth good,
"For the earth is the Lord and the fullness
    thereof" (Psalms 24:1 and I Corinthians 10:26)
Goodwill toward all, I pray, we should in
    this world.
Rather East, North, South or West,
His invisible freedom is upper-
    most best.
Look to each year, peace, hope, and
    inspiration,
For U.N. has confrontation with the
    Soviet.
In most lands grown cynically cold,
Hungry for power and greedy for oil
    or gold.
For U.N. of the delegate selected few,
Be a Gentile, Latin, Greek, Orient
    of Jew.
Of Faith, Hope and Love from our Father
    above,
His Son can turn man's sins from Hatred
    to Love.

John D. C. Estrella

> *Unlike grownups, children have little need to deceive themselves.*
>
> —*Goethe*

Sunshine Smiles On Children

Sunshine smiles on children in a special sort of way
it makes a golden halo around them as they play.
The winds of summer whisper to little girls and boys
in a voice so soft and light that it brings them added joys.
The flowers in the garden bow as children pass them by
while up among the soft white clouds, Bluebirds and Robins fly.
Trees spread their shady leaves for them above the grass so
    green
while far off in the distance a brook slips through the scene.
Summer sings her anthem to children everywhere
in a pageant of such splendor that perfection can't compare.
So with all of this in mind it is only fair to say
that sunshine smiles on children in a special sort of way.

Richard A. Leavitt

Ice Princess

A dandy man she chance did meet
And gave her heart away.
He gently gave it back to her
And told her he was gay.

A second time she gave her love
To one who was so shy.
Yet silently he slipped away—
She never knew quite why.

A handsome man was number three
With eyes of emerald green;
In him she thought that she had found
The answer to her dream.

He took her heart quite carelessly
And dropped it to the ground.
It shattered into fragments small
That much was left unfound.

To suffer up her heart again
When all had gone askew
Was something most assuredly
That she would never do.

She built a wall around her heart
As far as it would go
And locked away all love within
A tower of ivory snow.

Suzana M. Koehn

If You Should Smile

I smiled today and no one understood why, but I did.
I thought of your gentle face and your warm and tender touch.
I remembered the fun we had when just brief moments we were
the only two people on earth. I reminisced on the times we
spent just being silly, and the times we were totally serious. We
shared so much in such little time, for now I understand the
phrase "It's not The quantity, but the quality."

Where did the time go and will it ever come again?
Days go by and I wonder how you are and what you're doing.
I wonder also, are you thinking of me?

I ponder on what fate has in store for each of us.
Will our paths ever cross again or will there ever be a you and
me, together? It's possible, but not likely. It all rests on one
question. Do we want it enough to wait? I do.

My heart is warmed by the thought I carry day to day of the
special bond of friendship I hold with a very special person so
far away and yet so dear to my heart. That person is you.

And if today you should smile and not know why, it is because
at that very moment, I'm thinking of you, your gentle face, and
your warm, and tender touch.

Rhonda J. Constant

Happy...

Happy are those who can dream
From dreams they can try to redeem
Life's daily pleasures
And moments one treasures
Yes, all these can come in a dream.

Happy are those who can share
With sharing they show how they care
They find in this way
They often get pay
In a manner that cannot compare.

Happy are those who can love
They sense the sun's warmth from above
They glow from within
With a contagious grin
And it's living they're most fond of.

Happiest are those who perceive
From surroundings they often receive
Most of the pleasures
That anyone treasures
And all that the mind can conceive.

Marilyn Schnabl

Seasons

Can spring be the winter of my life?
I am old among the daffodils.
Uncertain I totter under the rose-arbor.
Breathing the fragrance of lilac
I sense its fading.

Will summer be my last memory?
Will I still see spruces spread their skirts
And willows flow in the breeze against the sky?
If lightning radiates distant clouds
Will it flash again?

Can there be another autumn?
Will I stroll under golden canopies
And caress the glossy skin of fallen buckeyes?
When skeins of wild geese point southward
Will they journey back?

If, for me, winter follows autumn
I shall let the white flakes kiss my cheeks
And see the world softly sink to soothing sleep.
Then spring may come alive again
Before the summer.

W. Edgar Vinacke

---

*There is no cure for birth
and death save to enjoy the
interval.*

—Santayana

Almost There

The valleys are wide the hills more steep,
A long way to go before I sleep.
   January, cold new fallen snow,
   February whispers, "There's a sunbow,"
March winds wail will not keep still
While a candle glows atop the hill.

A green morning breaks in April's arms,
May's in order with all her charms,
   June is waiting with a full moon
   While the mockingbird sings a lovely tune.
Sultry July brings a heat wave,
Shadows dance in an August haze,

Teasing September comes in today,
An October sunset is just a breath away,
   Beautiful November, always a thrill
   In grace steps aside, December's chill.
The valleys, narrowed, hills less steep
I'm almost there—I can sleep.

Virgie McCoy Sammons

Memories Of High School

My thoughts will often reminisce,
and suddenly remember this
one thing that kept my brain intact,
to catalog a simple fact.
Keeping up with all my peers,
I did my homework through blurred tears.

No study secrets for a test.
For knowing answers, only guess.
No longer question, Memorize!
To have a gift would tantalize.
If I could get one hemisphere
to shed some light and listen, hear,
a larger portion of my brain
would find the means to store, retain.
A promise to myself would be
some consolation, goal for me.

If looking over text my fate
I'd show no qualms to hesitate.
Then grades would fall, but wonder why
was never quite the failure. I
anticipate and with the fear
that I'd repeat another year.
But somehow making all ends meet
recover, landing on both feet.

Hester Gia Latimer

Mankind's Ingenuity

From a cleft in aberration,
   Man has forged the key, no less,
Which unlocks Impossible's riddle,
   With abstraction to digress.

He invades the upper strata,
   With an eagle's nonchalance,
Reconnoiters midst the planets
   And intrudes on the Moon's expanse.

He has made a potent scanner
   Which depicts his inner self;
Segments of the brain are labeled,
   Like the bottles on a shelf.

As a magical, surgical instrument
   He has loosed the laser beam,
Which removes tumors, etc. without cutting,
   Leaving ne'er a scar or seam.

T.V. the brand new adhesion,
   Pictures entertainment on a tube;
Radio adds jest to Life's excitement,
   With the chatter of a rube.

Ego gains no worthy promise,
   For desire abets no timely scheme;
Action earns the ready plaudits
   When ardor implements a dream.

Charles Ruggles Fox

Prisoners of War

The hope in the matter of prisoners, and prayer
For their immediate, unconditional release,
Ought truly to be
A simple act of humanity,
And will improve the prospect for peace.

The rendering of neighboring nations
Good conscience and expectations,
With strong brotherhood of realizations,
Should be uppermost at the peace talks.
Unceasing peace toward mankind will possibly be
To end the rumors of war and the prison camps.

Ambassadors of goodwill, and peacemakers,
Are the cornerstones for peace
Which, moreover, would be a lesson for all nations,
And the hope of brotherhood across their boundaries.

From a common bond to circle justice and our love
Would come peace and brotherhood.
It's time on earth for tender kindness
And for love to pass through you and me.

    John D. C. Estrella

From Where Came Such a Youth?

From where came such a youth
placed here upon the trodden path
leading past my house,
soothing the eyesore
with such simplicity
and obvious virginity?

And the glow that my outstretched hand
does unhesitatingly reach towards,
so soft, like summer cloud,
clean and sweet his smell
that I capture
as I nestle closer,
clearly my first real temptation.

I sent the young Swedish fruit away.
An older, wiser Juliet did play.
The lasting memory would be
the innocence of that day,
when I was more in love with Love
and what it does in silence say.

    E. Surina   *Canada*

THE CHATEAU OF PORNIC.

Finally Something Different
Dedicated to my son, Mario Antonio (Tony) Marinaro
Mommy loves you.

Started down hill,
With no fancy frills,
But I'm climbing up at last,
This time it's going to be a blast.

For I'm finally confident within myself,
To climb up high upon that shelf,
For I'm good, it's true,
Because I believe in what I do.

No more feeling sorry,
Or telling the same old story,
Because life is going to be great for me,
At last I'm finally free.

    Cindy Thomas (Prasad)   *Canada*

Daughter

She stands tall and graceful—sometimes slumping at the
kitchen sink—suds up to her elbows—toot—toot—hum—the
music blaring—as she whirls around the kitchen floor—ring—
ring phone—laughter—long lasting giggles—he said—she
said— Tip toe into her room—Walls—full of gorgeous—her
favorites— closet—pants—pants—finally—see the pink dress—
flowers—mirror—lipstick—pink—pretty—whoops—soccer
ball—nearby—magazines "seventeen"—keyboard—dusty—
Don't hurry time passing—growing up—tender smile—Love
Mom—

    Mildred McCluskey-Hilliard

Gingham Town

Gingham Town! Gingham Town!
On the road to Gingham Town!
On my way h-o-m-e
Down to my old, old home...

Been out in the world a-working and all...
Some forty years feeding my family and all...
Now I am old; my children have grown...
My friends are old, soon they'll be gone...

Dear wife, Bessie, God bless her soul,
    has long since been laid to rest...
It has been a long, long haul,
    my weary bones sure need a rest...
There's no more to do but go h-o-m-e;
So now I'm coming home...

Gingham Town! Gingham Town!
On the road to Gingham Town!
On my way h-o-m-e
Down to my old, old home...
    On the road to
        Gingham Town...
            Gingham Town.

Alexander Waino Ekman

Destiny

Constructed with precise geometrical spirals,
    every tenacious loophole glutinously covered.
Diaphanous threads enclose, my movements—signals
    to where the squat and deadly figure hovered.

I am enmeshed in glistening silver bands.
A web of fate holds me tightly in its grasp.
I struggle vainly against those silken strands,
    but am hopelessly encysted—'tis a forlorn task!

The ominous creature approaches with a victor's air.
A fatalism permeates my soul as my spirit dies.
I tremble as a cryptic voice bids me—prepare!
A diabolical, umbrageous shroud about me lies.

A lassitude of sublime repose and resignation
    enfolds my mind; all fear and horror leaves.
A euphrastic mood prevails—a curious anticipation
    as the ghostly terror carries me beneath the eaves.

Intuitively I know what will soon befall me,
    as the Darkness stirs; Kismet advances swiftly.
Clasped in a deadly embrace—I fulfill my destiny.
Desiccated, I lie abandoned amid the dead debris.

He lay for years beneath the eaves whereat he died.
Smiling peacefully from inside his gray-spun cocoon,
    his neighbor victims lying disheveled and dried.
For Nature is just: to Man, the worm or the baboon!

Theodore Femmel

The Coming of Age

I'm becoming what I've always been
A writer, poet, artist, musician
Now, at last, I've time
To indulge my every whim,
Fantasy, dream, within
And without the realm of reality.
Ah, the glorious joy of it!
I do, feel, communicate and know
The unbridled freedom
To climb the highest mountain
And enjoy the view below
Marvelous, varied, variegated landscape
Stretching from valley to distant seascape
Enveloped in the mists of Time.
So alluring, seductive, sublime
That I become part of the Primeval
Racing through ancient Eons
Above the land and below the Sea
Windswept or hidden,
Burning in the sun
Or a recluse in a cool dark cave.
Suddenly brave whenever and wherever I wish to roam
And best of all, to share
What I discover there with you!

Jessie Faulkner Cuedek
Included in **About The Poets** section

> ## All rising to great place is by a winding stair.
>
> —*Bacon*

Honorable Mention
In Line

Shadows in line sinewy and strained, in back
in a mother's arm a child lies
breathless,

now pieced is the pane, stained
glass blood outlined
now numb,

the last storm has passed and
no memories are left to speak about
once-upon-a-times,

letters scented and kissed and sent
nowhere,
none of old,
nothing to unfold,
dead rats drained, dried
ashen in envelopes tucked with
flamed tongues licked and sold,

no eye has the waveless sea
only blackness not even blind and
broken boned.
Next.

Stacy L. Ackerman

Wind and Waves

To be as free and careless as the wind,
whistling and wandering through the night.
The waves grow and climb,
as if to take flight.
Roaring and crashing upon earth's humble shore,
So powerful and mighty, then seen no more.
Now calm and still with a face of glass,
Then a gust of wind grows strong and fast.
No longer can I see the reflection of my face,
As I rise and fall without balance or grace.
Now the force has gone as fast as it came,
Left behind are the ripples growing calmer and tame.
So forceful and strong the wind and waves can be,
Yet gentle and taming, forever flowing free.

Neva M. Morgan

Attitudes of Nature

Nature is a forever changing force like a young spirit running
    wild,
Quick to change at any moment in time, to ravage, to devastate
    and defile.
As if to hide from watchful eyes, she slips along quietly to the
    depths of the ocean floor,
She lifts the waters to unbelievable heights, to batter and
    spread havoc
      to the helpless waiting shores.

She can move the land beneath your feet and reach to the very
    bowels of the earth,
To release the waiting menace from below, and earth quake
    giving birth.
With her many vivid tongues of fire she spreads destruction o'er
    the land,
Covering the earth with molten ash, leaving it so desolate where
    once
      so much beauty did stand.

Nature can also be as compassionate as a gentle falling rain,
That falls upon parched and barren earth, to spring fully into
    life again.
Where the abundance of brilliant colors as far as the eyes can
    see,
Hovers over the mountains, plains and valleys where nature
    expresses
      herself in total beauty and harmony.

She gently warms the earth and all that exist with her majesty,
    the sun,
The trees and flowers and all living matter entwine together as
    one.
She will send along a gentle breeze on a hot and stifling day,
You can almost hear her pleasant song as she journeys on her
    way.

For all the destruction and discontentment that she may leave
    behind,
New life appears to rebuild anew in the briefness of our time.
The attitudes of nature are a wonder to behold,
For everyday, somewhere on earth, memories of her are told.

Sheila Duprey

Brother to the Wind

I am brother to the wind,
As feral and uncontrolled as he.
I am a reckless adventure-seeking young fellow.
I am brother to the wind.

I am sister to the wind.
I am gentle—I am soft-spoken—very
unlike my brothers.
I come on gentle rains—I cool the Summer eves,
I am sister to the wind.

We are the children of the wind.
We sprang, full-grown, from our mother's womb.
We were spawned in the devil's nest on a
high craggy cliff.
we are the winds—we rule the world.

I am the grandmother of the winds.
I am fiercely proud of my grandchildren,
make of it what you will.
Zephyr tugs my heart—She is most kind.
I am the keeper of their heritage.
I am the grandmother of the winds.

Jane Pierritz

You Can Depend On God, Your Friend!

When he world seems to be crashing all around you,
When you seem overwhelmed by troubles and woes,
Remember there is a true friend you can count upon,
One to whom you can always for help go.

He will listen as you pour your heart out to Him,
He will laugh with you, when your heart is gay,
He will cry with you, when you are sorrowful and sad,
For He is right there with you, every minute, every day.

For if He sees each little sparrow,
As to the earth it does fall,
You know that He is always watching over you,
And will listen, when on Him you do call.

Depend upon Him as you would a beloved friend,
Lean upon Him, never doubt,
That your Holy Father is your very best friend,
A friend that you really cannot be without!

Thank Him for each gift that He does give to you,
Love, honor and worship Him, your best friend, each day,
He expects only from you, faith, honor and love,
If you give this to Him, He will be with you—for always!

Bernice Couey Bishop

Jo

A sad time has come
   To the children of Jo Howard Davis;
A time so hard to bear.
The tears flow so easily,
Both to the children and to those she was so dear;
For she has gone on from this life we are so familiar with,
   And we will see her no more.

So many would say she is dead; but it is not so.
for look inside yourself;
Can you not find ever so many memoirs there in your heart?
To bring a smile to your face,
   There she lives on in your heart.
Though you are sad her physical body is not with you,
Her memory from the times past are there
   To make you laugh or cry,
Depending on the memory you bring forth
   From the treasure in your heart.

So cry not at the thought of her not being there with you;
But be glad of the abundance of memories
   She has left for you for the days ahead.
For not all have the joy of so many pleasurable memories
   To carry them through the days ahead of them.

Glenn O. Davis

Epitaph

Weep not for me, oh sorrowful children
for I am not in what is before you
dry your eyes and look towards the heavens
for the rainbow or sun or blue of the sky
and there you will find the essence of me

My spirit is in the budding flowers of spring,
in the first snow of winter and colors of changing leaves
Look for my reflection in cool, crisp mountain streams
or in the fragrance of freshly cut grass carried gently on the
   wind

For what I am now is a true and free spirit
an energy of presence that whispers softly in your hearts
of all the joys and times we shared

Imagine the heavens, perhaps as I do
of bright and billowy mountains of clouds
of warm scented air and tall green trees
of flowers and always bright sunny days
and sparkling pools of warm healing waters
Could you really deny me this home?

Then draw a deep and cleansing breath
remember me in times of laughter
sleep with peace upon your hearts
then smile, turn the page and begin a new chapter

Marsha Williams

Short Encounter

She sat on a bench, awaiting her bus,
when he came, taking his seat
to her far left. She looked up,
their eyes met; there was a tic
in his face, when he said:
"How are you today?" "Fine," she said.
"How about you?" "I just had a set-back
financially, but I will make it,
I always did." Again, that tic.
"Then—there is more?" she asked.
"I lost my friend in an accident.
She's in the morgue, I must go there now,
I'm afraid," he said.
"Then don't go, she's dead, she won't know,
why not remember her as you knew her?"
"I have to see her," he said.
"Then you must go so you won't think
later, 'I should have gone'!"
His face ticked all over, his mouth
quivered, announcing tears,
He abruptly rose and left.

Jackie Berkson   Germany
*Included in **About The Poets** Section*

Insight

Freedom's intricate plan
We the people
Governed by law
Or controlled by man
Vices of political schemes
Or mortal men of dreams
The thoughts that remain
Ours just the same
Or a clever game
Do as you're told
Don't be so bold
There is no control
Power and money
A capitalist dream
Or socialist control
Puppets on parade
Elimination the goal
Unknown hands patrol
Our souls having been sold
Freedom's intricate plan
Destroyed by secular man
Greed's ultimate plan

Rayford Woodall, Sr.

Scarred

He stands there naked
Stripped of all self-respect
Left nothing but his tears
Battered—
He bleeds from wounds with no bruises;

There is no hand to comfort him
No kind words to rebuild him
No love to drive away the hurt
So, In his bitterness he lives;

Never was a hand laid on him
But the flesh heals faster
than the heart
And words can hurt, harm—
and haunt
Forever

Sheila A. Phillips

Untitled

That which is
to be accomplished
needs to be defined
from the inner
core of the joy
of creating.
Follow the Master
who placed the
wonder of His Gifts
for imitation.

Frances Santarsiero Ph.D.

The Forbidden Mind

The grandeur of the globe,
Like the globe of your mind,
Endless it may be,
For the end we cannot find.

There is so much within,
So much that remains unused,
And so much that we could share,
Left untouched, it seems abused.

Just as a creative child,
Has so very much to give,
If he is forbidden to grow,
He too is forbidden to live.

Dawn E. Rearick

It is a luxury to be understood.

—Emerson

Memories

I look up
Through the beam of sun
What I see
Is unreal
I see your face
In the clouds

Everywhere I turn
Your image is there
You left the world
Behind you
Why did it have to be you?

You are gone forever
But not forgotten
Memories were meant
To last a lifetime.

Daphne Weber

Loneliness

If you ever feel as lonely
    and as friendless as I do,
And I hear about your problem,
    then I'll shed a tear for you,

For I know the pain you're feeling
    and I know the pain you'll feel
Until you find a friendship
    that's honest, true and real.

I know how lonesome you can be
    though standing in a crowd,
And how it hurts to love someone
    when you are not allowed

To share one moment with her
    and to gaze into her eyes
While you tell her of her loveliness
    and listen to her sighs.

So come and raise your glass to mine
    and tell me of your woe,
And cry upon my shoulder,
    but then, before you go,

Allow me one small favor—
    and this I hope you'll do:
Just let me use your shoulder,
    for I am lonely, too.

J. O. Hillhouse

My Window

A charcoal colored night
finds a pale circle rising
shyly behind shadows
hanging dark and long
that fall asleep in
the coolness of the ground.

The lazy marble eyes
that sleep by day
await with hollow pain
for creatures crawling
past their way.

The coolness of the grass
finds the little black ones
in their glory
fiddles playing
for their prospective mates.

And the night
has just begun
for those that live
beyond by glass.

Loretta Ortiz   Spain

A Muse Meant

Sitting in this four-poster bed
  I muse on you, my muse that's fled
And wonder how with all our art
  we ever came to be apart
And though I know the answer
  Still I ramble over every hill and valley
of the blanketscape
searching for perhaps a clue, a hue,
  the scent of you
by now these things like you have gone
but Hope is with me and we trudge on.

Sitting somewhere in the sand
  we always are in desert lands
  even luggage gives us away
NOMADS—are we? Yes and so we stay
From land to land the sand will differ
  but your hand in mine will be forever

Sitting daydreams, gentle winds
  no stars—smiling day
    melancholy tiptoes by and keeps on going

  Anne Mulcahy Dower   *Greece*

Voyage To A Distant Harbor
*Dedicated to my long-time good friend, good shipmate and
loving neighbor; licensed master pilot, New York harbor. . .
Captain Tom Arena . . . 10/20/26-2/7/88*

When a ship has cleared the harbor, it's
indeed all set for sea
Wake from its propellers churn-up and
swirl murky harbor waters
Though soon gone—the ship a majestic
sight will always be...

Gentle swells roll away from its wash
toward the shore
To mere ripples they're diminished—then
one sees them no more;
Imbued serenity—a lofty, but gentle
silhouette: the ship, once blended to the
shore...

Watched, as it sails out of sight—one
may wonder anew;
Of exotic new harbors ere to visit—for
others it to view;
To places far away—beyond the horizon—
a sturdy ship, with but a single soul its
crew...

Alas! Though bon voyage lest we say—its
lofty, but gentle silhouette we'll see
again...perhaps, on some sunny peaceful
day...

  Daniel Kozak

"Mother"

  Once so, so young,
now so much older.
  While the past lends thoughts of
immaturity and innocence, there only lingers
wisdom in the present.
  While the past recalls times of foolishness
and carefree days, the cloud of responsibility has
come about in the present.
  But responsibility is something my mother
carries well.
  Along with responsibility though, comes
obligation; obligation to a husband and children;
making sure they are well cared for.
  Some may run away from this,
but mother I'm glad you did not.
  Oh, how you have changed dear mother.
  Hair once so golden, now tinged with
grey.
  Eyes once possessing a sparkle of
mischief, now hold a sparkle hinting at
fulfillment and happiness.
  Mother, you have changed for the better.

  Susan Podhajski

---

*Do not blame God for the
harvest when you yourself
do the sowing.*

—*Anon*

Blind Cats

There's something in a blind cat
that makes my stomach turn,
not with disgust, exactly.
Maybe it's the look of the eye—
that marbled glaze,
or maybe it's the trembling fur
that heaves itself along,
not knowing where it's going or where it's been—
that raw trembling that cannot still itself.

I long to still it,
to lift a steady finger and unglaze the eye.
But I know I can't.
It wouldn't let me if I could.
In the face of a blind cat,
hissing and clawing in the dark,
I am impotent and helpless,
a comrade trembler.

I know of one who doesn't shudder,
who looks upon blind cats
without disgust or fear
or nauseous churning,
whose steady hand unglazes even the dimmest eye
and stills the most voracious trembling.
To Him I commend all blind cats and comrades.

  Sheldon Smith

THE MOUNTAIN OF THE HOLY CROSS, COLORADO.

About the Poets

BALEY, GENEVE. Education: Masters degree in Piano and Composition, American Conservatory of Music. Chicago, Illinois; post-graduate studies in political science at Hunter Evening College. Aaron Copeland DO Scholarship Tanglewood Berkshire Music Center, studied two years in Paris at the Sorbonne with Mlle. Nadia Boulanger, and art at Chicago Art Institute. **Interests, talents:** Composition performed on WNYC radio, won Gold Medal in composition. Innovated an economic theory entitled "Horizontal Economics." **Writings and awards:** Listed in "Who's Who in Poetry, Who's Who in US Writers, Editors, and Poets," recipient of 3 Golden Poet Award Trophies and 26 Certificates of Merit. Wrote speeches for NY Human Rights Forum of Mayor Beeme and President Carter's Economic Conference Forum. Provided input on the economy to GAF and and Ford Motor Co. Participated in negotiations for Viet Nam POWs, Paris Peace '73, UN Mideast Resolution '67, Iranian hostage return '79 and Camp David policies. **Thoughts and comments:** My poetry is generally abstract impressionist "nonfiction." Most is written to record and depict issues of the day. Many of the themes involve actual proposals for the government, churches and universities.

BERKSON, EDITH. Education: Three years in school of acting in Germany; a high school diploma earned in one year in America, then college to study English, business and art. Member California State Poetry Society. **Writings:** Pen name, Jackie Berkson. Has written essays and one short story. Author of 26 poems, eight published: four in The World of Poetry, all of which received Honorable Mention and four in The People's Bible. In 1985 she received "The Golden Poet Award" in in 1986 "The Silver Poet Award." **Comments:** "I want to write my poems according to the world around me—what I see—with added wisdom of my own. I write about the fate of others but add my imagination, stepping into their shoes."

BERMAN, SONJA J. Education: Walter Panas High School, Peekskill, NY, with an interdisciplinary major in Psychology and English. **Occupation:** Educational assistant in New York City. **Interests:** The theatre, creative writing, art and singing. She is illustrating for her children's book at Glen Art Studio and doing live drawings for her poetry book. **Writings:** Wrote a poem for her college newspaper and wrote stories during her school years, receiving first place and an honorable mention. Has had several poems published in newspapers. **Comments:** "I like to portray characterization, feeling and sometimes a moral issue in my writing. My poetry shows a lot of images."

BISHOP, BERNICE CONEY. High School and 3 years at University of Georgia. Member Epilepsy Association of America, AARP, NCO Organizations. Formerly member of U.S. Navy Waves, National Geographic and Smithsonian Institute. **Occupation:** Retired office manager and bookkeeper. **Interests:** Has a prayer ministry; writes inspirational sermonettes, poems and songs; sings and plays the guitar and keyboard. A gourmet cook, she has won First Place in various local cooking contests. **Writings and Awards:** Golden Poet Award, 1988; poem to appear in Golden Treasury of Great Poets, Treasured Book of Poems and "You Can Depend on God" in Many Voices/Many Lands, The Poetry Center. Earned three Honorable Mentions from World of Poetry and appears in Who's Who of American Poets. **Comments:** "My poems are mostly from personal experience, both my own and the many for whom I pray daily for God's healing. Also, I have written about my childhood as 'railroad brat' on the Southern Railroad, also about memories and inspiration given me by my late grandmother, Hazel Miller Sonders, who instilled a love of reading and learning and gave me my religious beliefs. I have learned to channel my depression due to epilepsy into songs, poetry and music. I have 3 wonderful sons and 11 grandchildren who inspire many of my poems, and a wonderful and supportive husband."

BRADY, ADRIENNE. Education: B.A. Honors Degree in English/History at London University; M.A. in Creative Writing from Lancaster University. **Occupation:** Currently living and working in Singapore as a Lecturer in English Literature. Writings include poems in a variety of Anthologies and magazines. Edited "Teaching Anthology of Poetry" published in Singapore in 1988. **Interests:** photography, reading, travel and water sports. First Place Prize Winner in The Poetry Center's Spring 1988 Contest.

BREWER, CHARLES EDGAR. Education: A senior at Madison Plains High School, Sedalia, Ohio. Member of school newspaper staff. Membership in the Antioch Church Kingdom Seekers. **Interests:** Involved in the school's show choir, Quintessence; secretary of church youth group. Enjoys playing the piano and singing. **Writings:** Has written short stories, skits, is working on a book but enjoys writing poetry best. No awards but has had works published in magazines and is well-known as a writer in his school. **Comments:** "I know that I could not have written one word on my paper if it weren't for God being there guiding my hand. He is the true author. I am His tool. I really hope to succeed in my writing. I love writing more than anything...if it is God's will then some day I would like to be a distinguished author."

CAMPLESE, VIRGINIA A., R.N. 3 Year diploma, St. Joseph's Hospital School of Nursing, Philadelphia, PA (1973); A.A., St. Petersburg Junior College, FL (1981; B.S. in Nursing with minor in Anthropology, University of South Florida, Tampa, FL (1984. **Occupation:** 15 years of nursing, IV Team and Recovery Room. **Interests:** anthropology, metaphysics, writing, macrame. **Writings:** Various types of poetry, children's stories, and metaphysical writings. Would like to write for professional nursing journals. **Comments:** "Poetry is a great outlet for pent-up emotions. I started writing it when I was a teenager. It should convey great feeling touching the reader to the depth of his soul. Poetry gives one versatility in freedom of expression."

CABRINETY, PATRICIA ANN BUTLER. Born: Earlville, New York, September 4, 1932. **Married:** Lawrence Paul Cabrinety, August 20, 1955. Three Children: Linda Anne, Margaret Marie and Stephen Michael. **Education:** B.S. in Elementary Education and Music from University of the State of New York at Potsdam. **Career:** Music teacher and first grade school teacher in New York, 1948-56. Owner of music studios in Pennsylvania, 1960-1979. President of computer software firm and poet/illustrator in Minnesota, 1981 to present. **Interests:** Photography, philately and "love of Nature." **Memberships:** 1974-1976 gifted children's program advisor, Penn. 1979-80, gifted children's program consultant, New Hampshire. 1982-84 Minnesota Academy of Science consultant. **Awards:** Recipient of many awards and commendations, including Who's Who in Poetry 1986, Golden Poet Award for 1985, 1986 and 1987, Who's Who in Professional and Executive Women 1987, World Who's Who of Women (ninth edition), Cambridge, England; Who's Who in American Women, 15th and 16th editions; Who's Who in U.S. Writers, Editors and Poets (Second Edition); Who's Who in the East (Marquis 22nd Edition), Who's Who in the World (Marquis 9th Edition); 2,000 Notable American Women (First Edition). **Creative Works:** Composed sheet music titled "Paulett Fry" (Published 1965) and "Mi Cazone" (published 1983). Invented "Piano Micro" in 1979. Published total of 96 poems and 43 illustrations.

CARROLL, JOHN MICHAEL. Preferred not to publish personal biographical data and whimsically commented: "My interests include thinking about time (and watching Dr. Who). I want to be truly alive and to write a modern epic poem."

CASEY, BYRON C. Education: In addition to high school, he has spent time in Service Schools in U.S. Air Force. Associated with musical group that includes instructors from the music department at South Plains College in Levelland, Texas. Member and Vice-Commander of the South Plains Bashas of CBI/VA, a veterans' organization in Lubbock, Texas. **Occupation and interests:** A licensed airplane pilot and licensed real estate broker. Has traveled in 49 states and 15 foreign countries. A musician since boyhood, he has performed from church socials to nightclubs. His hobbies include growing a backyard garden and he is active in men's Bible groups. **Writings:** He has written poems and several songs; has won first prize in several contests and received a certificate of appreciation from a cruise ship for performances as a vocalist. **Comments:** "I write poems because of the pleasure I get from it. Writing seems a sort of outlet for my feelings."

CASVELLYN, TATJANA S. Education: Sheldon High School graduate, Eugene, Oregon. Particularly enjoys yacht racing and sailing. **Occupation:** graphic artist and poet. **Writings:** poetry and prose. Pen name, Tatjana S. Casvellyn. **Comments:** "My major goal is to be a model and fashion designer. Creative writing is a minor goal. I am rather a symbolic, visual writer. My poetry is mainly comprised of my experiences and about people I know. It portrays a part of my personality and how I see the drama of the world as it is. I try to make it absolutely original. I like to create imagery...to retain the magic. Writing poetry is like experimenting. I always go for the experiment and the result perhaps, but I never draw the inference. I leave that to the people who read my poems because, in a sense, I'm as much in the dark as anybody else is."

CENTANO, JESSIE. Education: Attended Grand Rapids Jr. College, Graduate of Holland High School. **Occupation:** Employed by the Nabisco Company. **Interests:** Bowling and tends to her movie collection. **Writings:** Has had poems published by American Poetry Association, Soft Connections, Green Valley, Yes Press and Suwannee. She has had short stories published both by Dick Starr and Carlton Press. **Comments:** "Writing poetry is more than a job or putting a lot of words together. It's an art. Poems are created as a way of satisfying one's personal desire. I have as a goal the writing of at least one hundred poems."

CUEDEK, JESSIE FAULKNER. Recently retired from NYC Civil Service. Other occupations include electronic and watch inspections and stock and disbursement clerk for airlines. **Interests:** Gardening, music, writing and painting—both house and art. Has three grandchildren and a Sheltie. **Comments:** "I've enjoyed writing since I was 10 years old. I usually write several poems a day, getting my ideas from newspapers, magazines, conversation and even TV. What else is there? Well, I'm always willing to find out."

DALEY, SHARON MILLER. Raised in Upstate New York in the foothills of the Adirondacks, where she learned to experience God in nature. As wife and mother, she feels a compelling responsibility to give something beneficial to her community, church, family and society in general. Through her daily activities as homemaker, piano teacher, church organist and avid Bible student, she seeks to express in a quiet and loving way the values of the Christian faith upon which she centers her life. **Comments:** "Through the art of poetry and the art of music, I seek to reveal basic spiritual values and to elicit guidance for positive living."

DAVIS, KENNETH M. Education: High school graduate, Flushing, NY. Course in air-conditioning and refrigeration, Apex Technical, NY and in television studio production and operation, Television Studio School of NY. **Interests:** Sports—basketball, handball, martial arts; singing, dancing, teaching, mechanics, audio-visual dubbing, editing and production, traveling, writing and religion. **Comments:** "I am writing two books: one a collection of my own poetry, the other based on theology, stressing spiritual and uplifting messages. If all I ever achieve is the creating of a wonder feeling within a person from having read my material, that alone will be rewarding to me. However, I welcome any other benefits that can be gained."

DEVINE, ARLENE PEARL. Education: High school graduate. **Occupation:** Seamstress. Mother of two. **Interests, talents:** enjoys playing the piano, writing poetry, drawing. Likes gardening, cooking and is a Memorial Hospital Service League Volunteer. **Writings:** Poetry and prose. American Poetry Association, Poetry of Life, Poetry Shell, Monterey, California. **Awards:** Golden Poet Award, 1985, '86, '87, '88. **Comments:** "I would like to write a book of poems. I hear and see so much beauty in this world that it overwhelms me. My love for music, I believe, is the reason why I write poems using rhyme and meter and I hope that my poems paint pictures with vibrant images. Poets and artists, I think, see with their minds, listen with their hearts and feel with their souls."

DRETA, DAME LJERKA. Self-taught, she is Consultant Management and Perspective. **Interests:** Life; The Reality of One. Member of 5-Star Music Masters of Boston. **Writings:** Theme of many are "Another Shore." **Comments:** "Welcome to you whom I know, your voice was heard, you are home."

ESTRELLA, JOHN D. C. Education: Los Angeles College of Business, B.A. Degree, L. A. University, Counselor and Computers; Theatrical Arts in Pasadena, CA. **Occupation:** Volunteer at various Private and Veterans Administration Hospitals, writes Newsletters at VFW Posts, Fleet Reserve Assoc., and many churches. **Pen Name:** Jonathan De Starr. Is a disabled Amvet with 8 years in U.S. Army and Navy. On USS HOPE Hospital Ship for 2 months. **Writings:** A variety of writings for Young Publications, Essay for Amateur Writers Journal Publications and essays and poetry for Veteran's Voices Publications. **Awards:** Laureate Award in 1985 from U.A.P.A.A. **Comments:** "I believe poetry can be a comfort in idle hours even in bed and uplifts my moods. Writing and typing helps me out of the bog of helplessness and despair. I write poetry and short stories and get them published...a reward in itself. It is in us to try for perfection, what a blessing from God. Poetry is the voice of the spirit, telling what is important to humans in times of trouble and disappointment. I love words and the subtleties of communication and I thank my God for creating people on earth as peacemakers. Amen."

FIELDS, MARY. Education: High School and nurse's training. **Occupation:** A professional nurse licensed in Illinois. Married, she has three children, 15, 12 and 8. **Interests:** A student of the martial arts, her style is American Ken Po. It is difficult but she enjoys the constant challenge. **Writings:** Has written many poems for greeting card companies. This is her first poem to be accepted for publication by a Poetry Association. **Comments:** "I like many kinds of poems—sad, happy, humorous, love. But my favorite by far is melancholy poems. That is why Edgar Allan Poe is one of my favorite poets."

FLEMING, ERIC LEE. Resident of Auburn, California. **Occupation:** Experienced in both retail and newspaper fields. **Other Interests:** Photography, long drives, people-watching, and collecting "almost anything": coins, pins, posters, postcards, etc. **Other Writings:** Has completed two children's books which he hopes to see published someday. **Comments:** "My poetry expresses my feelings about life. I usually get the idea for a poem after a specific personal experience which I want to share with others."

FROST, LINDA. Education: Graduate in Liberal Arts from Boston University. Earned Master's Degree in psychology and pastoral counseling. **Occupation:** Writing. Before multiple sclerosis put her in a wheel chair in a nursing home, she was interested in sports. **Pen name:** Jackie. **Writings:** Finishing a book, "No Child in Isolation," dealing with play therapy with a seven year old. A poem published in Who's Who in Poetry in the Northeast. **Comments:** "My dream is to make poetry exciting, full of life, vibrant; to get the reader to feel as I felt when I wrote. Some of my poetry is religious; some not in as much as nature and the natural world turn me on."

GARDNER, WANDA C. Education: Degree in Education. Member of National Association for Development of Gifted and Talented; Center for Anthropological Studies (a research foundation). **Occupation:** Writer, artist, homemaker (mother of three), student (presently seeking degree in biochemistry), teacher. **Hobbies:** painting, reading, horseback riding, hiking. **Writings:** Has had several articles and poems published.

GARDNER-WIMETT, GLENNA. Education and Associations: Belongs to the Poetry Society of New Hampshire, Creative Enterprises International Society for the Advancement of Poetry, and New Horizons Poetry Club. **Occupation:** Bookkeeper at B & R's Garage, a business owned and operated by herself and her husband. **Interests:** Knitting, crocheting, growing house plants, antique collecting, and researching her family history. **Writings:** Won Grand Prize of $350 in Creative Enterprises Contest for Poetry, Fall, 1987; a First and Third Prize from the Poet's Review Contests in 1988. Has won 4th, 5th, and many Honorable Mentions in other contests. Has sold three articles to Creative Enterprises and been published in their magazine "Write On. **Comments:** "Poetry is my greatest love outside of my family and I will be writing my poetry until the day I die, hoping to reach many hearts and souls along the way. **Goals:** I want to continue to give poetry presentations in local schools, encouraging and inspiring many young poets; to be published in many anthologies; and to sell some of my poetic works."

GAVAC, DONNA B. Education: M.A. and Ph.D., University of Michigan (History) and University of Portland (Educational Administration). **Occupation:** Writer and Educator. Served as Commissioner for Accreditation, Northwestern Schools, 1972-1978. **Memberships:** National Writers Club; American Historical Association (life member); Medieval Academy of America (life member); Renaissance Society of America; Alaska Historical Society; Cook Inlet Historical Association. **Professional Credits:** Who's Who in United States Writers, Editors and Poets, 1988; Directory of International Biography, 1982; Community Leaders of America, 1981; World Who's Who of Women in Education, 1978; Directory of American Scholars (Vol. I: History), 4th Edition. **Other Interests:** Hiking and Music; "major interests are family and education." **Writings:** University text on high school social studies teaching; TV script "Homemaker in History" series; Gresham Lectures on English Education; plus many studies on Erasmus, Pope Pius II, School Accreditation, Personal/Business Planning, Education of Women. **Comments:** "With children now independent and professional responsibilities lightened, I want to create and share thoughts on personal growth and belief; experience of the Far north; and continuities in human life I observe in historical records."

GIBSON, COLLEEN. Education: Bethany Nazarene College, Bethany, OK; Cal State, Fullerton, CA; Saddleback College, Mission Viejo, CA and Oklahoma City University. Has completed requirements for B.A. in Art and B.S. in psychology. **Occupation:** 20 years business experience in corporate finance, administration and writing for corporate publications. In recent years interests have become more creative. Has researched the relationship between mind and matter and is currently preparing a manuscript reporting the results. Talents include painting in oil and she has exhibited her work at John Wayne Tennis Club, Bel Aire Country Club and private corporations. **Writings:** In addition to writing poetry, she writes essays, articles, short stories and has written one play. She hopes to publish the book on which she is currently working under her maiden name, Colleen Struble. **Comments:** "I write poetry about things most meaningful to my life. In doing so I savor the experiences and reflect upon many lessons learned."

GOLDEN, CARLA. Education: Has attended schools of various levels in many places. Has been a good student but believes the most important things she's learned are about people, their actions, beliefs and emotions. **Occupation:** An interior communications electrician in the U.S. Navy, stationed at Naval Air Station, Keflavik, Iceland. **Writings:** This is her first published poem which she chose to write because she wished to think how she could change things that might not be as she wished them to be. **Comments:** "Writing has always been an interest of mine. Poetry took a little longer. Sometimes it's hard for me to explain my feelings, difficult to find the words, so I write about them and soon I find the reasons for them. I hope by putting them on paper others will benefit also."

GOODENOUGH, JUNE. Pen Name: Ricci. **Education:** B.A. in English from Mansfield University in Pennsylvania. Completed two years graduate work in Physical Education at East Stroudsburg University, Pennsylvania. Plus Air Command Courses, Staff Courses and Air Force Squadron Officers School. **Occupation:** Aircraft Maintenance Officer, U.S. Air Force (9-year veteran). Also partner in TCG Limited, a firm devoted to quarter horse performance. **Other Interests:** Volleyball, basketball and science fiction. **Writings:** Poems accepted by national and regional publications, including The Poetry Press, The New York Poetry Foundation, The Cambridge Collection and The Alcona County Review. Also published technical articles in The SAC Management Review. **Comments:** "The best poetry is an outpouring of the poet's inner feelings. I write for myself so I can be totally honest—but I share my poetry with others to let them know someone else has the same feelings...that they are not alone."

GOODWIN, REGINALD L. Education: Bachelor of Science, Engineering, Physics, North Carolina A & T State University, Greensboro, NC, 1984. Society of Physics Students, Alpha Psi Fraternity Inc., Service Schools. **Occupation:** Presently a Communications Officer in the USAF. At end of tour, he will attend graduate school at the University of Texas, majoring in physics. Hobbies are writing poetry and short stories, the martial arts. **Writings:** "The Highest Form of Madness," "Barbarian," dedicated to Black College Men, "Voices in the Wind," 1984, "Muse in Gluon," in Best New Poets of 1987. **Comments:** "This is the real me, the me that the cults and rites of manhood will not allow me to show with a degree of comfort. This is a page from my diary. With the changing attitudes on relationships, I hope to share more pages with you."

HANNING, ROSANNA. Occupation: Interior decorator, writer and counselor. Member Poetry Society of Oklahoma and National Writers' Association. **Writings:** "Poems for Every Mood," 1958 published by Greenwich Book Co.; "Poems for Fact and Fantasy," 1968 published by Naylor Book Publishing Co. The National Library of Poetry. Also listed in International Who's Who in Poetry, 1970-71. Is presently completing "Love Songs," her third publication.

HERRING, JAMES B. Education: High School and College. A.A., Kemper Military School and College. **Occupation:** Farming. About to add horses as well. **Interests:** Photography, reading, travel, collecting books. **Comments:** "I recently celebrated my twenty-fifth birthday, and I realized then that wisdom doesn't just come to you as you grow older. You think about things and your opinions change, as do you. And as will my poetry."

HRABCAK, VIRGINIA FREYTES. Education: High school graduate plus a secretarial course and experience to three years of college. **Associations:** Mental health groups, congregation members and neighbors. **Interests:** Writing, drawing, sewing and crocheting, bird watching, gardening, Bible reading and magazines. Scientific magazines a favorite. **Writing:** Prose, short stories and poems. Also writes lyrics for music and ballads. None submitted for publication. Pen Name is maiden name written backwards: Ainigriv Setyerf. **Comments:** "Most of my poems are based on true happenings, keen observation of nature and scriptures of the Bible which emphasize the time we are living. My general theme: World Around Us." **Goal:** "To be a published story author or poet."

HUTCHINGS, GAIL. Native of Utah. **Education:** Holds several certificates in professional selling, plus degree in self-defense. Continuing advanced studies in field of cosmetics to keep abreast of new product developments as well as makeup and fashion techniques. **Occupation:** Manager and consultant for several lines of cosmetics. **Other Interests:** Modeling, tennis, cooking and exchanging thoughts and ideas with other people. **Writings:** Have "written and shared so much poetry and prose over the years, I can't recall them all." Last published poem appeared in First Edition of "Many Voices/Many Lands" anthology. **Comments:** "My goal is to grasp the reader's thoughts and hold them prisoner to mine."

JACKSON, ROXANN. Education: B.A. in Psychology. Postgraduate work in addictions. **Occupation:** State certified and licensed Abuse Therapist, Family therapist and Accupressure Therapist. Clinical supervisor at alcohol/drug outpatient services. Member of Chemical Dependency Professionals of Washington State and other national and state professional associations. **Interests:** fishing, boating, plays, camping. **Talents and Hobbies:** dancing, ballet, oil painting, yoga and gourmet cooking. **Writings:** Has written many technical papers on the treatment of addiction, treating family of the addict and treating the adult child of a dysfunctional family. The poem appearing in this volume is her first poem. **Pen name:** Roxann Ruth Jackson. **Comments:** "I wrote this poem to my fiance as testimony of his love for me. My goals are to write non-fiction, self-help books for recovering families and, perhaps, a book of their poems."

JOHNSON, BRETT. Education: High school and continuous personal research. **Occupation:** pressman, second class. **Hobbies:** book collecting, reading and mountain climbing. **Writings:** Has written and published one book, Cinema Inferno,, Eve Star Publishing, 1988. **Pen name:** Broken Star, chosen for a star for every broken heart. **Comments:** "My poetry is and always has been. I do not know its origins nor do I understand it. My goal is to explore infinity, thus an eternal quest for immortality."

JONES-ROGERS, JOYCE. Education: Presently attends college working for a double major as a clinical psychologist and for a CPA degree in business. **Occupation:** Accounting Manager for Vitamins Mfg. and student. **Interests:** music, songwriting, writing poetry; collects clowns and Elvis Presley memorabilia, plays keyboard and sings in '50's and '60's country and country-rock band. **Writings:** Has won the Golden Poet Award for 1987 and 1988. "Know What?," "Forever," "Here's to your memories too."

KELLEY, WIN. Education: B.A. Pacific University, Oregon, M.Ed. University of Oregon, Ed.D. University of Southern California. **Associations:** Dramatists' Guild, Authors' League of America, Speech Communication Assoc., American Forensics Assoc., Screen Actors Guild, Actor's Equity Assoc., Veterans of Foreign Wars. **Occupation:** Actor, writer, emeritus professor of Communicative Arts, Citrus College, CA; former drama columnist, Talent Review Magazine; has performed on radio, stage, film and TV. **Interests:** Enjoys singing, oil painting, golf and other sports, arts and crafts. Collects plates, coins, stamps and writes songs. **Writings:** Waiilatpu (The Place of Rye Grass) pageant play, 1953; The Art of Public Address (book), 1962; Teaching in the Community College (book), 1969; Breaking the Barriers in Public Speaking (book), 1978; poetry: "Paradise Revisited," 1962 and others. Mark Twain Award, 1953; George Washington Honor Medal, 1973; D.A.R. Medal of Honor, 1981; second prize in National Play Contest for "Fades of Memory," autobiography, self-published in 1982. **Comments:** "I love classical poetry and tend to write traditional kinds. Poetry, like all writing, should be clear for the best communication. Hidden meanings tend to remain hidden, tend to confuse. I'm inspired by spiritual and philosophical aspects of my experiences, serious or light in treatment. I've spent years writing plays with only modest success. I've written poetry since I was ten years old. Now I'd like to share some of it with others by means of national publication. As a retired teacher, I have the time, and I trust I may have the necessary talent."

KNOWLES, VIOLET D. Resident of Nassau, Bahamas. **Occupation:** Co-founder and coordinator of Knowles Industries, a major, family-operated construction company. **Other Interests:** Writing and performing plays, song writing (especially lyrics for gospel music), gourmet cooking and gardening. Also experienced organizer of special social functions. **Honors and Credits:** Original recipes published in an American cookbook; several Honorable Mentions in poetry, including three Golden Awards. **Goals:** To become a famous poet, and to publish a collection of my poems in book form. **Comments:** "My inspiration comes from the heart; very early in the quiet morning hours, or sometimes while I am just driving along or talking to someone, God will inspire me to create a poem on a specific topic. My gift for expressing familiar thoughts, in addition to my Christian faith, has brought me much satisfaction in life. I have learned through day-to-day living to put God at the head of my life and to put my trust in Him in all things."

KOZAK, DANIEL. Education: Attended Public Schools and Maritime Service Training in New York. Writing courses at Empire State College. **Associations:** U.S. Reserve Officers Assoc., N.Y. Coast Guard; NYC Civil Service Retirees Assoc., Council of American Master Mariners, Pulaski Assoc., N.Y. Fire Department, Ukrainian National Assoc., American Military Retirees Assoc. and others. **Occupation:** Long varied career in Civilian and Military Reserve—Maritime. Rose from apprentice seaman to Civil Service Captain. Retired in 1986. Also served in 71st Infantry Guard as drill instructor, served in U.S. Coast Guard Reserve as Boatswain's Mate Curriculum Instructor, Executive and Intelligence Officer. Is now serving in U.S. Coast Guard Maritime Reserve. **Interests:** Deer hunting, singing and acting. **Writings:** 60,000 word novel, 'In a Safe Harbor,' as yet unpublished; a story published in Firehouse Magazine is currently used as a case study in marine fire rescue training in the New York area. Two writings awaiting publication are: 'Girl In The River' and an article: 'Forced Famine: Communist Tool of Terror.' **Comments:** "I find writing poetry very gratifying, in that I feel I can convey some significant thoughts and opinions in a pleasant entertaining way. I've written some 30 poems on subjects of health, defense, sorrow, criticism, age and patriotism. My immediate goal is to write 100 poems and become an American Taras Shevchenko, an internationally acclaimed 19th century Poet."

KRONER, LUCILLE M. Education: UCLA, Westwood, CA; Santa Monica City College, Santa Monica, CA. **Occupation:** Retired contract administrator. Her talents are voice, writing and painting and her hobbies incorporate these talents. **Writing:** Much poetry—"Elegos," "The Loss," "Mother," etc. She has received more than twenty-five awards and has been published a number of times. **Comments:** "I write about a variety of subjects, i.e. people, religion, the past, space, the seasons. I write as I am inspired and love every minute of it! My present goal is to complete a major work I am working on."

KUCHARAS, THELMA mb. Education: A high school graduate. **Occupation:** Does a radio show called Astrologically Speaking and has a real estate broker's license. She is also an artist and owns a one-room schoolhouse which she uses as a studio. **Writings:** "Psychic Exposure" is her first published poem. Shares her poetry with others by including a copy with a birthday gift. **Pen name:** mb. **Comments:** "I've used poetry as a release and expression of my ultimate feelings for people and God's reations. I wrote my first poem when I was seven and haven't stopped writing since then—it's a lifestyle for me."

LAGMAY, JOSE D. Pen Name: Pempe. Native of Philippines; naturalized citizen of U.S., 1972. **Education:** Bachelor of Science from the Philippine College of Criminology, Manila, Philippines. **Occupation:** Provider Services Assistant, Blue Cross of California. **Other Interests:** Singing and listening to gospel music; playing the guitar and ukulele; vegetable gardening. Also an "avid fan" of basketball (playing and watching). **Memberships:** Outstanding member of National Notary Association. **Honors and Credits:** Received gold medal for college graduation thesis, "Scientific Firearms Investigation." Held Editor positions with newspapers in both high school and college. **Comments:** "I write poetry for fun, but, more importantly, I am prodded by a desire to motivate and inspire my fellow man. My passion for poetry is truly indescribable; my writing expresses my ideals and aspirations—as well as my wisdom. My poetry is, therefore, one person's method of crystallizing his noblest feelings of love for his fellow human beings."

LAIR, HERBERT F. Education: GED College Level. **Occupation:** Retired from U.S. Government and Air Force, Alaska Air National Guard. Associated with the Washington State Head Injury Association and National Head Injury Foundation. **Interests:** Sports, Writing, Genealogy. Has traced his family's history back to the year 1543. Is presently working on his first novel. **Comments:** "I currently write my poetry, not for fame or fortune, but as a legacy for my children and grandchildren. I now have 4 with a 5th grandchild expected around Christmas."

LEIMONAS, MARYBELLE. Education: Bachelor of Social Work from Florida State University in 1967. She is a social worker and a member of the National Association of Social Workers. **Interests:** reading, writing haiku, animals and collecting postcards. **Writings:** A Haiku, "To My Favorite Seagull" to be published in 1988 in an Anthology of American Poems. **Comments:** "My poem in this edition of *Many Voices/Many Lands* was inspired by a comment from a friend on watching raccoons' habit of looking at the sky when eating bread: 'He's the Poet!' "

MANAV, VIMAL C. Education: Studies in Financial Management at Virginia University, Virginia. **Occupation:** Banker, now retired. **Interests and Associations:** Member of several professional and cultural associations, including Gita Bhawan (for Oriental Theosophists), Ayurved Club of India, and Authors Guild of India. **Credits:** Established Hindi Poet, with four published collections of poetry to date: Shakshatkar, Kagaz Ke Phool, Utpreksha and Abhyudgar. Has also translated many of these poems into English for publication in American magazines and anthologies. **Awards:** Winner of several awards and prizes for poetry, both in India and the United States. These include a Golden Poet award, 1987, and an Excellence in Poetry Award, 1988. **Comments:** "I compose verse about true love, moral beauty and natural charms as experienced in day-to-day life. 'Unscathed romance' is one of my specialties."

MAY, MARLENE. Education: Graduated Toms River High School, New Jersey. Studying to become a journeyman minister in metaphysics. **Occupation:** Homemaker and waitress. Main interest is in the study of subconscious awareness. Hobbies are dancing and music. **Writings:** "A Balanced Storm," "Your Justification and Mine," "Games," "Forever Stands" and others published in various anthologies. **Comments:** "I have always found it easier to express my feelings in writing; each of my poems/stories have evolved from emotions that were stirred from an experience in my life. My goal is to publish my own book of poetry. Not only so others will be able to relate their feelings through my poetry, but also so my children in later years will be able to see the depth of their mother."

McCLURG, DIANE C. Education: High school diploma (1968); college and university of life—20 years. **Associations:** Order of Rainbow Girls; member, First Christian Church for 35 years. **Interests and hobbies:** writing, creative cooking, piano, voice, gardening. **Special talents:** husband classifies her as a world class chef and world's greatest mother. (Pen name: I. D. Clare) **Writings:** Vanity published "Seasonings," a Personal Poetry Collection, 1976; Table-Top published "Recipe Monthly" Newsletter, "Good Nutrition On fixed Income." **Comments:** "Poetry is sentimental, mostly written to cheer those in low spirits. Frequently time myself when writing poems—'Missing You' took 13→ minutes. Currently working on a fact-based novel about obstetrical and judicial indifference and one victim! Me."

MEADE, LEE COOPER. Education: After high school special classes in art, music and cosmetology. **Interests:** piano, oil painting, dancing, writing and body building. **Writings:** "Song," "To Do It All Over Again." Nashville, TN. contract for recording with demo now in process for Nashville 50-50. Co-writers: Will Gentry, composer; Lee Cooper Meade, lyricist. "Once In My Life," "Star-Crossed," "88," "Thank You, Friend," "Remembering," "All Our Love" and many more. **Comments:** "Writing is one of my favorite professions, as is painting. I feel divinely inspired when I write and paint. I believe that once a writer is published, he has achieved immortality and that his work lives on forever."

MITCHELL, ENID. Education: Graduate of North High School. Attended Ohio State Univ. **Member:** The Humane Society of the United States. **Occupation:** Writer-poet. **Interests:** All the creative arts, especially writing and theatre; loves animals and supports animal welfare organizations. Hobbies are photography, reading and listening to music. **Writings:** Compiled and edited her mother's book: "Gift from My Mother" by Hazel Robertson Mitchell. Has had poetry published in American Poetry Association Anthologies, Scimitar and Song. World of Poetry, Golden Poet Award; Prize for "Challenger's 7"—Poetry Press. Biography in Who's Who in U.S. Writers, Editors and Poets, 1988. **Comments:** "I have just completed an epilogue for "Gift from My Mother." Also a collection of Mother Poems: "A Star in Your Hand." My poetry is metaphysical presenting the themes of God Within and the proof of life after death. "A Psychic Journal" describes Spirit communication between me and my mother, who is my Soul's companion, my best friend, my other self, and to her I dedicate my life and my work."

MITCHELL, STEVEN L. Pen Name: Steven Carol. **Education:** College student at present. Holds degree in Automotive Technology from Danville Area Community College. **Interests:** "Poems are my first love, but from time to time I also write short stories for my son Patrick." **Comments:** "I love to write. My poems are made of true feelings; every word comes from within. If anyone asks, I would say **that** is the secret of writing—you have to **feel** what you write. When you write, you've created something new, knowing that a part of you will live long after you've taken your last breath. All who read what you have written will forever have you in their memory."

MONESSON, HARRY S. Education: Continued studying toward graduation from the school of life. **Occupation:** Blueberry grower, archaeologist, mechanic, author and writer. **Writings:** Author of "Knibblers in the Sand" and "Sand Sharks in the Pines" which includes regional poetry of the New Jersey Pinelands, published 1988. Other poems include "Ye Old Bog Gate," "No Sech Hanimal," "A Bog Digging Man." **Comments:** "All things inspire. The urge to turn them into words comes in a rush. Themes go in all directions...everything from the enigmas of time, destiny and universe to poetic humor and political satire."

MUEHLECK, CHANCE. Education: Attended North Bay Marin High School and the College of Marin as a drama major. A student who enjoys writing, acting and drawing...hoping for an artistic career in the future which will combine these talents. **Writings:** Has been writing from an early age, experimenting with many styles and forms: books, short stories, non-fiction, and most recently, plays and poetry. **Comments:** "Poetry, as well as any art form, can give us a connection with our humanity so that we can truly live a meaningful existence. That is the best I can hope for in my creative expression."

NUNES-VENDETTE, BONNIE. Education: High school graduate, University of Connecticut. **Interests and Talents:** Loves Poetry and writes lyrics for songs as well as poems. **Comments:** "Originally my poems were written for my eyes only. Family and friends found out about my writings and encouraged me to get them published."

NECAISE, KEITH. Resident of Theodore, Alabama. **Writings:** Currently working on a collection of poems aimed at publication. Also interested in songwriting. Major creative goal, however, is to write and sell horror novels with a strong emphasis on realism. **Comments:** "My poetry reflects my personality and my attitudes toward life. I enjoy surprises—and my poems change with my moods: some are funny, some are tense, some romantic, etc. I feel that a poem should be a novel in 20 lines or less. It should tell a story and make the reader feel something he or she usually wouldn't feel."

NAPOLI, MICHELLE. Education: Presently a student at East Hampton High School in New York. **Interests:** Photography, music, dance and writing. **Writings:** "Brother," "Of what we were discovering," "Nature's Power," "This Night's Lightning." **Comments:** My poetry is a creative and emotional outlet. Through writing I can dream, release anger, work out confusion and express happiness and, at the same time, share these feelings with others.

PADILLA, SOPHIE. Education: Attended Sacramento High School and graduated from Mouler's Barber College. Attends poetry class once a week. Married seventeen years, has two daughters and six grandchildren. **Occupation:** Works as health attendant with the elderly in hospitals and home care. **Hobbies:** reading, gardening, writing poetry. **Writings:** Golden Poet Award for "Horse Shoe," World of Poetry, Honorable Mention for "The Hour is Late." Has written religious hymns and a few children's stories. **Comments:** "Many of my best poems were written so quickly, I wasn't sure if they were good...I pray to be able to write children's stories to bring joy, laughter, adventure and surprises to children everywhere."

PIERREUSE, EMMANUEL. Education: College; Ecole Normale de Lille, France. **Occupation:** Taught in elementary and kindergarten schools in Dunkerque, N. France, 1980-86. A member of San Diego Folk Song Society and San Diego Mandolin Society. **Writings:** "Atheistic Prayer for the Earth"; Many Voices/Many Lands, Fall, 1987. "Loneliness," 5th place, American Poetry Association, 1987. "The Guru," "Ideals," "Languages," "In the Kitchen of My Mind," "Marcel," "Portrait of an Administrator." Has been published in "Best New Poets of 1987." **Comments:** "I write about love and friendship and other feelings like any poet, but I want to give the idea that the world could be better, and to denounce its injustices and the people responsible for them. To me, the poet is more a columnist than a self-centered 'romantic'."

POWELL, WILLIAM. Graduate of Mississippi State University, State College of MS. Member, American Helicopter Society. Retired U.S. Army, served in Vietnam Conflict, 1965-1968. **Occupation:** Graphic designer. Interests include poetry writing, writing children's stories and songs. Hobbies are music, making greeting cards. **Writings:** Poem in National Library of Poetry—semifinalist. **Comments:** "The poem was written while on active duty in Vietnam in 1965. My goal is to become a recognized published author."

RICHARDS, DORIS. Education: College degree with a certificate in the social sciences. **Occupation:** Police Communications Officer, a position she has held for sixteen and one half years. Married, with three children and six grandchildren. Hobbies include reading and crocheting. **Comments:** "I have a habit of keeping notes and a scrapbook, something that I have done for years. It's filled with notes on happenings to my family, friends and co-workers. I hope someday to write a book of poetry, about my life!"

ITSCHE, EFFIE C. JENSON. Education: Bachelor of cience, University of Moorhead, Special Education with minor in music; teacher's certificate in piano, voice and theory, minor in rt, business management, bookkeeping and finance. Graduate of otel and Motel School. **Associations:** Civic and fraternal rganizations. **Occupation:** Office management, selling major ppliances for electrical firm for over forty years. Owned and perated a 17 unit rental apartment building and 40 bed resort. **nterests:** Paints in water color and oil, writes music, active in ivic and fraternal organizations. **Writings:** Has written several ovellas and recorded her father's violin music.

OBINSON, SHARON LEE. Education: Baltimore City and ounty Schools. Graduate of Sherwood High in Montgomery ounty, Maryland. **Occupation:** Mail clerk for the Federal overnment. Received awards at work for ten years service and r outstanding service. **Hobbies and talents:** gardening in ots, sweepstakes and contests. **Writings:** Writes poetry when epressed. **Comments:** "Use such themes as music or situations uch as death in the family or save the animals rights group. Vould like to become a writer."

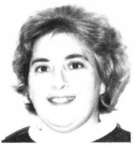

ROSSETTI, ANGELINA COFRANCESCO. Education: B.S. and M.S. degrees, Southern Connecticut State University; Certifiation as an English Teacher and Reading Specialist. **Occupaion:** Editor and Poet. **Memberships:** Poetry Society of Amerca; Academy of American Poets; Connecticut Poetry Society; Poetry Express Club; Southern Connecticut State University Alumni Association. **Honors and Credits:** Award as Outstanding Poet by Hamden Arts Commission; Commendation by Mayor of Hamden for Poetic Achievements; Poet Laureate Certificate and Honorable Mention Award for "Autumn's Final Fade" in international anthology, Many Voices/Many Lands, volume 2; Semi-Finalist in North American Open Poetry Contest. **Writings:** Many notable works, including "The Heart of America" in On The Threshold of a Dream; "Vignettes" and "Jessica" in Poets At Work; "The Plight of the Farmer" in American Poetry Anthology. Other poems in newspapers and magazines, many illustrated by her twin sons. **Comments:** "I am interested in poetry both as an artist and an educator. Employing language varying from simple to complex, I attempt to bring the magic and mystique of poetry to people of all ages and occupations. My work covers a wide range of subjects, and brings to the forefront themes involving conflicts in relationships, love of the land, patriotic themes and also children's poetry."

RUBENSTEIN, SHARON. Education: Two years at Pierce College. **Occupation:** Legal secretary. **Interests:** Reading, sewing. **Writings:** Tom Hendricks, 1975—Those We know (chapbook); The Poet, 1979; Feature poet 1984, 1986; Poetry Today, 1984-85; The Villager, 1981; Broken Streets, 1983-87 (Feature poet 1985, 1987); Prophetic Voices, 1986-87; Fine Arts Press, 1984-87; American Poetry Association, 1986-87; Who's Who in U.S. Writers, Editors and Poets, 1986-87; Certificate from Fine Arts Press for Excellence in Poetry, 1988. **Comments:** "My poetry focuses on youth, lost love, neighborhoods, schools."

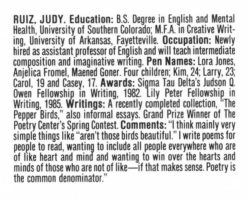

RUIZ, JUDY. Education: B.S. Degree in English and Mental Health, University of Southern Colorado; M.F.A. in Creative Writing, University of Arkansas, Fayetteville. **Occupation:** Newly hired as assistant professor of English and will teach intermediate composition and imaginative writing. **Pen Names:** Lora Jones, Anjelica Fromel, Maened Goner. Four children; Kim, 24; Larry, 23; Carol, 19 and Casey, 17. **Awards:** Sigma Tau Delta's Judson Q. Owen Fellowship in Writing, 1982. Lily Peter Fellowship in Writing, 1985. **Writings:** A recently completed collection, "The Pepper Birds," also informal essays. Grand Prize Winner of The Poetry Center's Spring Contest. **Comments:** "I think mainly very simple things like "aren't those birds beautiful." I write poems for people to read, wanting to include all people everywhere who are of like heart and mind and wanting to win over the hearts and minds of those who are not of like—if that makes sense. Poetry is the common denominator."

SCHAEFER, JACQUELINE. Education: A student at the University of Wisconsin, Eau Claire. **Interests:** As a student has discovered interests in political science and basic philosophy. **Writings:** Poem published in University Literary Magazine, NOTA. **Comments:** "I've always considered myself a fiction writer, yet it is my poetry that gets published. That should tell me something. I'll write about anything, if I can. I hope one day to make my living from writing. I've achieved my first goal, set when I was 15, to be published before I was 22."

SCHRIEFFER, BILL. Native of Chicago, Illinois; born 1965. **Education:** St. Benedict High School, 1983; Oakton Community College, 1986. **Other Interests:** Music and humor. **Memberships:** National Writers Club. **Other Writings:** Presently working on a humorous novella, "The Lost Midnight." **Comments:** "I think there is nothing like the brevity of a poem to get a feeling across...or a theme...or a thought...or a 'slice of life' moment. I try to capture as many angles of life as possible: the light, the heavy, the sad, the hysterical, etc. I feel that no other literary form can deliver such quick, powerful blows to get the thought processes running."

SCOTESE, MELPO DENNIS. Education: Attended Special Programs College at the University of Pennsylvania. Also studied theatre, choreography and ballet with Miriam Davis in Philadelphia. **Occupation:** Freelance artist working with interior design, architectural and fashion design and mural painting. Artistic director of cultural and performing arts at Cedar Brook Farm, New Jersey. **Interests and Talents:** Has taught ethnic dancing to many groups, wrote and directed plays for youth and adult theatre, choreographed musical numbers and swam with water ballet companies. She has appeared on television as a professional model, trained as a swimmer for the Olympics and danced with companies in Philadelphia and New Jersey. Winner of 7 local beauty contests, was one of 10 finalists in Miss Greater Philadelphia contest. Other interests include traveling, shopping for collectibles and a wide interest in the arts. **Writings:** Published in both first and second editions of "Many Voices/Many Lands" anthology, has written several original stage plays that have been performed, including "I'm Right for Right Field," "The Merry Muse," "Ballet of Poetry." Has written feature length movie and is currently working on "Booklet of Poems (Siamese)." **Thoughts and Comments:** "My poems are about cats since they have maintained their dignity through the centuries. They walk with confidence and live without consequence. Their calm is idealistic, as they set out on a path of exploration, glowing with a pretense of innocence. Writing affords the pleasure of unlocking creative treasures within, and through poetry, I find a positive declaration of life!"

SEAGER, STEVEN A. Education: Holds Associate in Arts Degree in Accounting. **Occupation:** Owner of a book store. **Other Interests:** Politics and literature. **Writings:** Collection of works titled "Songs From The Heart" published March, 1988. **Other Credits:** To date, 15 different poems have been accepted by a number of anthologies, including American Poetry Showcase, National Poetry Anthology, New American Poets, Rainbows and Roses, Misty Moonlight and Poetic Voices in America. **Comments:** "Most of my present poetry is concerned with romance and its various emotions of longing, loving, pain, confusion and uncertainties. I plan to continue with these themes, while moving into other areas as well, possibly a work of historical fiction."

SHARON, IDAN. Education: B.A. SUNY, Albany, Medical student at Tel-Aviv University, Sackler School of Medicine, Israel. Second Place Prize Winner in The Poetry Center's Spring 1988 Contest.

STRITTO, ANNA DELLO. Born 1968, Caserta, Italy; now resides in Worcester, Massachusetts. **Education:** Attended Venerini Academy Elementary School and St. Peter-Marian Central Catholic High School. **Writings:** American Poetry Anthology, 1987; On the Threshold of a Dream, 1988; New York Poetry Anthology, 1988; Sparrowgrass Poetry Forum, 1988; Second Edition, "Many Voices/Many Lands," 1988. **Comments:** "I think this great piece of wisdom best sums up my attitude toward my poetry: 'If a man does not keep pace with his companions, perhaps it is because he hears a different drummer. Let him step to the music which he hears, however measured or far away'."

SUMMER, CLODAH G. Resident of San Antonio, Texas. **Education:** Primarily self-taught in early years, with college work in Art, Music and Photography—as well as special studies in Concept-Therapy. "However, life itself is the *real* education; all knowledge resides in our subconscious mind, waiting to be contacted when needed." **Other Interests:** "My curiosity leads me to many interests, including music, art, photography, science, psychology, philosophy and religion." **Honors and Credits:** Has been writing poetry since 1945, and finally started getting recognition in 1985. Received Golden Poet's Award in 1986 for "Cackling Hen," and again in 1987 for "Revolutionary Revelation." **Comments:** "Variety being 'the spice of life,' I aim for a balance of thoughts, from serious to humorous. Humor is very important to help keep people from being too serious. My poem in this anthology, 'Cackling Hen,' is short, but its humorous message helps people smile or laugh a little—which feels so good when it happens. I am a teacher more than a poet, and I must teach to help God evolve humanity to a higher state of consciousness. My knowledge of what God is—scientifically—helps me love the one life in all things, even as I hate the negative aspects. You can't have the positive without the negative pole of electricity. This is the Scientific Age and many details must be updated for mankind to evolve any higher."

SVEHLA, JOHN. Education: High School graduate. Some college courses at Los Angeles City College. **Occupation:** Senior typist/secretary. **Writings:** Poetry (A Small Book "Sun"), Thom Hendricks Associates. 1975 Pigiron Press. 1976: Spafaswap. 1976; Look Quick, 1977; Wind Magazine 1979-1988; Cambric Poetry Projects, 1980-85; Portland Review, 1983; The Poet/The Fine Arts Society, 1979-86/87; Earthwise Literary Calendar, 1983; Fine Arts Press/Anthologies 1983-88; The DeKalb Literary Arts Journal; American Poetry Association's Anthologies, 1985-88; Wide Open Magazine, 1988; Second Edition, Many Voices/Many Lands. **Awards:** California Federation of Chaparral Poets, 1977, Second Prize. Honorable Mention Awards from Pennsylvania Poetry Society, 1977, 1981; Finalist Award Negative Capability, 1986; Honorable Mention, The American Poetry Association, 1987; and Excellence in Poetry Award for Rainbows and Rhapsodies. **Comments:** "I am putting forth a new idiom in nature poetry."

SWANSON, IDA ADELL. Pen Names: Dell Hartzell; Dell Stevens Hartzell. **Education:** B.A. in Education, Western Washington College of Education; Arkansas Teachers College, 1928; Graduate Studies, University of Washington, Seattle, Washington. **Occupation:** Elementary public school teacher, now retired. **Awards:** Certificate of Appreciation, Jefferson County Public Schools, Washington, 1966; Merit Citations, 1983-84, Ladies Auxiliary to the Veterans of Foreign Wars of the U.S.; Presidential Achievement Award, Republican Party, 1987. **Comments:** "I published my first poem in the Arkansas Gazette in 1935. I write poems whenever an event or idea strikes me as having good poetic possibilities."

WELLS, CARRIE M. Pen Names: Marie, Maria, Blackdiamond and LadyFree. **Education:** Currently a junior at Kirkman Technical High School. Also enrolled in writing correspondence course. **Other Writings:** Has completed several short stories and hopes to have them published "one day." **Comments:** "I have completed over 100 poems. One of my goals is to have a complete book of my poems published one day."

WENZEL, EVELYN M. Education: Graduate South River High School, South River, NJ. **Occupation:** Working as live-in Nannie; cook-assistant and manager at Carmelite and St. Francis Retreat Houses in Illinois. Enjoys reading, writing, travel, crossword puzzles, nature, music, crocheting, cooking. **Writings:** Poems published in various anthologies and listed in 1988 Who's Who in U.S. Writers, Editors and Poets. **Comments:** "I've always loved writing but only recently have been inspired to share with others. I'm thrilled to see my poems in print and blessed to share them."

WILLIAMSON, LORI. Education: College degrees in business and writing. Plus extensive study and performing experience in the fields of dance, choreography and drama. **Occupation:** Public relations and professional sales endeavors. **Other Interests:** Modeling, photography and "all the theatrical arts." **Honors and Credits:** Many national awards in poetry; district, regional and state awards in drama; special recognition for public relations achievements. **Writings:** Now in process of publishing a series of non-fiction works, including an autobiography titled, "Reflections of You." **Comments:** "My theme for life's accomplishments: To be the best I can through gained knowledge and experience, with the courage to keep moving up the ladder to success."

WOOLUM, GLENN. Education: Two year technical degree in electronics. A student of Eckankar since 1978. **Occupation:** computer programmer. **Interests:** Loves to write poetry; plays guitar and keyboard; is always seeking deeper spiritual insights on the path of Eckankar. **Writings:** A poem, 'Love's Joyous Return' to be published in On The Threshold of a Dream. **Comments:** "My poetry usually has a theme of communication of love and spiritual principles."

WOOD, DELORIS. Education, Associations: MA, Southern Illinois University, Carbondale; BS, University of Tulsa and BSE, Southwest Missouri State University. Overseas Press Club of America, Society of Professional Journalists, Hemingway Society, COSMEP, Association for Education in Journalism. **Occupation:** Co-publishes and edits *Lost Generation Journal*, an international literary journal about Americans who pursued their literary careers in Paris in the 1920's. Has taught at Temple University, American University in Cairo, Egypt, and Salem High School. Past editor at the Arkansas Democrat and the Egyptian Gazette. **Interests:** After writing, her first love is photography. **Writings:** Writes mainly on contemporary themes in free verse with an occasional rhyme. Began writing poetry three years ago with publication in anthologies and magazines with a few poems submitted for publications. **Comments:** "My goal is to become a noted literary figure who makes a mark in literature merging poetry and prose in a new literary form called 'Fiction: Poetry & Prose.' I have just finished my first work using this form entitled 'Striking Gold!'"

WOOD, DR. THOMAS W. Education: Ph.D., University of Oklahoma; MS, Northwestern University; MA, University of Tulsa; BA University of Tulsa. **Associations:** Overseas Press Club of America, Association for Educators in Journalism and Mass Communications, Hemingway Society, COSMEP, Society of Professional Journalists. **Occupation:** For thirty years a professor at Temple University, University of Arkansas, Little Rock; American University of Cairo, Egypt; Southern Illinois University, Carbondale, and the University of Tulsa. "I was also a reporter-editor photographer for 35 years." **Interests:** The preservation of American history. Co-publishes the Lost Generation Journal, a literary magazine of Americans in Paris starting their literary and artistic lives. **Writings:** Recent honors and awards: Poetry: The New York Poetry Foundation; Amber Beetle Press, "Aureole," limited edition. **Other writings:** Arkansas Press Women, Pennsylvania Press Club, Missouri Press Club. Has written for the Tulsa World, City News Bureau of Chicago and Egyptian Gazette. **Comments:** "The poetry I have written should stand the test of time. I have written about nature, love and emotion. When I read my poetry it reflects any of the 68 years I have lived both yesterday or today."

Index